PENGUIN B

SEMI-DETA

Griff Rhys Jones was born in 1953. He was educated at Brentwood School and Cambridge University. He has worked as a security guard, a petrol-pump attendant and a television star and has written for hundreds of radio and television programmes, and in the press. His *To the Baltic with Bob* was published by Penguin in 2003.

Semi-Detached

GRIFF RHYS JONES

PENGUIN BOOKS

For my mother

PENGUIN BOOKS

Published by the Penguin Group
Penguin Books Ltd, 80 Strand, London WC2R ORL, England
Penguin Group (USA) Inc., 375 Hudson Street, New York, New York 10014, USA
Penguin Group (Canada), 90 Eglinton Avenue East, Suite 700, Toronto, Ontario, Canada M4P 2Y3
(a division of Pearson Penguin Canada Inc.)
Penguin Ireland, 25 St Stephen's Green, Dublin 2, Ireland (a division of Penguin Books Ltd)
Penguin Group (Australia), 250 Camberwell Road, Camberwell, Victoria 3124, Australia
(a division of Pearson Australia Group Pty Ltd)
Penguin Books India Pvt Ltd, 11 Community Centre, Panchsheel Park, New Delhi – 110 017, India
Penguin Group (NZ), 67 Apollo Drive, Rosedale, North Shore 0632, New Zealand
(a division of Pearson New Zealand Ltd)
Penguin Books (South Africa) (Pty) Ltd, 24 Sturdee Avenue, Rosebank, Johannesburg 2196, South Africa

Penguin Books Ltd, Registered Offices: 80 Strand, London WC2R ORL, England

www.penguin.com

First published by Michael Joseph 2006
Published in Penguin Books 2007
3

Copyright © Griff Rhys Jones, 2006
All rights reserved

'Semi-Detached Suburban Mr James' written by Geoff Stephens
and John Carter © 1966 Carter-Lewis Music Pub. Co. Ltd.
Used by permission.

The moral right of the author has been asserted

Typeset by Palimpsest Book Production Limited, Grangemouth, Stirlingshire
Printed in England by Clays Ltd, St Ives plc

ISBN: 978–0–141–01287–2

Contents

Acknowledgements

I would like to thank everybody who helped me try and remember some of this stuff, especially Graham, Charlotte and Geoff, also Louise, for being so patient, Cat for being so good, David for being so attentive and Jo, without whom nothing at all would be possible, ever.

So you think you will be happy, taking doggie for a walk
With your semi-detached suburban Mr . . .
Semi-detached suburban Mr . . .
Semi-detached suburban Mr Jones

Suburban Mr Jones by Manfred Mann, 1966

1. Into the Woods

The first thing I can properly remember is having breathing competitions with my father. I can recreate the sensation of lying up close to him, in my parents' bed, waiting for him to come to properly. We would have been under that pink eiderdown – the shiny satin thing, with the arabesques. It ended up in the spare room, the stitches going, fading in sunlight, but at that time, slippery and cool to the touch. It was thrown over the lot of us, crammed into the one bed on a Sunday morning. My older brother and little sister, across the landscape of imaginary hillocks, beyond the Kilimanjaro of my father's stomach, were there too, huddled up against the cold. It was cold in houses in 1960s mornings. That's why we were all in their bed. I must have been about four.

There had been previous lives in Cardiff and in Banchory in Scotland, where my sister was born. I had had a bobble hat with flaps and a pretty impressive sledge, because I have seen the photographs, but a starting point which is mine and not part of a diary or hypnotic recall is that Sunday imprisonment in my father's hum. I can feel the walrus enormity of his presence, instantly reimagine the sure, steady rhythm of his inhalations, as he dozed on, drifting in and out of sleep while I waited for him to get up.

My father never slept like a baby. He slept like a piece of agricultural pumping machinery. It was quite impossible to out-breathe him. I got dizzy trying to fill my lungs in his ponderous way, particularly when the slight fizzing whistle started up and the honking suck of a snore began somewhere in the back of his throat. I remember worrying too, because listening to him used to make me acutely conscious of something that otherwise I did all the time without ever thinking about it.

To get back to my beginning, one weekday in March I returned to West Sussex. It was an unfamiliar route, which was good. There was a sense of exploration, which is what I wanted. At Hindhead the traffic lights in the middle of the A3 had a pre-war craziness, which was apposite. Turning left towards Haslemere, I began to pass the estate cottages, with their doors and windows in the jaundiced yellow of the Cowdrey Estate, turned off at the top of the downs on to the mile-long drive towards 'the Sanny' and plunged into a thick, wet mist. What could be more appropriate? I was visiting this place through a Powell and Pressburger special effect. My dad worked at this sanatorium as a junior doctor. We lived in 'the Lodge', sometimes known as 'the Engineer's Lodge', just before you got to the hospital itself. I went to a kindergarten school called Conifers down the hill in Midhurst. When I was seven he got another job, and we moved away. But the truth is I always remember Midhurst as a paradisical half-dream. And now that world of woods and paths and the little house amongst the Douglas firs was coming at me through a watery vapour condensed about dust particles, a fog of associations and half-glimpsed realities.

To the south of our house, through the trees, lay the mansion of the eminent Australian chest doctor who ran the place, Sir Geoffrey Todd ('the Old Man'). So if it had been a Sunday, after my father had dragged himself out of bed and complained loudly about how he hated socializing, we would have gone down there for pre-lunch drinks.

Our hair would have been plastered down to our scalps

with water. (Run the comb forward with a harsh, agonizing scrape and then flick to one side.) Our grey socks would have been pulled up tight to the bottom of the knees, anchored there with tiny elastic garters, so that no more than an inch or two of white-scarred and sometimes black-pitted leg showed below our long, pleated shorts. The shorts were held in place with a snake-belt, again striped and elasticated, the ingenious 's' buckle slipping through a twisted metal hole. On top of this we would have worn a tight, woolly v-neck jumper, grey flannel shirt and, in all probability, a tie. And this was our day off.

All the grown-up males dressed in an adult version of the same get-up. Not shorts, but long grey slacks (gathered high, in pap-scratching mode), tweed jackets and tiny striped or tartan ties. Somewhere between schoolteachers and scientists, the doctors were the post-war *Punch* middle classes. They talked lawnmowers and smoked pipes: sometimes bold modernistic ones, with a corner-angled bowl. The mem-sahibs wore hooped, fullish skirts in bold patterns. And everybody drank gin and tonics, probably in special gin and tonic glasses. It wasn't an affluent time, but it was an aspirational time. They dressed like the Royal Family – like Prince Charles still dresses.

We children had to stand properly in a little row until Lady Todd had paid us due attention. Like all the grown-up ladies she was rustly and powdered, but slim and angular in her Australian way, and with Antipodean shorter hair, bolder earrings and the twinkle of sophisticated, amused condescension in her eyes. And then we got a Coca-Cola. It was a measure of how far into the stratosphere these people were that they dispensed real Coca-Cola from a deep fridge somewhere in 'the servants' quarters'. These were bare and functional, compared with the glittery, shiny Todd front room with its French windows opening on to an achingly bright lawn. Real Coca-Cola was something we never saw anywhere else. Not simply because it was an expensive luxury, but because, like American comic books and ITV, it was something inherently corrupting, although not apparently to Australians. At Sir Geoffrey Todd's house it was served in little metallic cocktail beakers in a translucent blue, or a glittering pink, which went cold with their contents. Oh! The icy perfection of it.

Once, the Old Man himself took my father and me up to his attic. We had to mount a ladder which he pulled down from the ceiling and crawled through a hatch under some dark planking to emerge in the middle of a model railway system of stupefying complexity. Hundreds of feet of rail snaked past gasometers, stations and signal boxes, not just in single measures, but sometimes laid six in flank. And then he flicked a switch and plunged us into darkness, and his entire marshalling yard landscape lit up. Each train was illuminated, obviously, but so were hundreds of free-standing lights on tiny gantries. The Pullman carriage windows revealed little lampshades inside. Sir Geoffrey sat in the middle of his network, rattling his personal fairy-lit trains hither and thither though the gloom, and puffed on his pipe.

What was it about doctors and do-it-yourself enterprise? In Blake Morrison's book *When Did You Last See Your Father?* he writes about his GP dad and his ever-handy tool kit. My friend Rebecca Hossack's doctor father built his own house in the Australian desert, decorated throughout with homemade murals. Perhaps the other doctors and their families, a little squiffy from their G and Ts, spent the rest of the afternoon playing tennis together on the sanatorium's private courts, but not my daddy. He would have got bored, falling asleep in the middle of tea and snoring embarrassingly. He preferred to sequester himself in the middle of his own territory, using his family as a sort of human shield, and then make things.

Elwyn, my father, was the youngest of four siblings after a five-year gap. 'Some sort of mistake, it seems.' He had been brought up by his older sisters, Megan and Gwyneth, his mother, 'Nain', being rather too grand in a Welsh, pompous way to bother with him. 'Spoilt,' was one verdict. He was certainly indulged, nannied and babied in a manner that the matriarchal Welsh enjoy. He seemed to me to spend an inordinate amount of time in the bath. He loved sweeties, and sought out ice creams with which to treat himself. He looked like a baby, too, soft, pink skin, a large, growing belly, pale, scrupulously scrubbed, chipolata hands, with the doctor's fingernails always trimmed to nothing. (There were nail scissors everywhere in our house.)

He would sit at Sunday lunch with a napkin tucked up into his shirt front, knowing that he would splatter it with my mother's nursery cooking. Casseroles and chops and frozen peas were favourites. Rissoles, shepherd's pies, big cream puddings or trifles followed. He was happiest at his own table, in his own house, where his indulgent habits and self-centred shyness could be annexed from the demands of any normal social order. He never went to any party without grumbling. In later life, despite working at three different hospitals, he came home every day for lunch. Other people and their English social rituals frightened him. Once at a wedding, a dreaded occasion, he advanced towards the greeting party and kissed the bride's father by mistake. With strangers he could be curt and offhand, wanting, I think, to escape human confrontation and its attendant boredom.

He drank little, gave up smoking when it was discovered that it caused cancer, never played golf or joined any clubs, and had few close male friends, particularly in later life. He never seemed to have an affair. (It would have been unthinkable, actually, impossible to imagine.) He never seemed to join any committees, or even the adult world. He supported himself on a trolley of his own dignity. He was like Arthur Lowe. I can never catch a glimpse of prickly, slightly fat, shy, silvery-haired men, men like Edward Heath, without being reminded of him. They are a type: sexless, defensive, often intelligent in a boffinish manner, self-important, and I always rather love them.

We can't really get to know our fathers as other people until we are almost grown up ourselves, and by then they have become that immutable bundle of fixed opinions and uncurious appetites – the middle-aged man. But in Midhurst, Elwyn would have been in his mid-thirties: young, ambitious, a bit of a comer in his own way, I suppose. He would have been part of a close-knit hospital fraternity, modelled much on the army – quite a difficult man for me to get at through the fog.

I parked my car in 2005 opposite where we had lived. Even though the mist still hung around I could see that a lot had altered. For a start the woods were a car park. I had arranged to meet the communications and PR manager of the hospital. She showed me into her office. I trailed mud over her white carpet. I apologized. She passed me a history of the sanatorium as I sat down. 'Your father was the engineer here?' she began briskly.

'No, no. He was a doctor.' I was disconcerted by this. I nearly said consultant, but that was still some years ahead.

'He was the only one with membership in the place,' my mother had explained only a week before. She meant membership of the Royal College of Physicians, an extra qualification he had worked hard to get. 'If they had any problems they would all come running to him.' He had asked her to show the head chef how to feed diabetics. She had invented a lot of recipes to his instruction.

I came upon a photograph of the 'World Conference on Tuberculosis' in the history book the PR manager had handed me. 'That's him!' I nearly shouted. But I was relieved to find him there, looking perhaps a little tense in the back row compared with the exaggerated bonhomie of the senior consultants who were slouching at the front, but he had been young then, a junior medical assistant.

Now a general hospital, with a cardiac unit which treats morbid obesity amongst other things, the sanatorium where my father worked was built at the turn of the twentieth century to house TB patients. They had no idea then how to cure the 'Bluidy Jack', but they sought means of mitigating its effects. There were expensive clinics in the Alps, like Davos (the inspiration for Thomas Mann's *The Magic Mountain*) and whole townships in the balmy air of the South of France. While the Kaiser ordered up dreadnoughts to compete with what he had seen in Britain, Edward VII struck back with a consumption hospital. The Germans had hundreds of showpiece treatment centres. Britain was falling behind in the medical race. With money made available by Casells, his financial advisors, the King personally supervised the project and stayed in the grounds, in 'our' house, which had been painted red and gold to make him feel at home.

Apparently he entertained his mistresses there. If he did it would have been in unaccustomed pokiness. The place was a miniature Arts and Crafts cottage with tall chimneys, high gables and tiny rooms. Not much room for King Edward's renowned copulation harness in the Lodge. Nonetheless, if you drove a pedal cart at speed into a skirting board, the

white paint would flake off and reveal red and gilt trim-
mings underneath.

My mother explained across the kitchen table how we got
there: things I had never known, never really sought to find
out. After the war there had been too many doctors leaving
the army. Originally my father had done extensive research
in diabetes and its effect on eyesight for his PhD. But his
consultant had asked to borrow his results to use in a lecture
and then published them in the *British Medical Journal* as his
own. He thanked my father in his acknowledgements, 'for his
help', but the research programme had become useless. 'He
was very upset,' my mother told me. The simplicity of the
words and her direct look showed me how she must have
helped him through it. I knew his capacity for worrying. 'We
carried his notes around for years. They filled a tea chest and
in the end I made him burn them.' After that he was advised
by another senior doctor, angry on his behalf, to specialize
in chest medicine. He had gone to Banchory, a hospital near
Aberdeen, which coincidentally featured on a television
programme I presented in 2003.

'Shall we show you round?' the PR manager at Midhurst
asked.

The sanatorium had recently gone into liquidation. 'The
best thing for it', because it had enabled a rescue package to
be put together. The rescue was of the building itself. All the
space and light that the architect Percy Adams had deliberately designed into the wide corridors, the Arts and Crafts
staircases and the shuttered balconies (recently declared unsafe
for patients) would soon go into up-market apartments. They
would certainly take me to the Lodge, but would I like to
see the San first?

It is difficult to walk down the corridors of your past in
the company of a tour guide. I had to apologize and leave

them waiting as I stopped and stared into the hospital stores. The hospital stores! We used to be taken there for sweets, but I tried to remember. There was always something strangely forbidden about it, wasn't there? Was it some memory of the anxiety? We had to be extra good because it was inside the hospital.

We walked out. There was the cricket pitch. My father hated having to play cricket. But that would have been the only time we were ever allowed in these Gertrude Jekyll gardens. I could remember him in the whites and being given his gloves to hold. I could remember playing on the dry-stone walls with those purple flowers which hung out of them in great swags. 'And over there,' I said, pointing across to the trees. 'Isn't that where Sir Geoffrey Todd would have lived?'

'Oh yes. Of course, they're all private houses now.'

I hoped our house would provide clues or starting points. But I toured behind Tricia, and David Hayward, in a semi-anaesthetized trance. If I pushed, just a little, I could remember the texture and colour of two grey blankets, with a red check in them, and the glow of the tiny Christmas tree in a wooden tub, and even the holly-berry-red curtains, but only in my mind. Nothing in the shape of the place started anything. I stood there hopelessly. I couldn't even say which bedroom had been which. The shape of the fire-surround was familiar, but it had been painted over. The place had anyway been used as an office. 'It can be very cold in here,' said David. 'There are three outside walls with the windows facing north.' At the base of the staircase the gloss white had been knocked away to reveal red paint under-neath; the only evidence that this was in fact the same house.

In due course we had to have our own train set. My brother and I slept in a tiny room with a sloping roof, though

I could not identify which one in 2005. Our beds were shoved up against the wall, because one corner gradually became occupied by my father's version of Sir Geoffrey Todd's railway empire.

The railway was constructed on a made-to-measure platform, which lifted on one side so that you could clamber in and sit in the middle. It was much less detailed than Sir Geoffrey's. It ran on grey rails instead of individually sleepered tracks, but there were Airfix stations and a brown WH Smith newspaper stand with the books and newspapers on sale in incredibly tiny writing on the side, which added a splash of authenticity to the grey plastic platform.

But wait, wait, wait! Here we go. This is doing it. This is opening the file in my memory. The speciality act was the mail coach. Some sort of hook arrangement hung by the side of the track. There were several tiny red plastic lozenges with a loop at one end, supposed to represent mail-bags. You hung one on the hook, set the train in motion and it would pick it up, carry it on to the body of the red mail coach with a satisfying click and, because it was so small and the terrain proportionately was travelling past so quickly, it all happened at super speed; a quick whizz-click and it was in. No matter how hard you concentrated it was almost impossible to spot the mechanism in action. It just happened. Whizz-click. And better than that, it disgorged the same mail-bag lozenge into a special black plastic collector chute further down the track, as the train rattled on, around my father's frankly rather lurid landscape.

His hills and tunnels were rudimentary affairs, but my father liked to paint them in blazing oils. It was the same 'pointilliste' manner he had once used to do the view from his house in Cardiff. Perhaps he was going through a Churchillian phase at the time. There were splodgy impastos of trees and walls, as if the major inspiration of Monet had been 'Yes, I could probably manage something like that, too.'

But Elwyn was mainly transfixed by woodwork; sawing and glueing at the kitchen table, to the despair of my mother, never changing out of his 'good' clothes and carrying sawdust through the house. The boys got the railway platform. My sister got the doll's house (not quite as good as the one he made earlier for my cousins in Gloucester, which had an opening front, stair rods on the stairs and an array of clunking great electric switches hidden in the lean-to round the back); Helen's was a flat-fronted, four-storey cupboard with a dormer roof, but it was painted a sticky white with a poisonous green creeper up the front, spotted with cabbage roses; a Kees Van Dongen, Post-Impressionist influence for a change.

Later came a full-sized puppet theatre and puppets, animal hutches, shelves, cupboards, record boxes, garden fittings, walls, garages and an entire boat. Meanwhile in Midhurst he moved on to a tree-house in an oak tree up at the back of the clearing. It had Tyrolean peep-holes, and a real pitched roof. Having got that far, he set to work on a section of the woods themselves. He got into brick-laying (more Churchill?) and built himself a giant barbecue which could have doubled as a field kitchen for a battalion (mind you, I suppose there were an awful lot of Australians around the sanatorium). Others might have settled for an old oil-drum, but we got a pit. He laid foundations and constructed a sort of Vulcan furnace. An old wash-pot was inserted into a brick surround which climbed up to a towering, oblong chimney. It vied with the kitchens of Hampton Court.

In 1988 the hurricane had come at the south-facing slopes of Easebourne Hill like Thor with a strimmer. The entire pine forest behind the house was mown flat. It had quickly been replanted, but nearer to the Lodge than before. The new wood had grown up in thick, serried lines. It was already about twenty feet high when I plunged into it in 2005. I was back in a metaphor. My widely spaced, wooded, open playground had been smothered with an overplanting of reality. I stepped over a chicken-wire fence and found myself in a beige, dead world. There was no path at all. It had been obliterated. Within minutes I lost every sense of direction. Instead of finding the things I wanted in memory-bank wood – the pet cemetery, the tree-house, the barbecue – all I got was a thick, claustrophobic maze. I quickly got lost. I began absurdly to panic. I literally couldn't see the wood for the trees.

When I suddenly burst through back to the edge of the garden right in front of the house, almost by accident, I kicked into a brick. It might have been a brick from the barbecue, covered in a thick green moss. I noticed there were others around. I felt like a detective in a Polish film, searching for evidence of some past atrocity. It was damp and cold. What did it signify anyway? What had I expected to find? Bones?

Did we ever use the barbecue much anyway? Elwyn certainly built himself a picnic area to surround it, using massive half logs, dipped in a preservative that never quite dried. The accompanying benches were anchored to the ground, just a stretch too far away from the splintery tables. He was very proud of it. We were too. He must have ordered a patent glass cutter from a magazine, because I remember the trees were hung with half-bottles in wire cradles, holding candles. Everybody was called around to drink gin and tonics, eat the burned sausages (how could they be anything but incinerated in the improvised blast furnace) and swat the midges, until my father announced, as he habitually did, 'Well, I don't know about you, but I'm off to bed now.'

What a dad! Except of course he was always a little remote, busy at something, perpetually screwing or sanding, glueing or painting, and when he wasn't, he was down the hill at the hospital, where we seldom went.

We went everywhere else. Perhaps because my father was so diligently occupied, and my mother so understanding, we were released into the wild as no parent would dare do today. There were strict times we had to be back: for lunch, supper and bed. We must have gone to school, but I only remember my time in Midhurst as a pre-lapsarian paradise of feral gangs.

The Lodge sat on a little promontory above a drive that led a few hundred yards down the hill to the main hospital, hidden from view by the woods. The trees crept up on the other side of the white road too, fronted by a few mountain ashes and the occasional giant chestnut.

Behind the house was a little fenced garden; beyond that a stretch of grass, traversed by a path; and beyond that more of the enclosing trees. They were tall Douglas pines with red, scaly trunks. We thought they were useless, because, although they had branches, the branches started twelve feet above our heads and they were impossible to climb. Miles up there somewhere, they formed a canopy of dark green fir, which groaned in high winds.

The floor of the wood was thick with pine needles, soft underfoot, even and clean and slightly bouncy. 'The buxom, rosy-faced and high spirited patients' were discouraged from drinking and given the gardens to till. They also went for walks, which were 'measured' so that just the right amount of exertion could be prescribed. The walk past the back of the house was one of these. This was where we buried the family pets: in the middle of it. The hamster went into a shoe-box coffin with a wooden cross made of twigs. There was

Winston, an angora rabbit. (My father claimed my mother shaved it for its fur and it died of the cold.) We liked our graveyard so much that we took to searching for other corpses and carried dead birds and squirrels to be buried in state, and once, triumphantly, an adder squashed down the road next to the fuchsia bushes. Thus the passing-away of a loved one became bearable to the infant psyche. Or rather we became all too keen for our pets to hurry up and die, and took to examining the tortoise with the blue cross on its back, the guinea pigs and Bella the dog for signs of imminent mortality. (Wasn't there a donkey too? Now that would have been a funeral.) We liked our ceremonies and the jewels and cotton wool in the caskets, but best of all we liked revisiting the plots for a touch of disinterment. We dug up a woodpecker over and over again to scare ourselves with the shiny white maggots, until my mother caught us at it and chased us off.

We'd have run on down the path, now eradicated. One second and you were in the woods, thirty seconds and you were gone. The undergrowth was surprisingly dense, good for camps and ambushes, but scratchy to push through in shorts.

Just along the way, heading west, the path crossed a ride cut through from the back of the main hospital building, lined with massive rhododendrons. There was some unwritten rule that we were never to be seen by the hospital staff, and most particularly the patients. It would give them some sort of fit, apparently. So when we decided to climb the giant larches, we had to scoot across to get to them.

A family gang, as opposed to a school gang, involves a variety of ages, including an unwanted baby figure, who has to be held by the hand, one of the boys from the Benicky family, several girls and an older brother who goads the younger brother (me) into life-threatening situations.

'We could get to that branch.'

'I can't reach.'

'You're not scared are you?'

The lower branches were prone to snap off, but they were frequent, rather too frequent, in fact, because we had to take risks to wiggle between them. Nobody had ever climbed this tree before. That was obvious. We kicked off clouds of green dust from the tops of the branches. It was so thick we were not really able to see anything, except if we looked down, the upturned faces of the girls, now too small to register as anything but a smudge of concern. But I distinctly recall, when we finally got right to the top, that this was the highest tree we had ever climbed, high enough to see right over the top of the hospital, beyond the cricket field on the other side, down to the valley of the Rother. In truth, it was rather higher than we wanted to be. It began swaying. And after the moment of triumph, a wash of panic came sluicing up. The whole superstructure suddenly seemed fragile. So I gripped tighter to the only bit that really seemed substantial, the trunk itself.

'Put your foot down.'

'I can't.'

Then everybody started panicking. The branches seemed an enormous distance apart. It was impossible to stretch down to the next foothold without releasing the iron hug on the trunk. And that was the only thing that stopped me falling.

'I'm stuck.'

'You're not stuck.'

Not that he knew. He started crying before I did. He was the one who was going to start shouting at me, because he was the one who would have to tell my father that he left me at the top of a hundred-foot larch tree.

'Let go of my foot!'

'Let me put it down. You'll be all right if you can get your foot on to this branch.'

After about five minutes, I was. But the way down was horrific. The scratches from the twigs began to really hurt. There was inevitably a horrible slip on a green-covered branch, which wrenched an arm socket and crashed me on to my crotch, so it brought tears stinging.

'Don't start crying.'

'I'm not.'

Then on the ground you actually could start crying.

'He made me do it,' was a useless excuse. 'If he told you to put your hand in the fire would you do it?' This didn't require an answer except to shake the head and stare resolutely at the ground, but the honest answer was probably 'yes', especially if he had got away with it without hurting himself.

We once went to some house further up the hill, and I was sent off with the son, a brand new acquaintance (while the adults drank gin and tonics). He took me through the farmyard and stood me in front of a long barn with a row of upper windows, yards long. It was a dappled-sunshine day. He leaned down, picked up a stone, said, 'This is fun,' and threw it straight through a pane of glass. It was fun actually. They were big panes and collapsed with an exemplary destructive implosion, so we worked our way along the building, taking it in turns to demolish the lot. As we reached the end I glanced up to see my pal's father stomping round the corner of the barn. There is a sort of level at which you can understand, even excuse, the fury of your own parents (blood counts for a lot) but there is an unspoken rule amongst the badly behaved that dads don't bawl out other people's children. Your own parents, hot with embarrassment and shame, can usually be counted upon to redouble any hand-me-down annoyance. But here was my friend's father in the throes of a full screaming fit at me. Me! It must have been bad. I was left quaking for the rest of the afternoon, though I noted that the scion of the house got over it fairly briskly.

Is it only because these traumas are lodged like burrs in my hairy subconscious that it felt like our lives were one scurrilous outrage after another? We ate all the peas in the vegetable garden at Jimmy Summers' house. When I was three, I chopped the heads off every tulip in our front garden. I went on the run in Chichester. I broke my arm attacking a swan. When I was six I reached up and pulled down a poster stuck on a tree in Bosham, just for the thrill of it. I had seen it done in a film. It was what cowboys did to 'wanted' posters. Nobody ever found out.

We must have been good sometimes. After all, the fury of all adults, and my father in particular, was something to be avoided if possible. A good spanking was hardly as common as in the *Dandy*, but I remember once being offered the choice between missing television and having a smack. My father laughed when I chose the beating.

Forty years later, in the end, I found the path again. I walked up the road, skirting round the new plantation, and turned south. A few yards through some overgrown rhodo-dendrons and there was the unmistakable view of the back of the hospital. So the little track leading west must be the path, the path where I learned to whistle. It was nothing. The larches had gone. Twenty yards through what was now overgrown scrub and I was standing on 'the cliff'.

The hospital was built to be a sustainable community, which in the 1960s meant a self-contained community. There was an incinerator block with a tall chimney and a hooter that sounded at twelve for lunch. Round the back and down a set of steps were the kitchens. My father used to take me there to meet 'chef', who liked to escort me into his cold room and feed me scraps of over-cooked pork or cold chipolata sausages. I have grown up with a dread of hospitals and especially the greasily polished kitchen departments. This was the real morgue: the heavy door that threatened to seal you in the gloomy, yellowy-grey room with its metallic shelves and hanging carcasses. I didn't like the noisy clatter of battered baking trays, the pale, fleshy hands of the largely Italian staff who grabbed my hamster cheeks and pinched them hard – to get a reaction presumably – out of a sudden welling of affection probably – but all alien and noisy and utterly unappetizing.

There had been fields of Brussels sprouts and pig sties too, which must have been part of the total operation, I suppose. My brother William was old enough to be taken down to see a litter of piglets born. I only remember the morning after and being led down to where they lay, like us with our father in bed, in the smelly straw under a hot lamp. The pig shit and dirty, low-ceilinged hovels were more appealing than the hospital.

And there was a hay barn. This was on 'the cliff' which overlooked the offices of the sanatorium. The cliff was ours.

It was here we discovered something smelly in a milk bottle and took it in turns to go and look at it. I think it was probably a premature pig, at least I hope it was. But up there in the undergrowth, where we were in charge, we could keep an eye on the comings and goings and take our own time over exploring things, including boys and girls things.

Though I left this place before I was seven, I had already taken part in some complex games of Doctors and Nurses in the elder bushes behind the hay barn – unusual scenarios of a melodramatic nature that needed one of the little girls to injure herself, requiring 'doctors' to examine her bare areas beneath her dark-blue knickers, sometimes using a twig or leaves. I forget the names of the girls, or who initiated the games, but they fired up the pangs of curiosity and added significantly to the layer-cake of guilt. And the girls were much keener on the play-acting than we were. It was almost as if the chance to satisfy curiosity was the price we exacted for taking part in the silly play-acting games in the first place.

We much preferred to be inside the barn. It was totally forbidden, but never seemed to be visited by anyone. It was piled full of straw-bales. At the risk of white ridges in the fleshy parts of the fingers, these could be lugged around in the half-light by the two strands of thin baling twine to make first a tunnel and then, after hours of work, secret inner caves. We had hardly settled triumphantly in one room of bristly benches before somebody would start yanking at another bale.

Later, when the recriminations came, it was pointed out that the entire heap could have collapsed at any moment, smothering us, in a tragic disaster from which our mothers in particular would never have recovered. We had not, apparently, been thinking about them at all. That was true. We had worked our way through the straw building blocks until we came up against the planked wall of the barn. The sunlight struck through the slats and a knot gave us a spy hole through which we could see the woods, and the path snaking away through the pines. For once, there was actually someone coming along it.

We spied on an old man (probably in his forties) pushing a bicycle. It was laden with panniers. There was a large basket filled with parcels at the front and a wooden box fixed to the rear. He propped his bike up against a tree and walked off down the hill towards the sanatorium offices. He had sideburns. Like a cowboy.

I blame television. He was inadvertently acting out the scene of the man who thinks he's on his own in a clearing in *The Last of the Mohicans*. Virtually every day we sat in front of the black-and-white television in the brown, shiny bakelite box with an armoury of 'Lone-Star' cap-revolvers and Winchester repeater rifles close by on the sofa, in order to shoot down the 'baddies'. On long journeys, we would attempt to drive our young and exasperated mothers out of their minds by humming the six notes from the theme from *The Alamo* under our breath, until the mummies suddenly boiled over, brought the car to a halt and turned on us with undisguised fury.

The man was a bicycling grocer. We were Apache. So we raided his pack. We sneaked out of the barn and were probably just going to have a quick look, but the basket was packed with sausages. This was too much. They were beautifully pink and squishy. We had to hang them in strings like Christmas decorations all over the nearby trees. What else could we do? Well, we had to stick pine needles in them first, obviously, to make them prickly. I know this because, as I write this, I can suddenly recall sticking the thin, bifurcated spikes of pine needles into pink, yielding sausage meat somewhere, and when else would I have done that? I can still remember the pungent whiff from the packets of tea in the panniers, oblong boxes with pale blue markings. Inside there were grease-proof paper bags. We tore them open. It was ordained. We had to scatter the useless stuff all over the pine needles then and trample them about a bit. We stuck all the cigarettes in the trees. We didn't steal anything. We simply vandalized the lot. Then we went back in the barn and waited. The excitement of the exercise was the opportunity to appear from nowhere, wreak havoc and then slip away to watch the result. It was a real adventure raid, not a pretend. That's what made it good.

I don't even remember whether he railed, jumped up and down or looked mystified; probably the lot. But it was easily worked out, by a process of elimination, who did it. Apart from the kids who once set a dog on me, there was no one else it could have been.

Weeks later, we overheard a scrap of comment (while they were drinking gin and tonics and giggling about it). When my mother offered to buy the stuff, the man pretended that we had destroyed far more than we actually had. Not only that, but after she paid for it, he wanted to keep it. 'Probably going to sell it,' my mother said, and the other mothers snorted. So, he was untrustworthy, and we were on the right side, and that was all right. But we still knew it was better to say nothing.

The naughty child knew that if he could just endure the lecture, stand still, wipe the smirk off his face, look abashed, even squeeze out a tear, then the raging parent would fall prey to exasperation soon enough. A mournful walk across the garden, head down, and then as soon as you were safely round the bamboos, run! As long as my brother didn't seek retribution, the matter was forgotten, the woods closed around again, and it was straight back to the camp for a few moments kicking dirt while the shame evaporated and someone suggested something else, like 'an explore'.

The barn has gone. The piggeries have gone. There is a new housing estate where 'the staff' lived. Sheltered by the nursing home, some of the huge firs have survived, but the whole place looks suburban and containable now. What had seemed a continent was little more than an extended back garden, even then, though we still managed to get lost easily enough.

Once, somebody had been given a tent for her birthday, and this warranted a proper trip. We took sandwiches. My mother probably helped make them: Marmite, that black line of salt on the smear of butter, or sandwich spread, a vinegary dice of vegetables in mayonnaise, or Shipham's fish paste – in several different colours but one basic fishy flavour, out of unscrapable jars (you couldn't get the bit out from under the shoulder) with the green screw tops and the pink plastic sealing ring that needed plunking open. When we were all packed up and laden with bags for our 'expedition', she probably waved us goodbye, imagining, as any mother might, that we would come back in a few minutes to borrow the kitchen table and turn it into a boat. But we trudged off, dragging some really tiny ones along with us, out beyond the barn in the woods, beyond the piggery, up the hill on the other side where the sprouts grew, past 'Aunty Edith's' house, with the goldfish in the front garden and the budgie in the kitchen, and off through the fields, out on to the heath that crowned the downland area. Here we pitched camp for the night.

The weather changed. The sky grew cloudy. There was a considerable argument in favour of going back, but, logically, that was quite impossible. First, the youngest children wouldn't walk and seemed to have given themselves over to lying on their backs and crying. Secondly, my sister had put on her Wellingtons and disturbed a bumble bee, which had stung her. And thirdly, it was now quite dark and we had no idea where 'home' was. The solution, forcefully outlined by my brother, was to sit in the tent, shut up crying all the time and wait until morning, morning being but a few moments away, since it was already night. In the meantime a delegation was sent across to knock on the door of a nearby farm cottage and beg, as travellers did, for bread and water. The owner of the cottage was naturally startled to open his door to two eight-year-old children 'just staying the night' across the field.

We were equally surprised about half an hour later to see a phalanx of parents pounding up the hill, waving sticks like a village mob in a vampire film. It is an image as vivid in my memory as the opening credits of *Bill and Ben the Flowerpot Men*. The dark shapes of the adults and the flashes of their torches, bobbing towards us, against the clouds of a late-summer night. As they approached, the entire tent burst into tears. And then, instead of the expected wrath, they scooped us up and hugged us. How can that image sit so fixed in my consciousness? It is utterly fuzzy at the edges – no real 'before' or 'afterwards', but like a Mivvi bar, ever more concentrated at the centre, frozen into a gooey sweet jam of pure recollected emotion.

2. Weston-super-Mare

My mother was eighty on a Sunday in 2004. It was a convenient day. We could organize a celebration at my house in Suffolk. About forty people had been invited. They were mainly old and respectable and many seemed peculiarly anxious to remind me that they had seen me last at my mother's seventieth birthday. My sister's children were all, I noticed, suddenly quite large. My son was nineteen. Was he? I had renovated these barns. I had moved into them. There had been television programmes. We had taken holidays. But the headlong rush must have stopped somewhere. 'Ten years ago'.

If we noticed we were getting older on a daily basis we would do nothing but squat in the dust and fret.

'It's mainly a state of mind,' a girl once told me. 'You know, there are some societies where people don't age at all, because they eat the right things.'

'Really? I find that hard to believe.'

'Yes, their hair doesn't go grey either. They just stay with black hair, because they are in tune with their environment and they all live to the age of over a hundred.'

And this was a nurse talking. She seemed happily entranced by what was, by anybody's experience, preposterous twaddle.

'Look at me. I am grey. I am old,' I said.

'Yes,' she agreed. 'But that's because you have actually allowed yourself to age.'

I nodded. I was only talking to her in the first place because she was a sexy, smiley nursey. And she must have been in her early twenties. Was she? I couldn't really tell any more. The nineteen-year-old peering out of my flaccid fifty-year-old body didn't want to.

I got no reassurance from all the game old biddies at all. Most of them had lost their husbands, or the ones still trailing along dropped hints about how happy they were to have survived their scare, or took me aside, like the old GP and family friend, who wanted to seriously tell me how he had only just survived the same thing that carried my father off – prostate cancer. He wanted me to make sure that I was ready for it, to ensure that I got all the tests, because the cancer was genetic and I should be taking the greatest care now.

Now what? Now I was getting old, he meant. Which test did he mean? Would my doctor do this thing? Could I ask? But I was whisked away to serve up some meringue.

How could all these old men face their passage from the world with such equanimity! 'Gosh! That's great, I've got another five years at least.' Five years! My God, didn't they understand, the last ten years had passed in an out-of-focus whiz? My mother was eighty.

It is quite difficult to write about your mum. I can't be judgemental. I was, still am, a Mummy's boy. If I look at the few photographs that seem to survive from my early childhood then there she is – young, beautiful, with handsome Welsh features and long black hair, usually tied in a bun. (A catch for my dad, I should think.) But I also see what she is now: trusting, enthusiastic, loving, laughing, simple – good.

There is one Madonna-like, black-and-white snap of her, cradling my sister, where she gazes at her baby with such intensity. It can be no surprise that she submerged herself and her life in her family. My feelings for her now are some sort of refined version of the great blob of emotion that I felt for her then: a blob because it has no definition. I only know that at a young age I hated to be separated from her. To pick out moments from that blob is impossible. There are only memory snapshots, like the horror when she cut off her long hair. (My father was mortified, and we children were no help. Like all under-tens we were as conservative as the Pope.) Her girlish enthusiasm, driving up the hill to Singleton one summer day, with the car full of all of us, and suddenly skittish, squealing at the little Morris as it laboured up the last of the steep bit through the beeches, banging the wheel, 'Come on, come on, you can do it, you can do it!' Or the silliness of her yodelling 'coooee!' when she walked into somebody's unlocked house, a tone which even we knew she had picked up from her new posh friends. But how can I forget my mother coming in to say goodnight on a summer night? Perhaps it was one of those annoying evenings when we had to go to bed ages before it got dark and they were 'going out'. The rustle of her silky dress and the waft of scent when she leaned down to kiss me, and later waking in the black, as the headlights flashed across the ceiling and I knew they were home, and making some noise so that maybe she would come in and whisper about going to sleep now.

My mother became severely ill when I was six. This was a rarity. You weren't allowed to properly become ill in our family. 'Disturbing the doctor' was a sin. Any attempted days off school resulted in a thermometer bunged in your mouth and an expert finger probing underneath the chin for swollen glands. The only suffering ever experienced was apparently by the hard-working medical staff. (Ever since I have apologetically claimed to be 'perfectly all right, Doctor', while exaggeratedly feigning fatal symptoms.) This applied to everybody except my father. Ill, he staged a performance worthy of a seamstress in an Italian opera, with a strictly enforced silence and tinkling upstairs bells.

But if the doctor did come out, then we were suddenly encompassed by the fraternity. We got a glimpse of my father's real world. The doctors openly banded together to discuss our symptoms and their diagnoses.

Years later, after I had passed beyond the green baize door, my wife developed complications in labour and I found out what it was like to be outside the brotherhood. Then nurses came and went, machines were fixed up, housemen were summoned and I was pushed to one side, a useless and un-acknowledged passenger. I wanted to stand and say, 'Look, you don't understand. My father was a consultant. I can be included. I want to be talked to in measured tones and seri-ous semi-whispers. I want to stand and nod at the foot of the bed. I want all the adult confidentiality of the initiated. I can take it. I am from a medical background. You can't just bustle past me as if I were some fractious child.'

I was somewhat too young to be consulted on the kidney problems that my mother suffered. She had to go to hospi-tal in London. My brother was shipped out to stay with my maternal grandmother in South Wales, and my sister and I got to go to Battersea funfair. I can remember the stalls in the half-light of the coloured bulbs, and one in particular that recurs in dreams still: a basin of water covered with small, floating red and blue miniature beach balls. Each had a number. I was given a net and had to fish one out to see if I had a prize. Why that memory should stick I have no idea. I didn't win anything.

It is a matter of family record that my brother went away a normally sized little boy and came back from Granny and Grandpa's fat. (They were so called to distinguish them from 'Nain', my father's mother, whose origins were in North Wales and who thus merited the full Welsh cata-logue.) They owned a greengrocer's in Ferndale, near the top of the Rhondda valley, and William was allowed to roam the shop.

Evan had been a miner. His father, Grandpa Pegum, came from Pegum, and his real name was Griffith Jones. 'I was a Jones before I was married' is one of the catch phrases of my mother's routine. He and Evan ran a successful tobacconist's in Bargoed, and as I write that I can see Grandpa's wedge-shaped, arthritic hands at the end of his life, the blue fingers stained with yellow. But they lost the shop in an economic depression. Evan went down the mine, not to dig, but in some supervisory capacity. He came back up to start a greengrocer's with Louisa in Ferndale.

I must have been to the grocer's myself, but not when I was old enough to notice. Recently, when I was working on the first series of *Restoration*, they told me we were going up into the valleys to visit a pit village where a chapel had been restored. 'My mother comes from up there somewhere,' I started, and then the name of the place escaped me. 'Green, wood something . . .' I went on. 'It will come to me.' I looked down at the script. It was written at the top of the location call sheet: 'Ferndale'.

The next day we stood on what had once been a slag heap, looking down on an untidy grey huddle of streets, and then dropped into the village, with its busy main road, where small boys on bicycles played chicken with construction lorries. It was lined with shops: butchers', tiny grocers', tea shops and a video rental palace.

'They're building a motorway through the valley,' I was told. 'When it's finished, then people will be able to get to the big supermarket and all these shops will go.'

The chapel, facing on to the bend, where my mother won a shilling for singing in a local Eistedfodd, had been restored for a local charity. And we were there to film it. But the rest of the village was remarkably unaltered, unlike a suburb in the South-east of England. Decay takes its own time.

I went into number eleven. It was a charity shop. I asked if they knew about the Joneses who lived there forty years before. The old ladies who ran the place looked at me blankly. It was a stupid question. My father had been 'Jones ten' at school. It was one of the reasons why the Welsh middle classes appended extra barrels to their names (Rees-Mogg, Parry-Williams, Rhys Jones). But Mrs Williams was summoned from out the back.

'Yes,' she said with that positive tone that old ladies use when they find something too obvious. 'Evan Jones and Louisa wasn't it? It was a fruiterer's.'

'A froo-tar-rers,' she said. The word had an authentic, valley tang. She seemed completely matter-of-fact about it. 'If you ask across the road in the "caffy", they were here then.'

So I crossed to the fish and chip shop, where the family led me to their mother, sat at a table up the back, listlessly drinking 'coffy' and smoking a fag. She raised a quizzical eyebrow above a smackingly red, lipsticky mouth. 'Oh yes. There was Gwynneth, the daughter, wasn't there?'

In a fever of off-the-cuff ancestral research I got my mother on the mobile phone and induced them to talk to each other. I was surprised by everything. Surprised to find every-body still there, surprised that we were joined now by Megan, who had worked at the fruiterer's and remembered looking after my brother (and presumably stuffed him with ice cream and cake). I was surprised when it finally occurred to me that this old girl must have been a young girl then. Gosh, younger than my mother still, in fact. But the old lady in the back of the caffy, Megan and my mother really had nothing much to say to each other, other than to point out that the Italian family had arrived in Ferndale a few years before grandparents Evan and Louisa had left for Weston-super-Mare, and their retirement by the sea. They seemed unmoved. What had been surprising to me – that people stay in one place for forty years – was utterly unsurprising to them.

Weston-super-Mare was a dreary exile. I would have been happy to be fed sweetmeats and get fat in my grandfather's fruiterer's. Instead I was only ever sent once or twice a year to the limbo where they had elected to wait to die. The bungalow, although new, was a gloomy mausoleum inside. The net curtains were never drawn. A pallid light illuminated the heavy brown furniture, the piano, the polished mahogany table and the Welsh clock that ticked and whirred heavily in the gloom. It was prison. Granny seemed to have become a little old woman at the earliest possibility. Grandpa was struggling towards drawing his last agonizing breath, his lungs filled with coal dust and cigarette smoke. He must have been a strong man once, but he was bent with arthritis by then. And he struggled to get in and out of cars. 'Dew, dew, fucky!'

'Grandpa! Children!'

But movement clearly hurt, so he didn't move much. Days were often spent just sitting in the gloom, visited by other decrepit old people like Aunty Betty, with her frizz of grey curls and currant eyes, and Uncle Jan, whose idea of amusing children was to let them look at his pocket watch. Most of the games we played in Midhurst have gone from my memory. I was too engrossed. But the few 'holidays' when my parents dumped us at Granny's, by contrast, are lodged in a yellow jelly made of furniture polish: the laborious preparation of tea; the clink of cutlery against a plate; the shuffling feet in the corridor; the endless, inert waiting. It was the antithesis of life. I have been left with a horror and impatience for the petty rituals of home ever since. Nobody goes off to change their shoes 'for going out' when I'm around.

We were by the seaside, but we only went to the front on special days, and anyway, when we got there, the water had inevitably gone into retirement too, disappearing miles out into the Bristol Channel, way beyond the end of the mile-long pier. So we had to sit and wait for that as well. Most days we were pushed into the deadly boring strip of garden for the morning, as long as we behaved quietly, with the shed smelling of creosote, the hybrid roses in the yellow clay soil, the cement paviours along the side of the house where snails faced lingering, fizzy death from my grandfather's salt attacks. Our main entertainment was running down to the embankment at the bottom of the garden and waving madly at the trains. Sometimes the passengers could be induced to wave back.

Driving to Weston-super-Mare in September 2005, I found myself wondering whether anything would have survived to fire up any memories. Had the approaches been as slatternly then as they are now? There were so many signposts and safety instructions winking in the sharp autumn light, I feared that the Weston-super-Mare I had known had probably been swept away by a quango.

'We have to find the floral clock,' I told Jo. 'That, Timothy White's and the trams are all I remember about the centre of the town, and I presume the others have gone.'

It had been that dull. The floral clock was considered a form of light entertainment. The big minute hand would judder its way through the rockery plants and a bird would pop out with a wheezy 'cuckoo'. If we arrived ten minutes early Granny and Grandpa seemed perfectly happy to sit and wait expectantly for the hour.

To give it its due, the centre seemed a glamorous destination then, if only by comparison with the bungalow. I remembered a Lubitsch–like prosperity: dark, shiny shop fronts, window displays and discreet red and dark green liveries.

Now we parked in a cleared lot. It was one of many. A single Regency building stood marooned in the asphalt with a boxer dog roaming its fenced roof. It sported a big sign: 'Biker-Friendly'.

The old lady in the car next door decided that the floral clock had probably gone. 'Weston's not what it was, no, it's not.' I liked her Somerset emphasis. It wasn't. After a foul seventies shopping development – 'Multi Value' – and a set of flats that tried to define the word 'block', we walked past another empty lot facing directly out on to the promenade.

But not all of it. 'Look up there!' In front of us was a neat populated hillside closing off the bay. 'I don't remember that elegance at all.' But I did suddenly remember the Winter Gardens, where we used to go for tea, just past the pier.

It is a conference centre now, next to the Wonky Donkey gift shop, but still a noble seaside building. The manager showed us round. We went into the main ballroom. It had a wooden sprung parquet floor and a raised balcony running right around it. Here the tables used to be laid with super-conductor silvery metal tea pots, too hot to be poured except with asbestos gloves, and ice cream scoops that you chased around those metal bowls on stalks.

'The Beatles played here,' the manager told us proudly, but I was equally affected by the poster outside which announced that Robert Pratt and Mark Howes, in association with Derek Franks, were about to present 'the Troggs, P. J. Proby, Herman's Hermits and the Ivy League' on their fortieth-anniversary tour. God, I'd like to have been there for that.

I ache for proper British seaside. I even associate it with proper British pop. After all, Herman's Hermits, Dave Clark and the Beatles always ended up looning around at the seaside in their films didn't they? When we were taken off on our middle-class holidays on our middle-class sailing boats, we kids had to solemnly negotiate with my father for R&R days in Walton-on-the-Naze. I loved the pier and the crowds. The Mighty Waltzer on Walton pier was a shocker. It still is and, as a fifty-year-old piece of machinery, is genuinely scary now. At seven I became enormously excited by the posters advertising the arrival of the secret *Daily Mirror* man in a trilby. 'He will be in this town on Tuesday.' This was real intrigue.

Once we stumbled on the *Radio One Roadshow* on the beach and glimpsed Pete Murray on a big temporary stage. (I saw him stand in the wings and say in a different voice, 'Ladies and gentlemen, give a big hand for Pete Murray,' before walking straight on to a big round.) We were deprived children. I wanted to be inside the barbed wire surrounding the famous Butlins in Clacton, spending all day on free rides, instead of having to listen to my father making jokes about prisoner-of-war camps on the pebbles outside. You could get vouchers for Butlins worth three pounds in the *Hotspur*. Unlike where we lived, the seaside was cosmopolitan. I still visit resorts now, whenever I can, with an unhealthy addiction to their melancholy. 'Strangers on the Shore', the Acker Bilk clarinet theme, starts playing in my head. It was one of our first forty-fives, with a holly-green label. The television show opened with that shot of a beach, and that mournful tootling. It was the theme.

Weston was proving a marvellous dose of decrepitude for me, a proper husk. 'My sister used to dance on this floor!' I pointed at the parquet.

'Mmm,' said my wife. 'Can we get lunch near here?'

The manager pursed his lips. 'What sort of lunch?' He looked doubtful.

'She would run down the stairs there. There would have been an orchestra. We must have danced here together, my sister and I, just to ingratiate ourselves with the old people. "Ah, there's lovely!"'

Before we left the Winter Gardens I peered closely at some blown-up sepia photographs of Weston in its flouncy prime. Surely it was, historically, as important as nearby Tyntesfield House, which had been saved for the nation at the cost of a small fighter plane, except that, instead of being the private playground of some fertilizer manufacturer, Weston was the playground of huge numbers of factory workers from Birmingham and Cardiff, who effectively built the place out of their wages following the Bank Holiday Act of 1871.

I pieced together the grains of the lumpy, blown-up gelatine and suddenly thought I identified some donkey carts, which had operated near the pier. A parking attendant confirmed my detective work. 'That's right,' he said as I nodded proudly. 'They had a stagecoach and a train and a space rocket.'

I was pleased with myself. This had made the whole trip worthwhile. I distinctly remembered the hard, red-painted seats and the complicated clip door on the space rocket, a Flash Gordon affair, pointing upwards at a forty-five-degree angle. And, yes, it was slightly incongruously drawn by a donkey. That didn't matter to us. You had to jump in quickly before other kids took all the places. 'And look!' I had made another archaeological find in the sandy valley. There was the oval pool for sailing boats, still there in the middle of the beach, still filled by every rising tide, where I launched one of those bright red miniature yachts with the woolly sails and the figure-of-eight cleats that, astonishingly, sailed very well, and which, even more astonishingly, you can still buy.

But most of all I suddenly got flooded with a vision of a sea swimming pool. It was somewhere along the front. I trotted off in search of a blinding snowy light, reflecting off the cream-painted walls of the lido, and the bright blue tiles of the pool itself. Was it still there?

It was boarded up now, behind a green-painted hoarding. Inside, someone was pumping water through a pipe into the main sewer, but I couldn't find a way in, so I went around the side, and found a set of steps down to the beach and a rusty side entrance.

'Look at this,' I grumbled to Jo, moving away some temporary barriers. 'They've tried to stop us getting down there.'

But in fact they'd just built new steps. I put my hand on the rail and covered it with an orange tar that took six days to get rid of.

But I still lay on the sand and peered under the rusted gate. The great parabola of the diving boards, the nose of the place, had been surgically removed. Not a trace remained, but I could just see, over in the corner, beyond the sweep of the cracked plain of pavement, which I was now looking across from a child's viewpoint, the wedding cake structure of the fountain. That fountain had been the essence of a trip to the pool. It was white on the outside and seaside blue inside, with a rough-finished non-slip circular lip. It had a scrapey surface, and my sister, who used to wear a ruched pale-blue swimming costume, would clamber through a sheet of falling water holding hands with me until we were inside, splashing in the shallow blue pool and looking out on the Technicolor world through a water lens.

'There's a plan to revive the place as a Caribbean Paradise Disco Resort,' the car park attendant explained.

And that was that: the fountain, the mini-stagecoach and the concrete pond in the sand. All brought back to the frontal lobes. Later, in the interests of further research, I directed my wife through the back streets to where the houses backed on to the railway, to Coleridge Road.

'This seems to be some sort of sink estate,' she said, but we came round the bend and there were some houses with peculiar second floors built into mansard roofs. 'Stop. This could be it,' I commanded.

'I thought it was a bungalow.'

'Yes, but these places were once bungalows. I'm sure of it. Look, they must have built these silly roofs on later. That's exactly the same crusty grey pebble-dash. Those are the concrete slabs of the path round the side. And look. I remember those prefab garages.'

I rang my mother. 'I can't remember the name of the street,' she said. 'My memory is going for all that sort of thing. Anyway,' she went on, remembering after all, 'I was never there for more than half an hour. We'd dump you lot and high-tail out of it.'

'Where were you going?' I sounded abandoned.

'Oh, just off on holiday without you for a change.'

'Oh. Well, this is where you dumped us.'

'No, it wasn't.' She remembered more. 'It was a cul-de-sac.'

'They probably extended the road later.' I took a last look at the horrid little house we used to hate.

When we were back on the motorway my mother rang back. 'It was Brewster something. I've just remembered. Brewster Road, or Close. You see, my memory isn't so bad.'

We'd been nowhere near.

3. All About Me

Between attempts to prostrate my poor mother by 'disappearing' in public places and 'appearing' in even more public places, I was gaining a reputation as a forward child: cheeky, of a 'sunny disposition' and a nuisance, sniffing out the advantages of my position. I was one year ahead of the vulnerable, girly baby, Helen, and three years behind the aged William. He had to take responsibility for all three children, the dignity of the entire family, and the duty of carrying dicta to elderly relatives, while, as 'Griffith, Griffith Bach', I was allowed to simper and wriggle.

'Don't shift the blame on to Griff, you're the oldest.'

'You can stay behind and help your father . . . because you're the oldest.'

He was also the biggest, so he could hurt me. His function, apart from absorbing parental flak, of course, was to act as a mobile punch bag.

My own son had nobody but a little sister to fight with so I had to wrestle with him, but fathers say, 'Not now,' and laugh at key assaults, whereas brothers, given a hefty kick getting into the car, respond in kind and get themselves into trouble. You could karate-chop an older brother to see if it really hurt. He in his turn didn't just 'play' at fighting. He liked to win. ('No punching! No biting!') If he shouted, 'Submit,' there was always the last resort of pushing him to the limit so that he actually hurt me. I could yowl seriously then, provoking Mother to leave *Mrs Dale's Diary* and demand furiously why William, *who was the oldest*, didn't know his own strength. And look, he had actually hurt his brother, and we had better stop fighting and go outside, otherwise our father would hear of it. Temporarily gathered up into a bosomy, powdery hug, I could be the brave one. Then I could follow him outside and whack him with a stick.

I was put up for things: songs, recitations, kisses. My mother recalls a visit to an end-of-the-pier show in Bognor. The family sat up with glassy-eyed attention when, during a break in the musical light entertainment, the cast were joined by a four-year-old boy who came on and sang 'Twinkle, Twinkle Little Star'. The grisly child was me.

I knew how to suck up. Our earliest holidays were at a place called Goran Haven in Cornwall. We stayed in a flat above a crab-fisherman's locker and played on the beach, while my father paced about in a distracted fashion on a cliff until it was ice-cream time. Here, I recall, I made a paper knife out of a spider crab's leg and a bit of charred driftwood. I solemnly presented it to my mother. It hung around the house smelling noxiously for most of my childhood.

Occasionally we travelled to Cardiff, on a deathly visit to Nain, my father's mother, the white-haired matriarch of the family. She was spoken of in awed if not quite respectful tones. From the perspective of the back of the car, as it rumbled through the four thousand traffic lights on the way from Sussex to Cardiff, she seemed to be a powerful brake on the independence of our rulers.

We were ordered to say 'please' and 'thank you', to keep out of the way, to make no noise, not to fight or argue, and to make use of our two Welsh phrases, 'Nos da', good night, and 'Boredar', good morning. This wasn't because she spoke Welsh herself (though all the ancient crones of Wales usually had it in them somewhere). Nain (North-Waleian-Welsh for 'Granny') had long been settled in

English–speaking Cardiff. The Welsh was only designed to make us look cute.

It would appear that we children were the principal reason for the excruciatingly long journey in the first place. And she, Nain, despite being sensitive to the slightest flaw in our upbringing, like some ant-eater able to sniff out wriggly behaviour, was also apparently frail, not used to young children and in need of long periods of complete inertia in her gloomy house in the suburban street in Pen y Lan, the quiet, posh bit of north Cardiff.

Her husband, Taid (North-Waleian Welsh for grandfather), had originally come to Cardiff to supervise the Western Region for Jesse Boots, always a slightly mythological presence in my father's side of the family. (There were 'shares', spoken of in hushed tones.) William Rhys Jones the Elder was a chemist who had worked in London and Southampton, having originally come from Betws-y-coed. He was a Senior Deacon of the Calvinistic Methodist Chapel and preached himself. He always entertained the visiting ministers. Three times every Sunday my father was forced to walk the mile to the chapel, and they always discussed last night's film on the way. Whether the film did for coming back, too, my mother couldn't tell me. Taid was a charismatic man who died at the age of sixty-five, when my father was still at university, but my father was the runt of the family, ten years younger than his older brother, Ieaun.

Nain and Uncle Ieaun took over the running of the Rhys Joneses. This seemed to have included a fierce duty to prevent the two daughters marrying. Any man who came back to Elan Road was virtually run out of the house. My aunt Gwyneth had to pretend to take my father, the little one, for a walk to get down to the tennis club and eventually escaped to Gloucester with a minister (although I can't think that he played tennis). But Megan had to stay. I sat with her in the Park Hotel towards the end of her life, when I was touring to Cardiff and its impossible New Theatre stage, and she remembered the dances she had been to there with tears rolling down her face.

As children, we always arrived in Cardiff after dark. Wales is forever associated with inedible salad. It was 'impossible' to have a 'proper' supper, because nobody could guess when we might arrive, so big, weeping chunks of boiled ham were laid out with hard-boiled eggs, bitter 1950s lettuce and blobs of salad cream: that vile yellow gloop that puckered the mouth and just about smothered the taste of the over-ripe tomatoes. My father loved it. To us it seemed a poor reward after sitting for six hours in the back of the Morris Traveller. And worse, after Megan had cleaned the plates away into some smelly back bit of the gloomy, under-lit house (though it was Nain who did all the cooking, my mother assured me) it would be announced that it was immediately time for bed, even for my brother, who, although he was the oldest, must be tired out after the long journey.

So we were lined up to kiss the old woman with the long, bright-white witch's hair, a passable imitation of my father in drag, and then, God help me, I remember hugging her and piping up, like Shirley Temple in *Wee Willie Winkie*, 'There's a kiss from Mummy, there's a kiss from Daddy, there's a kiss from Helen and a kiss from William.' And the old dear raised a withered hand to stroke my bulging baby cheeks and wipe a tear from her eye. 'Ahh, Griffith Bach' (meant this time – my father only used it as a prelude to some expression of severe disappointment). My brother looked on with undisguised disgust.

It had not been puritanism that influenced my uncle's

protection of his women-folk, it was snobbery. My mother is convinced he believed that Elwyn had married beneath himself, and in turn she disapproved of Ieaun and his play-boy ways. Her deepest distrust was reserved for Joan, his wife. 'When we first went there with William and they came down to the car, Elwyn passed the baby to Joan, who said, "Don't give it to me."'

Joan was admittedly a pretty stupid woman, but the pair were dead sophisticated for Glamorgan. They had a Bentley and a sequence of houses decorated in excruciating South of France taste, with lurid patterned wallpapers and gold-encrusted bibelots. They modelled themselves on the Duke and Duchess of Windsor, even down to their smelly, noisy, asthmatic pug dogs: all pretty glamorous for a consultant anaesthetist from Cardiff. My uncle came across as a Welsh cross between Rex Harrison and Bertie Wooster. He was a squadron leader during the war, and was the only man I ever met who actually said 'what?' at the end of his sentences.

There was a picture of him when he was in his twenties, stood on the top of a cliff, in a trench coat and plus fours, next to a low sports car, wearing an outrageous jumper. He was the polar opposite of my father. Naturally I found him rather interesting.

My mother can still work herself up into a fit over the indignities of their visits to our humble dwellings. 'I didn't think you lived in anything like this,' was Joan's comment on first seeing their house in Epping. Ieaun was driving in the car, quite possibly his Bentley, and turned on us chil-dren. 'We'll have to stop this car unless you lot can be quiet.'

'But you used to say that all the time,' I countered.

My mother snorted. 'You were perfectly quiet at the time.' She giggled. William had been turned out of his bed to accommodate the visiting potentate and stood in front of him and said, 'When are you going home? We're fed up with having you here.'

What my mother resented was their concentration on luxury when she and my father were struggling to bring up their children. All their lives Ieaun and Joan danced attendance on a rich old aunt called Dolly, at the races, at Claridges and in the South of France. Dolly had married a French banker. She had become estranged from her own daughter and gave Joan a dress allowance and paid for her to come up to London once a month to have her hair and nails done. My mother liked Dolly. 'Oh, she was a lot of fun.' A measure of her wealth was that she always booked two seats in the theatre – one for her mink.

Ieaun and Joan never got the money. The French inheritance laws intervened. I felt my mother was quietly satisfied. She had never forgiven Ieaun's silly assumptions about the superiority of surgeons over physicians. It had led to a row the night before my father's funeral. Ieaun, already getting woolly-minded with the onset of Alzheimer's, had claimed that Elwyn probably did not understand, during his final illness, what was happening to him.

It still caused my mother to flare up fourteen years after the event, with Ieaun long dead too. 'What nonsense you speak,' she had told him. 'Of course he knew. He was a Fellow.' She resented the way that Aunty Megs had tried to shush her, as if she were some junior even then. But she could also pity Ieaun now. For Mummy, her family was everything, and his lack of children left Ieaun to die lonely and forgotten, whereas she sees her children every week, would do every day if she could.

My father obviously felt oppressed by his brother and would have nothing to do with his Glamorgan snootiness. He had plans, even before we left Sussex, to move me from my posh kindergarten and once took me for a frightening glimpse of the noisy local state primary school.

Perhaps he was worried about the fees. He told me he thought there were too many girls at Conifers. I got out the school photograph to check. What was he on about? There were plenty of boys. There was Charles Hume and Graham Stott and my best friend, Jimmy Summers, who lost an eye in an accident after I left. (I was deeply upset by the news and went up to the back of the garden to cry.)

Perhaps Conifers was a bit girly . . . I rather liked it. There was a 'Wendy house' in the grounds of the tiny school, where only girls played during the break. Once we managed in a moment of heightened excitement, deafened by squealing and blushing, to 'penetrate' this forbidden bastion of femininity, and I remember, as we rushed through, that, to our surprise, behind the clapboard walls and the dirty curtained windows there was just a bare, planked room and nothing to see at all, the conclusion of most sexual curiosity at that age.

Otherwise, we boys did everything that the girls did. We played rounders rather than football, so I never matured into blokeyness. (I still loathe the beautiful game.) We did an awful lot of skipping and we learned to sew (excellently useful, though I've forgotten how to do the chain-stitch). I made a scarlet swimming-costume bag with a bright white rope pull in one of the sunny upstairs classrooms in what was, after all, little more than a suburban house near the outskirts of Midhurst.

I can bang away at the doors of memory here, but nothing really comes out. Images, perhaps: the new gym built round the back, with the beautiful, varnished, yellow wood climbing frames and the clean, new smell of the suede-covered vaulting horses (not sensations commonly associated with school gyms). I presented a current affairs project on the independence of Sierra Leone there. And rows of Wellington boots under the awning on the veranda. But I only know that because they were still there when I drove past a few years ago; as was the conifer tree that gave the place its name, with a big bowed branch where we used to sit at breaks. All other lessons, personalities, friends, teachers, pottery classes, infant school food and serious application have gone, except for *Hiawatha* and the *Little White Bull*.

The school presented an elaborate pageant every year. *Hiawatha* was memorable, not because of the Itchigumi and of the fur he made him slippers of, but because it involved dressing up as Indians. We wore sacks, chopped with ragged fringes at the bottom and tied with coloured belts. We wore head bands. Our faces were daubed, gratifyingly, with war-paint, made from those great jars of children's pure floury colour.

The next year Longfellow was supplanted by Tommy Steele. Tommy must have already abandoned his good-rocking persona and adopted the cheeky nudge-nudge narrative style which was to become his forte for the rest of the twentieth century. He 'sang' the story of the 'li'l why bawl!' (Chorus, loudly and with a note of mania: 'Little White Bull!!') And the bull, which was deficient, in some ugly-duckling way, scored a comical triumph in the bull ring (before being slaughtered, I assume).

It is the first pop song I remember, because we had to listen to it hundreds of times. I was the back legs, my first major part. The bull itself was made out of chicken wire and that infant-school staple, papier-mâché. We legs wore big white trousers, and it was an early experience of the unexpected trails of theatre as spectacle. Naturally, my brother, who was older, was the front. After weeks of rehearsal, of clutching his waist and gaily tripping hither and thither in time to the music, the dress rehearsal was a fearful shock. No Mexican penitent, shouldering a painted Madonna, could have been less prepared for the actuality of the performance than I was. My brother seemed to have all the advantages. It was preposterously unfair. He could at least see. He could actually breathe. He was upright. His big bull's head gave him relative freedom of action. He was not continually pronged and lacerated by the razor-wire edges of the inexpertly trimmed chicken-wire carapace. He could also assess the inevitable discrepancy between the routine as devised over months in the tiny gym and the routine as performed on the expansive prairie of the school playing-field across the road. So he romped away with frisky white bullish spirit. Admittedly, this was to keep up with the toreadors, matadors and picadors who were skipping spiritedly away ahead of him, energized, as is often the case, by a rush of adrenalin.

'Shut up you,' and 'Keep up you idiot!' were of limited assistance, and a Chinese burn and dead-leg didn't help much afterwards. The utter misery of the experience was only matched by the three-day tech-run for *The Wind in the Willows* at the National Theatre thirty-five years later, when I realized for the first time that most of Toad's dialogue would have to be shouted over hordes of violin-playing rabbits bounding across the stage and a full-sized gypsy caravan trundling into view.

My father could just about be persuaded to turn up to these occasions. He made a point of avoiding speech days most of my life. By then he was already engaged in the great do-it-yourself project of the Midhurst years.

His closest friend on the staff of the hospital was a man who went under the slightly alarming nickname (from a patient's perspective anyway) of 'Jab'. J. A. Boulton wasn't a doctor. He was some sort of administrator. These were still the days when doctors ran the show. All ranks of hospital staff, and most certainly the general public, were subordinate, expected to bob in the wake of 'Doctor', a super-powered dreadnought, cruising through ward and sitting room alike, one hand permanently extended for notes.

They got hold of a loft, above a shed with a green door, just across the road from the piggery and its hooter-chimney, and down the lane from the hay barn fortress. Below housed the sanatorium fire engine. Up above, they began a marathon of wood-working.

We were sometimes taken there by an exasperated mother trying to shoo her biggest charge back to dinner. I can recall the two men, at men's work, with black slicked hair just fallen forward in a dishevelled lick, in their braces and shirt sleeves, which were white under a single naked light bulb. There was a low roof, and the red curls of mahogany on the floor gave off a strong acid smell. Gradually, an Enterprise sailing dinghy filled the entire space. It seemed huge to us. It would have seemed pretty huge to Uffa Fox, the designer. Jab's navy connections meant they got their wood from an MTB company in Portsmouth who provided everything with an extra quarter of an inch allowance all round, to allow for later honing and planing. On hundred-foot ships, the margin was negligible. On a twelve-foot dinghy the margin was a liability. The racing dinghy became, like my father, a little heavier than was strictly necessary.

Heaving this solid lump across the 'hard' at Bosham in Chichester Harbour became the first of many minor tribulations of the yachting experience that my parents failed to rise above.

Quite why my father, not naturally inclined to react to

minor set-backs with equanimity, and, indeed, slightly neurotic about heath and safety factors (such as the ease of death by drowning, significant injury from flying tackle or disease from polluted waters), decided to take to the high seas is still a bit of a mystery. I suspect it was the wood-working that lured him initially. By the time that Jab had discovered that the cumbersome hulk was bound to lose races, my father had realized that his new hobby could set him adrift from polite society. In fact, apart from bumping into other boats (only necessitating the tersest of exchanges) he need never have anything to do with anybody else at all, ever, except his family. So from the earliest days we were roped in. (Literally, to begin with.)

The dark blue Enterprise didn't really last very long. They must have lugged it up and down the hard at Bosham and into the Itchenor river a few times, and we must have got in the way, because little children always do. So I can remember being plumped down in the centre of the boat next to the centreboard casing and being able to reach out and tweak the swollen mandarin oblongs of plastic buoyancy bags lodged under the thwarts. They were tied in place with bright white webbing strands that smelled new and later, when sucked, were salty to taste. Or we played with the sheet ropes and pretended they were snakes.

Normal rebellious infant behaviour just evaporated. We knew this was a different state of existence. Not just because of the racket, but because the parents had become other beings. My mother, dressed in rather too tight slacks and a short-sleeved shirt, had the urgent look of a determined Cossack on a Russian propaganda poster. She was attentive to my father's every wish. It showed in her expression. And he had taken on a fervent watchfulness, his eyes darting around in a lively imitation of a startled squirrel, gripping on to the tiller, suddenly turning and looking behind him, reaching forward to whip off a rope while issuing curt instructions to Mummy, who responded with impressive speed. 'Pull her up now! . . . let go the rope. Get back.'

It was probably from those earliest moments of sailing, with three tiny children crammed in the bilges, with my poor mother steadfastly accepting that it was not her place to fully understand what was going on, that my father adopted his lifetime habit of Jonah-like exaggeration and hyperbole in order to rule his ship of doom. 'Keep your hands in. You'll have them off. Don't rock the boat! You'll have us over!' All designed to frighten children into wide-eyed submissiveness, until such time as we were safely past the few moored boats and we could be allowed to sit up with the adults. 'Hold on! Sit still! Get ready to go about!'

It was captaincy by paranoia. And having effectively dragooned us as scugs, he never abandoned the habit as we grew older. 'Mind the gybe! The boom will have your head off! Keep your fingers well clear of the anchor chain, now! Don't go too near that boat, we'll hit her!' And though the wind was slight and the gybe would have been well signalled, although only a village idiot would stick his hands in the chain box and the said boat was two or three hundred yards away, we grew to accept that this was the modus operandi. He saw potential accidents and disaster everywhere. Later, in motorcycles, ladders, pints of beer and long hair; for the time being in boating, swings, roads, bicycles and staircases. He was a doctor. They were all lethal. But this was more than wariness. This was control. Daddy saw the consequences and Daddy needed to point them out. We never capsized. I remember once he banged a finger and I recall the misery of a small child seeing his father-hero in pain, borne bravely I may add. But otherwise we sailed through it all, as a slightly less hysterical man might have expected to do all along, given that we were, after all, in a sailing boat.

It was interminable stuff. Sitting on the floor lasted several years at a time. Sailing down the river, keeping still and out of the way, took a couple of decades. But eventually we reached our paradise: West Wittering.

Wittering was little more than a spit of dunes at the mouth of an estuary. You could walk to it, if you were dogged (and to begin with my mother was ordered to do so, 'pushing that bloody pushchair'), but it was largely the playground of the water-borne. There was a steep shelving beach of sand ('Be careful now! I don't want anyone drowning themselves'). On sunny weekends the curve of the bay filled up with boats, until it became a complicated, not to say fraught, business to anchor there. Ashore, we would huddle under the shelter of the dunes attending to what united the Rhys Jones family most: lunch. Tupperware boxes of sandwiches, gala pie, sweet and slightly gooey liver sausage, home-made Scotch eggs and a faux-wicker-patterned tubular thermos of asparagus soup. This was one of those treats of industrialized grub that tasted better than any fresh original (sardines, canned tuna, tinned peaches and baked beans being the others). To the children the picnic fulfilled the requirements of being sweet and mushy 'food' – not gristly parts of a sheep's anatomy, or those 'cabbages on stalks' with the wet, slightly sulphurous taste (Brussels sprouts) that we got at home. I utterly refused to eat cabbage until I was past ten.

Then after lunch there was a visit to the red ice-cream boat. Luckily, my father's interest in ice cream was a match for any four-year-old's. He seemed not to care that the belching 'Mr Whippy' machine excreted a fluffed-up spew of aerated lard that could have greased a Russian half-track. The more synthetic the confection, the more it reminded him of his childhood and Glengranogg on the Cardigan coast, where his family had a holiday cottage and where the 'ice-cream' was made of powdered milk and baking soda. When, as a teenager, I went to Florence and raced back to England with the news that ice-cream could be made of real cream, with proper chocolate and hardly any salt, I never really felt that my enthusiasm paid off. He wasn't seeking the ultimate ice-cream heaven, he was looking for the nursery.

I got lost once in the dunes. It was a great place to play, somewhere that adults could hardly be bothered to go. I would wander off. The sand creamed up between the toes and crumbled around the ankles, silver and hot on top, cooler and darker underneath. Sometimes the dips were disconcertingly deep. Once, far up the seaward end, I crested a dune and came upon a grown-up lying totally 'bare' in the spiky grass. He was arched on his back and my eyes were drawn to the massive pink flushedness of his jutting erection. It was quite a surprise. Did I, at six, feel anything sexual about it? I think I did. Was he lying there waiting to present himself to a passing little boy? Possibly. He didn't seem to want to cover himself up or roll feverishly over on his front, as any self-respecting, embarrassed wanker might. So I suppose he was showing it to me. I never reported the event to anyone. I was complicit in it, just in passing by, just in looking, just in being there. It was certainly not something I would want to explain to a grown-up.

After all, we all liked to look. We had a maid or au pair at one time. She was blonde and had a round face and wore full-bottomed fifties skirts. She fell asleep on the lawn one day, in hot sunshine, and I distinctly remember the huge excitement brought on when Jimmy Summers and I tried to peer up her skirt. What were we doing? We had no idea. My first sex education was years ahead. Even the rudimentary details were years ahead. She woke up and chased us away.

The argument over 'the rudest word' that took place between my brother and myself must have happened much later. It was overheard by my sister, who threatened to tell my mother. We persuaded her that 'c★★t' was indeed the rudest word you could say, but only meant 'Wellington boot', not a particularly inspired improvisation, and she inevitably told my mother she was putting on her c★★ts in the rain.

Had we had any grasp of any reality, I would never have lied so badly in the affair of the man on the bus. Every day, after school, we took a big green bus into the centre of Midhurst and then waited, opposite a handy sweet shop, for the coach that took us the few miles up the hill to the sanatorium.

Sometimes we bought sweets at the sweet shop while waiting for the second stage. But on this particular day I had half a crown. It was a huge sum of money – twelve and half pence, in decimal currency.

So we bought stuff. Half-penny chews were big, but penny chews were enormous blocks of ridged edible plastic. There were probably sherbet dips, a yellow paper-wrapped drum of sherbet with a stick of liquorice that you dipped in the stuff and licked. Gobstoppers changed colour as you sucked them, and had to be taken out all wet and sticky to look, until you finally got the aniseed taste when you crunched up the little bit right in the middle. We bought all these and crossed the road to the bus stop with full blazer pockets.

While we were waiting my father rolled up in the car.

This was highly unusual. He must have had an afternoon off or gone to visit some patient in another hospital. He was very pleased to see us, as fathers always are when they are doing nothing and can drive their children with no trouble to themselves. We all jumped into the back of the car, where my brother and sister blithely carried on munching and chewing.

'What have you got there?'

'CHEW, SUCK, ummm . . . sweets! CHEW, STUFF, RUSTLE.'

My father tried to glance back over his shoulder. Fathers, especially fathers of a medical persuasion, have a low opinion of sweets and generally make comments about fillings, and making sure that you clean your teeth, except, of course, when they are eating them themselves and handing them round, which anyway they only do as an afterthought.

I had already tried to stuff my sweets out of sight.

'Ha ha. So where did the money come for all these sweets, then?'

There were more chomping and thwacking sounds from my brother as he tried to loosen his overladen mouthful of goo, but my sister managed to find enough of a gap in her maw to articulate her innocent evidence.

'CHEW, SCRUNCH, CHOMP . . . Griff had . . . CHEW, SWALLOW . . . half a crown.'

Even though I had no idea what to call it then, I could feel the nemesis approaching.

'Half a crown? Where did that come from?'

The answer was simple. It came from Charles Hume's money box. We had been playing up in his well-appointed bedroom filled with envy-inducing toys and he had shown me his frog, which had a slot in the top and a screw plug in the bottom and was full of half crowns. When he took them out they fell on the shelf. He had piled them up in at least three towers. Then his mother had called him downstairs and I had simply, in a dreadful impulse, taken one of them and put it in my pocket.

I felt it unwise to tell my father this. Despite all his frequent protestations that it was always better to tell the truth, and that no harm could come to you if you did, I sort of knew that this was utter hogwash. I had stolen the money.

Charles was most unlikely to raise the alarm. He had no idea how many half crowns he had. Charles was a Fotherington-Thomas sort of playmate who rocked back and forth humming at his desk in school. He clearly had no idea what he was worth. If it had been me I would have counted my half crowns every day and calculated what exact proportion of a super-death-ray-blaster I could afford. But Charles seemed manifestly otherworldly, hardly a fit custodian of a frog full of dosh, so I had taken one of the half crowns. The opportunity had come to me on the crest of a rip curl of envy. No little demon had appeared in a puff of smoke at my left shoulder. I had simply taken it, very swiftly and almost without thinking. But the half crown almost instantly became a liability: a massive, unheralded amount of money. Buying sweets for everybody, including my older brother, was far from being an act of generosity. It was an attempt to dispose of the incriminating evidence as quickly as possible and, woe, oh fatal happenstance, my father had borne down upon me in the bottle-green Morris Traveller, just when I least expected him.

So, anyway, I lied.

'It was given to me,' I said.

'Given to you?' Something in his tone gave me the impression that he was not going to let it go at that.

'Yes.'

'Who gave it you?'

I was wildly groping now. 'A man on the bus.'

There was a silence. Clearly he was next going to ask me 'What man on a bus?' But he didn't seem to ask it immediately, as you would, which was a relief, because I couldn't think of any man who might have wanted to give me half a crown, but it was disconcerting that he seemed to want to chew over this information for at least a quarter of a mile, and a noisy gear-change.

'What did he look like, this man on the bus?'

And this was where my powers of invention took flight. I gripped the loose leather loop which was used to pull the door of the Morris shut and glanced at my brother, who was still chewing. 'He had a bowler hat on,' I piped.

People did wear bowler hats in those days, although I am not sure that at the age of five I had met many guardsmen or city workers, but it must have seemed a handy flag of identification. Instead of reassuring the pater, or even prompting a snort of derision at the very idea that a bowler-hatted man would dispense valuable coins on public transport, as one might have expected, my father fell to brooding. A worried frown appeared on his face. He became oddly solicitous. 'What sort of man? Did he ask you to do anything in return?' This struck me immediately as some sort of cunning ploy. But there was no indication of any guile. Guile did not anyway come naturally to my father. He was generally a book in which emotions were printed in big print and underlined to assist the partially sighted. 'No,' I answered firmly and when we got home I was sent away to my room, to await further developments.

My father summoned a policeman from Midhurst. Ordinarily, I might have been rather fascinated to meet a real detective face to face, but it was clear, even to this embryo criminal mastermind, that this was all getting a little out of hand. I heard of boys whose fathers threatened to take them to the police-station to see justice done, but we knew this was transparent hyperbole, a hollow threat uttered by an

exhausted garrison which had long ago used up all its ammunition. This night was different. It had grown dark, and, as
ever when serious matters are under consideration, nobody
seemed to have bothered to switch on the lights in the hallway. Supper had been hurried and eaten in silence. My
brother and I were waiting in our room at the top of the
stairs. We were summoned one after the other. I went second.

This was all far beyond expectations. The policeman was
not wearing a uniform, but a double-breasted suit. He was
really quite stout and flush-faced and he had a lot more
grease in his hair than the other adult males who usually
visited the house. Clearly, I was about to become unstuck.
All the elements that had been carefully prepared to put me
at my ease, to ensure that I felt secure enough to tell these
slightly smelly men – tobacco and wet serge – who were
now leaning down to my level and thus breathing on me a
little heavily, had the effect of scaring me rigid. Tears were
already starting in my eyes; which only seemed to make my
father even more concerned. The policeman gently asked me
a series of probing questions, and I stuck to my story. The
bowler hat was mentioned again and was joined, I think, by
a mackintosh. After a short while he paused, and I was asked
to leave the room.

When I had gone, he briskly told my father, 'I am sorry
to have to tell you, Doctor, I don't think your son is telling
the truth.' It was, for some unaccountable reason, a bit of a
shock, accompanied by exquisite pangs of embarrassment,
that the policeman had come all the way from Midhurst in
order to come to this elementary conclusion.

In fact, listening from the room at the top of the stairs, I
rather wished that the policeman wasn't quite so easy-going
about it: 'No, no, Dr Rhys Jones, it was quite right of you
to call me out . . . I was more than happy to drive out here

. . . that's very kind of you, but I am on duty.' The door banged shut. The front door knocker rattled as usual. There was a significant pause as my father lingered by the door. It was _The Winslow Boy_ in reverse. He was thinking up a cruel and unusual punishment, and who could blame him?

If the family had stayed in Midhurst would we gradually have fitted in more? Would I have felt less like an outsider, less willing all my life to be a voyeur, looking in on the lighted window across the square, or the gravel drive, and the Georgian house glowing in the sun, or the clink of glasses and the bray of public-school certainties? After all, in the local kindergarten one of my classmates was Lucy Cowdray. Her father, Lord Cowdray, came and stood with a red face and flat cap at the sports days watching us do somersaults. Jimmy Summers, my best friend, had a maid who wore a uniform. Their house was huge. When we played at Jimmy Summers' house he could reach into a toy chest and pull out a set of lead toy boats which, astonishingly, included scale models of every ship that took part in the battle of Jutland – Germans too. It took us hours to lay them out across his vast playroom floor. It must have come from some family connection. The sort we lacked. There were fancy dress competitions at the local church fête where I was dressed as a Mexican with a burned cork moustache, but they were always won by some damned people who had the same elaborate costumes every year and fooled the visiting judges. I sang the treble opening to 'Once in Royal David's City' at the local carol service. 'Jab' and the Benicky boys and the general Tory heartland benevolence of this pre-war English Eden easily sucked my mother in. She loved the social whirl. Who knows, it might have even broken down my father's natural defences. I would have gone to a public school, like my boyhood friends. We would have had chintzy furniture, and my father would have had to learn to like cocktail parties.

But when I was seven, my father started looking for another job. In some shadow world, down at the hospital, there was another, rather different father, the dedicated, stern and diligent chest physician who had toiled, between wood-work projects, to get more qualifications and who was now expecting promotion but not getting it, in the cloistered and class-ridden atmosphere of what was after all an ex-RAF hospital. It was time for him to move on. My mother's friends could hardly believe it. It was not just the idea of promotion, throwing up the world of the sanatorium and the close-knit society to which they were all so firmly attached. It was the location. 'How will you cope, Gwynneth? It will be too awful.'

We were moving to Essex.

4. Swimming in Essex

The M25/M11 intersection, a colossal masterpiece of road engineering visible from Mars, lies slumped in the bottom of the valley of Epping Green. Wendy Davies' architect father had a house there, where I first listened agog in the semi-darkness to Leonard Cohen. I'd be lucky to hear him now. The traffic whistles in all directions at once, but the nearby hill is still topped by a castellated beacon: Epping's water tower.

I see this turret of my old home virtually every weekend, but I never ever venture off to look at where I lived for fourteen years. When I did, I didn't know how. 'You presumably have to come off the M11 early,' I explained to my wife, Jo, who was driving. The map-book was under the dog, and the dog was asleep. 'You'll have to come off where it says Loughton.'

'If you want to come off for Epping,' chimed in my mother from the front seat, 'you'll have to come off for Loughton.'

My mother is a little deaf. The noise of the car made it more difficult for her. She obviously heard things, but confused them with instructions from her subconscious.

'It's just up here, the next exit.'

'It will be the next exit, I should think,' said my mother.

There was nothing familiar at all about Loughton in the damp autumn of 2004. Like planned post-war housing estates everywhere, it managed to look utterly haphazard. We could have been in Bremen or the outskirts of Leeds.

'Just head north,' I said, following my nose, and we did,

until the blank international rubbish suddenly gave way to more familiar, mock-Tudor rubbish. We were in the outskirts of Theydon Bois and beyond that was the soggy fuzz of Epping Forest, my playground around the age of ten. It is peculiarly watery. These days, the once private, once enormous, royal deer shoot is little more than a thick beard of trees on either side of a high road on a crest of hills, but there are bits of bog everywhere. If you walk it, you'll plunge into a chocolate, composty gloop soon enough. I certainly did. I fell through the ice when I was nine. A little unhelpfully, the other kids with me stripped me off and tried to warm me up in front of a fire made from my sketchbook. It is quite easy to spot the fishing lakes and their sandy parking areas, but less so the spiky-headed needles that mark patches of marsh. Why it doesn't all slide off down the side of the hill and swamp Waltham Abbey I have no idea.

We were climbing up to and into it. In a few moments, after we had missed our turning, we would go down and out of it.

We sluiced up to a roundabout. 'Which way now?' called Jo, and though I recognized the roundabout (revered the roundabout, indeed, as one of the key roundabouts of my youth), it was familiar like a dream. But perhaps any roundabout in the middle of a wood, with trees all around, would have been familiar in the same way.

As a family, we dropped parties along the road to Epping. My brother William stayed in the Midhurst grammar school where H. G. Wells once taught. My sister, metaphorically, stayed behind there in the comprehensive school. Harlow was a new town and a new experience for us pampered southerners. 'We're not going to live here! *It's not even detached*,' I said as soon as I saw the terraced house my father had been allocated, until he got himself settled in nearby Epping.

School in Harlow wasn't much solace to the young master. In Conifers I had been one of fifty or so. In 'The Downs' there were many hundreds. Did I make friends? Was I bullied for speaking posh like a twat? Probably. Most of my memories of the six months we lived there are of being alone, playing self-absorbed fantasies out amongst the big beds of spiky plants on the windy pavements between the huge recreation grounds.

For some weeks I became a detective, with a toy spy kit. I had an FBI pass in a plastic wallet and a fingerprint kit made out of drinking chocolate. I wandered the streets in a mac with a tightly drawn belt, 'spying' on people. I was occupying myself with myself, while my parents searched around for a house to match my father's new status as a consultant to three hospitals.

One of his hospitals was in Harlow, where we had been provided with our temporary residence, one in Waltham Abbey, fifteen miles to the south on the other side of a spur of Epping Forest, and between them was St Margaret's in Epping, where it was almost inevitable that we should settle, on the right side of the main road, just up from the underground station, in White Lodge, Hartland Road.

We went round the roundabout twice.

'I can't remember where it is,' my mother chimed in.

'No, I've just said that.'

'But if we go straight on we'll probably find it.'

'I just said that too. This will take us down to Waltham Abbey.'

'This will take us down to Waltham Abbey. They've demolished the hospital now. Daddy once decided he would cycle here. He only did it once, though.'

I remembered Waltham Abbey, because we always went to the cottage hospital on Christmas morning. As soon as we'd opened our presents we'd be bundled into the car and taken on a little tour of my father's wards. Sister (the unmarried one) had marooned herself in her staff room, almost hidden behind a colossal display of sweet sherry, peach brandy and ginger wine. She and an unshaven priest with a red face would be steadily knocking back this Christmas largesse, from grateful relatives, in a stifling, over-heated atmosphere, waiting for soggy turkey. They relished the opportunity to force a couple of mince pies and some warm lemonade on to us. And then my father would go and wish his charges 'Happy Christmas' and have a little chat with the poor old ladies with no one to take them in. (The ideal was to send the walking back to their fami-lies for the festive season.) We didn't want to go. The hospital was smelly. We had a new Slinky, or the Dan Dare Helicopter Gun that launched red plastic spinners up on to the top of the wardrobe waiting back at home, and we'd hardly played with them at all yet.

The sister would want to hug us too tightly and slobber over us too wetly. And the poor patients were yellow. After I'd been held up to give one of the old crones a kiss, I remember my father walking away down the nearly empty ward and quietly saying in a matter-of-fact tone to my mother, 'She'll be dead by New Year's Eve.' But, you see, he was a good man, who did good, by performing his duty. We would go straight on to St Margaret's – bigger and noisier – and do it all again.

He took us, I think, because we were life. His medical work was mostly with the chronically ill, wheezing their way towards death. There were few glamorous cures. But I have met a surprising number of them. In unexpected places people seek me out, and sometimes I make the mistake of thinking they want my autograph, but they want to tell me about my father, and his care for them. Chronic illness and private practice don't match. He was a National Health doctor all his life and watched the erosion of the discipline of doctor-led medicine with despair. When he retired he solemnly made us promise that, if he were to fall ill, we wouldn't take him to his own hospital.

Personally I only rode as far as the roundabout. It was definitely part of the cycling years for me. What age was that? I had a yellow bike, and later a blue one, with drop handlebars with special pale blue racing tape wound around, like a plastic bandage, for extra grip. I bought a water bottle carrier to attach between my legs and a very beautiful square chromium-plated bolt-on mirror.

There was one long, five-in-the-morning trip down to a pond somewhere near Woodford, to go fishing. (Why? I never fished.) Even at that time in the morning, the lorries thundered out of the night in an intimate rush: one tiny wobble, lose your nerve and . . . kerrang. It was downhill the entire way, all thirteen miles on a slight disabled-ramp of an incline. Too scary for my dad, I suspect.

But more usually we cycled off to High Beach.

'Is it because of the beech trees?' Jo asked.

'Yes,' said my mother. 'Though I've never been there.'

'You have been there.'

'Have I?'

'Yes.'

'I don't remember it.'

'And I think it's spelled the other way – "High Beach" – because of the gravel or something.'

We came to a sign, and it said 'High Beach'.

High Beach was a Victorian place of resort with a huge pub and a stretch of open heathland dropping away to the Lee valley below. John Clare was thrown in a loony bin here.

Tennyson had lived near by. John Betjeman's father used to take his work's outings here.

'That pop star lives down here now.'

'Rod Stewart.'

'He lives somewhere here.'

The surrounding villages of the Forest had the ancient rights to farm the wood, but strict enjoinders to leave the deer alone. So the beech nuts were collected for pigs and the trees were coppiced for firewood. The trees today owe their magnificent squiggliness to all this. Then Queen Victoria gave the whole thing to the Corporation of London, and it became where East Enders went for a day out.

'When Aunty Betty heard we were moving to Epping she was horrified,' my mother told us. 'She said, "You're going to the place where the murderers bury their bodies."'

'We used to come here in the summer to swim in the huge pool behind the pub.'

There were steps up and the remains of buildings. I clambered on and looked through the close-boarded fence. I was looking at another pool from my childhood. It was still there. I didn't recognize it at all. Surely it had been much bigger.

'It's bound to look smaller,' said Jo.

'I know that.' But there had been huge diving boards, the biggest in the region. I remember finally plucking up the courage to go up to the top board, which meant a very narrow and slippery ladder, and, once I got up there, it was much higher than I'd ever been before. Higher than Loughton and Harlow, and they had proper boards for show-off twisty divers in Olympic-sized pools. I stood shivering, clutching the metal side rails for several minutes, before I decided that I couldn't do it and ignominiously had to climb down. But the pond I could see through the crack couldn't have sustained such a death jump. And there had been changing rooms too. Where were they?

Londoners don't come to drink at High Beach much any more. The breathalyser has killed the trade. In the woods, the litter stopped a few feet from the road. It was probably quite a good place to bring the bodies now. We drove on.

'Your father proposed to me on the Isle of Wight.'

This was all new. 'What were you doing there?'

'There was a special hotel for nurses. He was studying for his Membership, and I was going away, just for a short holiday, and he came running down the platform and shouted, "Get a hotel room for me."'

Yes, that sounded both romantically delightful and presciently typical.

'Why couldn't he book it himself?'

'He was very busy. He didn't want to come away at all. They had dragged them off just after qualification, for the War. He always said that when he came back it was as if they had to start all over again. He didn't feel that we could get married until he had his Membership.'

'Of the Royal College of Physicians.'

'He was made a Fellow, you know.'

'Yes, I know.' But she was just going over his achievements, in his honour, paying him his due, as she always did.

Until later that morning, when I stood on the corner of the crossroads where Hartland Road was bisected by Kendal Avenue, plunging away down a hill fringed with red-brick walls and dripping evergreenery, I had never really been aware of how comfortingly suburban our house was. I decided I would quite like to live in one of these dignified Edwardian mansions now: not the new ranchero-style maisonettes, with their steep drives, fake clapboard and hump-backed minia-ture lawns squeezed into the former gardens of the grander homes, but in one of the grander homes themselves, of course. Suitable for middle age, security and routine, I suppose that was why my father liked it. Naturally, I found it suffocating at the time.

'He was a retired dentist,' my mother was telling Jo about the neighbour. She was as interested to see the road as I was but a good deal less showily sentimental. 'He kept a gun by his bed.'

'Did he?' I asked.

'He had a very large collection of valuable snuff boxes. He said he'd shoot anybody who tried to get in. But he wasn't a nice man. He was always complaining about the dog. He would send letters claiming that the dog was encouraging other dogs to come into his garden.'

The dog, like most dogs do, entered the family under false pretences, obtaining a fake visa as my sister's pet. She chose him because he was the shaggiest of a litter of Norwich Terriers. For a century, Norwich Terriers had been bred to be bright, attentive little short-haired frisky yappy things, but then something went wrong and this throw-back, flop-eared genetic mutation popped out. He looked like a two-inches-off-the-ground walking draught excluder, a type favoured by Victorian sentiment, which naturally found an echo with my eight-year-old sister. She had to have him. She called him Harold. For a week she shuddered in ecstasy over Harold the miniature Aberdeen Angus and then never paid him the slightest attention again. So my father fell besottedly in love with him instead.

Never very profligate in the hugging and kissing department, Elwyn lavished every emotional excess he could muster on the dog. They had much in common: vile tempers if rudely awakened from a day-time nap, unquenchable appetites and severe territorial obsessionalism (to get the dog or my father out of 'their' chair required daring and cunning). And they both disliked the cat too. My father allowed Harold to kiss him, sleep in his bed and use him as a mattress. In return, he accompanied the dog to the end of Hartland Road for its comprehensive investigation of every kerb, stick, lamp post and bush in the street. Hours could be spent in mutual love-ins. The dog took precedence over everyone. Towards the end of my father's life Harold was replaced by Judy, a Jack Russell, which snapped at my babies. My father seriously suggested that the children should be locked away upstairs to avoid annoying the dog. I have, incidentally, grown to have exactly the same relationship with my Labrador, 'Cadbury' (chosen and named by a twelve-year-old).

Across the bottom of what was a steep hill for supposedly flat, uninteresting Essex, but a thrilling one to freewheel a bike down, I could see directly out on to open, arsenic-yellow countryside and a row of massive pylons. The suburb was skin deep. Out the back, behind Mikey Everard's house, there had been the fields and copses where we played kick the can.

Today, the front of the house in Epping looks stark. It has two bays with Tudorbethan timber-framed gables and is painted grey, despite the name 'White Lodge' that shines out on a brass lettered plaque in the porch looking suspiciously like my father's handiwork. There is a small ledge above the door.

I had climbed up on it once when I came home un-expectedly after some sort of Footlights summer tour and found the place locked up. I had been able to see a light on in my grandmother's room and, indeed, her shadow playing on the net curtains, but no matter how much I hammered on the front door or stood in the front garden and bellowed at the window I couldn't penetrate her deafness. So, mad with frustration, I had finally clambered up the front of the house and knocked on the bay window.

'You shouldn't have done that!' My father was aghast. 'You might have given her a heart attack.'

She didn't see me. I was standing on the top of the front door, six inches from her face, yelling at her. She looked out into the darkness and addressed me throughout as if I was a hundred yards across the street. 'Who is it?'

'Granny, it's me. Griff!'

'Griff's not here!'

'No. IT'S ME. I AM GRIFF!'

'Griff?'

'Yes. Let me in. I've forgotten my keys.'

'Why don't you come in?'

My mother was away up the hill towards the town, not particularly bothered to explore the house we lived in for twenty years.

She only really paused when we got round the back, by the alleyway that led out into the high street. She pointed out the pair of houses. 'We sold the land,' she told Jo, 'to pay for the repairs to the house because the man who owned it previously had started stripping the place, taking out the fireplaces . . . there was a huge hole in the roof when we arrived.'

The hole, I remember, was magnificent – quite frightening even – with jagged edges, in a sloping bit of ceiling just at the top of the first landing on the stairs. My brother and I liked it. It made the place look like a ghost house from a film, or *The Munsters*. Almost the first thing we did, when our cast-iron bedsteads were put up on the bare floorboards in our room, side by side against a rough, unpainted grey plaster wall, was carve 'home sweet home' with a pair of dividers in what we thought was a good approximation of prisoner's graffiti. My father exploded, in a good approximation of a chief warder's fury.

White Lodge changed over our years of occupation, but in what order I can hardly recall. The hole must have been patched up pretty quickly. The rudimentary servant's quarters with big glass-fronted butler's cupboards, which had to be shown to visitors, were opened out into a modern kitchen with a bar thing cutting it in half where a wall had once been. My mother and father applied themselves to fitting out their new sixties home with William Morris wallpaper upstairs (rather appropriate since Morris' workshops were just down the road in Walthamstow) and bold Sanderson fruity stuff in the dining room.

I rather enjoyed the element of surprise involved in this. We never seemed to have the money to do the things that other families did. We never went abroad for our holidays. Suburban Epping utterly closed in around us. But I was quite excited once to discover two brand new step ladders, standing in the garage. What big things to buy without telling us. The lack of conspicuous consumption in those years seems surprising now. My parents were part of a generation still reeling from the War. We lived in a perfectly adequate manner but frugally. And we were the posh ones as far as our mates were concerned – in the big house.

With a new boat in a muddy creek, my father seemed to have exactly what he wanted: his house to fiddle with, his hobby and a strict routine of work. He took up brick-laying and walled in a section of rose beds behind the kitchen. A gardener called Lofty came, and went, after he propositioned my mother. The sofas were covered in dark-blue squeaky fake leather. A big brick double garage was built next to the house. Daddy erected shelving in the living room. He built a puppet theatre. He bought a Cortina. Granny and Grandpa came to live.

This must have been a stop on my father's independence,

though he never openly complained. Grandpa didn't last long. But Granny hung on in. She moved into that room upstairs when she was in her early sixties and died at the age of ninety-eight, three houses later. 'I think he just expected them to stay for a short while,' my mother said ruefully. 'I don't suppose he imagined she would outlast him.'

My mother's sense of post-partem proprietorialism even extended to houses built by a speculative builder on land she had sold forty years ago. 'Well, they seem to have let that house fall into a state.'

And it was in a state, with a shopping trolley bunged up against the side wall. I was prepared for change. How could I not be? It was effectively thirty years since I had been in Epping – at least ten since I had last had any reason to go there.

The alleyway was still functioning. A billboard advertised 'Holistic Massage' on Wednesday, 'Thought Field Therapy' on Thursday and 'Spiritual Healing, Shiatsu and Reiki Teaching'. When I was last there, every other shop in the high street sold shoes. Nowadays the holistic clinic was joined by two acupuncture centres, a Chinese herbalist and 'Positively Healthy, the healthy living shop' (in our old doctor's surgery). Nobody came into town for white stilettos any more. They came to get their auras read.

'It's all restaurants now,' said the man in the 'Oriental Rug Shop'. It was all oriental rug shops too. But 'Coles the Tailors' was still flogging what looked suspiciously like the same stock, beneath its familiar sign (a man in inflated breeches wielding shears) and 'Batchelors', the smelly riding tackle shop, was still there. 'Church's the Butchers', where, if stuck, you could almost guarantee to find your mother ordering pork pies, was there too.

I stood transfixed at the corner of the high street. They

had moved the zebra crossing twenty yards, but . . . 'Look, look,' I squeaked. Sitting where I had sat, over forty years ago, was a row of little boys waiting for the same Saturday-morning shearing in the same barber's shop. 'Just a little off the sides and back, please.' They certainly didn't listen then. Whatever you asked for, they scraped you down to the bone. Did they still get the long strands of cotton wool out of those chrome dispensers poked down behind the collar? Did they use those puffers that finished the job with a squirt of talcum powder? Were these kids going to glower at their own fat faces emerging from shaggy disguise, beg not to have any Brylcreem and rail at their mothers for sending them there?

To escape the depredations of the Demon Barber we had moved to 'Nigel's'. He was my mother's hairdresser. My father refused to be seen going to a women's salon, so Nigel started coming to the house for private sessions. He ended up cutting all the local doctors and the vicar too.

'You probably won't remember me . . .' she began.

'Gwynneth, you haven't changed a bit!' Nigel himself, older and stouter, his business thriving, was misty-eyed for the old days when Epping's entire medical community had sat in my mother's kitchen waiting for their trim.

'I used to get through a whole bottle of gin in an evening,' chortled my mother.

Across the road I had worked the pumps one Christmas, falling for the old 'check the radiator' gag in Volkswagens and waving goodbye to customers with their petrol cap still in my hand. Shell had gone. A car showroom occupied the forecourt. But the Methodist church, the big plane trees and the picket fences were still in place.

On my first day in St John's Primary, standing in assembly in that huge hall with the high windows and the gloss baby-blue wall paint, amongst another six hundred strangers,

I had suddenly felt hopelessly lost. After moving from Harlow to a second school in the space of one year, and, at the age of eight, when I should have known better, I wept publicly and humiliatingly.

I was over it by lunchtime. I was perfectly happy at an ordinary school, where you were safe enough as long as you kept out of the way of the nutters. We had a lavatory block that you avoided. It was better to do it in your pants than have to use the oozing facilities, with the unlockable doors, crashable by prowling junior sadists. We had the boy in class who got increasingly covered in scabs and got to smell so bad that the teachers had to step in. We had the church hall on the other side of the road, round the back of which certain of the more bossy girls would organize 'you show me yours if I show you mine' assignations. There were monumental playground games of British Bulldog. We collected Civil War bubble-gum cards, with 'death on the stakes' a prized rarity.

Whatever time was left over from school was occupied in the pursuit of war. Obviously I had a massive collection of armaments which included, after much badgering, the black plastic Armalite rifle from Woolworth's with real clip-on, knife-shaped bayonet in slightly bendy grey plastic. (It effectively out-gunned any silvery Colt cowboy gun in Epping because of its up-to-date murderous reality.) Although I was rather fond of a fine matching pair of matt-black long-barrelled six-shooters, now I come to think of it.

I also had a massive army. At some time in the late sixties Airfix hit on the spectacular wheeze of the 'little men'. They came in boxes with a Cellophane window: nicely detailed half-inch-high personnel pegged to plastic trees. They were cheap. A two-and-six pack provided two dozen soldiers. To begin with we got the British army in khaki, the German army in a bluey-grey and the Afrika Korps in a sandy yellow and ended up with thousands of them. We tipped the lot out on to the bedroom floor, grabbed a blanket which could be roughed up a bit to make a convincing landscape and spent whole days plonking them down in mammoth conflicts. Our main pleasure was lying with our faces pressed close to the carpet, closing one eye and going 'Peyooow!', 'Pooorgh' and 'Acka, acka, acka' while visualizing extremities of carnage.

Mostly, these were years of routine. Out of the house, around the back, through the covered alley, past the newspaper and sweet shop, down to the pedestrian crossing (manned by the old bat who got in the papers because she was a devout Catholic and objected when her hand-held traffic sign was abbreviated from 'Stop children crossing' to 'Stop children') past the church and down the road to the school. To begin with we even came home for lunch. It was a Church of England primary school, which owed much to the folk-myths of the pre-war education acts: pageants, country-dancing, queues, reciting, rote and willingness.

Empty on this wet Saturday in November, the school was astoundingly familiar. We walked straight in. The main entrance door was painted the same eau de nil colour. There was a big new block where the prefab infants' school had been. Everything else was unaltered. The red bricks were spalling in just the same way, the high building labelled 'Cookery School 1915' was still the art room. I could see the paint brushes stacked against the window.

'Come around here.' I led Jo on. 'Look at the back playground.' There it was too, bounded by high walls, unremittingly tarmacadammed like a prison yard, exactly as it had been forty years ago. It lacked children, but somehow that made it like a visit to the silent past; as if some bell had just summoned everybody away.

There was only one major change. Above the playground was a close-boarded fence. I clambered up. It was slippery and raining. I was peering at yet another abandoned swimming pool. There were tall weeds growing through the concrete tiles on the other side of the empty bath. The paint was flaking. This wasn't winter storage. It was finished. And we had built the place ourselves. I remembered the fundraising drive. We had sold apples from our back garden in the corridor during the lunch break for two pence – 'tuppence' in fact.

The highlight of the summer had been the races, won by the fat bloke with astonishing water-borne agility, who flung himself in, emptied half the contents and darted through the remainder like a walrus. But we were always standing by the poolside. It was always swimming. There had been swimming back in Midhurst, where I learned: getting one foot off the floor as I slipped towards the deep end of the little hospital pool (closed this year for health and safety reasons).

In his book *Waterlog*, Roger Deakin charts the decline of the swimming pool. The health and safety lobby have successfully closed all the plunge holes and untended pools across Britain. Roger defiantly swam across the country, jumping into locks, closed lidos, canals and quarries on the way. I went with him for a reedy dip in the Waveney. But I wonder whether the lust for it has gone too.

I walked back to St John's church, where I'd left my mother. When I was nine she had fancied that I ought to be able to sing because I was Welsh and sent me off to join the choir. There was practice in the cold church on a Friday night, and I was expected to attend at least one service a week, preferably two, under the tutelage of a particularly twitchy, greasy vicar with a taste for High Church parade.

Was it the hours I spent listening to his ponderous biblical readings that turned me into a life-long opponent of organized religion, or was it the boy führer of the choir, who jumped me during some spat, pinioned me across the shoulders with his knees and dug his extended middle knuckle into my temple screaming, 'Repent, repent'? Either way, the place had seemed horrible, the ruffs and cassocks uncomfortable, the services interminable. Even the extra two bob that could be earned on a Saturday morning for turning out at a wedding never made the thing worthwhile. And now I thought the church was quaint with a beautiful pale-blue coffered ceiling and an estimable rood screen. The Harlow Choir were rehearsing. They were enchanting.

When I took the bus a few weeks later, back to Harlow itself, it ground through the back ways, as buses always do, skipping the obvious express route to the centre (raffishly called 'Second Avenue') and took me on a tour of the new town and its world-beating collection of mini-roundabouts. I looked at it anew. Harlow wasn't a brave new world after all. It was a brave new Hampstead Garden Suburb. Many of the houses had pitched roofs and tile-hung fronts. The blocks of flats were neat and unthreatening. There were dozens of recreation fields and hundreds of rhomboid green corners, seemingly designed as targets for used plastic Coke bottles and cans.

In the seat opposite sat a girl wearing pink stiletto boots. She had bright white trousers held up by a pink belt, with a shiny pink anorak trimmed in fur and a pink baseball cap. I wanted to capture this genuine Essex Girl's overheard conversation, just like Alan Bennett, except that he must have sharper ears or quieter buses. As I spied on her, she met a surprising number of former school friends. They were on their way to Harlow too, for a bit of mid-afternoon action.

It had been the same for us. London had been an hour away; a giant step.

In the centre of Harlow the original spare, tinky-tonk ethos has not aged well. All the geometric details – the concrete octagon half-roofs, the shell designs, the raised walkways and the sweeping underpasses – only work if kept spanking new. We have more affection for the fantasies of Gerry Anderson and Ken Adams, the designer of James Bond, than we do for the concrete realities of Basil Spence. Yet Lady Penelope could have married the Saint in Harlow church with its bathroom glass windows and copper-coated needle spire.

The bus put me down in the usual place. It was the bus station! We ate Wagon Wheels outside this very newsagent, 'Newswell', chocolate-covered marshmallow biscuit sandwiches, waiting with sodden towels. And we flicked through Marvel and DC comics on the revolving wirework rack. Green Lantern and Captain America, Spiderman and even Superman were forbidden. My father disapproved. We never seemed to have the money to buy them anyway. We had subscriptions to improving comics like *Look and Learn* and *The Eagle*. American comics had to be taken furtively. Like the noisier, bigger toy guns 'that would only break', like ITV, like American series, like pointed shoes and long hair and foreign holidays, they were not for us. There was a line around our family taste that must have been placed there by osmosis, since my father never paid membership fees to any social group. But it was vaguely puritanical, vaguely in favour of British things and vaguely attached to good taste: 'nothing too garish'. In Harlow, however, there were no barriers. This was an East End overspill after all. Hereabouts, American would have been good. Bubble gum would have been very good. Colourful would have been extra good.

The crowds did not look very colourful today. Next to

his van in the market with a virtuoso vertical display of raw
meat, a butcher was spookily whispering into a powerful
speaker system. 'Good prices today, ladeeez.'

This was our nearest cinema. Sometimes we came into
this piazza and joined a queue stretching right the way around
three sides. Well, not that often, I suppose, but definitely for
Summer Holiday with Cliff Richard, and for most of the
Norman Wisdom films too.

A man stopped me in astonishment ('What are you doing
here?'), but he couldn't tell me whether the cinema I was
looking at was the original one. It felt wrong. There were
surely some new buildings.

'It's all change in Harlow. It changes every day. They're
taking the market out,' he told me.

I was surprised. It seemed the only life in the town.

In one of those corners had been the Chinese restaurant,
an utter foreign novelty when it arrived, but, unlike Marvel
comics, one which our family took up – because my father
loved the nursery, sup-sup food, I expect.

Perhaps it was after *The Wrong Arm of the Law* (Norman
played a would-be copper too short to get on the force) that
I shook the soy sauce over my helping of egg fried rice and
the top came off, drenching the plate in salty black liquid.
I can vividly recall my despair, and then my parents laughing it off and salvaging my meal, sharing everything out
again. Ironically, there seems to be no Chinese restaurant in
the centre of Harlow now. Now that they are everywhere.

But, standing facing the cinema, I knew that the swimming pool was somewhere near. I turned on my heels. It was
over there, wasn't it? I set off towards an underpass. Harlow
was supposed to be a bicycle city. But you couldn't make the
British into the Dutch. There was no danger walking along
the cycle lanes now because no one was riding a bicycle. The

cycle storage area, with a corrugated roof covering at least fifty cycle supports, was being used as a car park.

As I passed underneath a wing of flats, towards 'The Hides', I was feeling increasingly like some cat, dropped miles away from home, that manages, somehow, to find its way back unaided. I ignored the fact that I had not the faintest idea where I was going and allowed little subconscious clues to press me onwards. And then I stopped.

What was the emotion here? The French must have a word for it. It is not nostalgia. Synapses that had been dormant for decades were suddenly fizzing. Not for the little houses, with their new mock-Georgian doors, not for the street signs, though I certainly remembered 'The Dashes'. No, I stopped dead in the underpass itself because on either side there were large lumps of flint laid into render at the top of the wall, just some black pieces of irregularly shaped stone, and, like a face spotted in a crowd, I knew this place exactly. This dip under the flat bridge had had some huge significance to me as a nine-year-old. It must have done, because it affected me now so tangibly, like nothing else in Harlow.

I wanted my sister to be with me, to feel it too. I wanted her to rack her brain and put the connecting bits in place, as if, like that set of Christmas lights that used to infuriate my father with the conical screw-in bulbs we could replace the missing dead lamp and the whole chain would light up.

As soon as I walked on, all the electricity evaporated. The rest of the street meant nothing. And if I tell you that I didn't recognize a single bit of it, you'll have to agree that it was peculiar to turn left suddenly, as if on mere impulse, and find myself facing Harlow swimming pool.

It was the familiar, handsome facility built in 1961 and opened by Christopher Mayhew. The manager, Mr Fidget, had expected to be overwhelmed on that first day. He had organized a secret entrance so that 'local big-wigs' could come and have a look without having to queue. When he threw open the plate-glass doors it was to a single swimmer from Royston.

Business soon picked up. In order to get the same experience as that Royston swimmer (the huge thirty-three-metre length with its four-metre deep end, a shimmering, empty three-dimensional playground) we had had to come here very early. Sometimes we left our bikes out there in the asphalt car park at the bottom of the bank at seven-thirty in the morning and waited for the pool to open and to be first in.

If we were very lucky we had the place to ourselves. The white-trousered attendants marched across to take up their languid positions, over by the gigantic ceiling-height windows. We came through the footbath, always the first cold shock, dodging the showers and their fine spray, and took our time to pierce the surface and surrender to the glassy buoyancy.

More usually, we arrived when it was already full. We queued to get in. The changing rooms reeked of chlorine and thundered with noise. The pool was choked with bodies. The water was a continuous maelstrom, stinging the eyes with chemicals. Everybody swam in all directions at once. You had to twist to avoid collisions. And the great barn roof threw back a constant, never-lessening, hollow shriek of adolescent clamour.

It is a measure of its size that, whereas everything – forest trees, town centres, school halls, houses, streets and people – seemed smaller than I remembered, Harlow Pool still struck me as massive. I had taken a safety nappy pin with a key attached from the locker downstairs where I changed and felt rather foolish trying to poke the blunt needle through my shorts. Did they really mean me to make a hole? It seemed oddly dangerous. We had had rubber arm bands, in different colours. They were uncomfortable and rode up the arm when you dived.

And it was diving we came for; or jumping, mainly. We swam the odd width entirely underwater to show off. Sometimes we had races. Now and again we would splash furiously off in a burst of crawl like a boy-racer gunning the engine, but mostly we jumped, plunged and bombed. There was a long springboard to the left with an adjustable roller. Not too far back, or the whole plank became vibrantly alive and unpredictable, but just right, and it got you up and sailing through the air to crash into the water. You submerged in a rush of bubbles and then kicked out towards the edge. The trick was to swim underwater as close to the steps as possible so you could bound out and skip straight to the queue to do it again.

'No running!!'

It was at the next height that all the consequences became more serious. The second springboard was some twelve feet above the ground. We usually moved the roller as far forward as possible, to avoid any unnecessary wobble. Nobody wanted to hit the water in anything other than a planned way from up there. But the surge was better. The sudden sick feeling in the stomach as you went up was excellent and it was followed by a much more satisfying horrible drop and a thunderous immersion. The first time you did it, you wondered why you bothered with the lower board at all.

It was a big event to mount the final set of stairs and take on the highest platform. This was a wide, blank, oblong area. There was no spring at all. The whole surface was flat, the lip was wide and the back and sides were ringed with high railings. It was quite possible for five or six boys to gather up there. On a big day it was a club. Some just resting, enjoy-ing the view, leaning against the railings, getting their breath, waiting until the trunks began to get cold. Some were there hanging on for life, plucking up enough courage to venture forward and approach the brink. 'You'll love it when you've done it.' 'Don't look down.' 'Just jump.' But it was a long drop. The soaring, sinking, sick-making descent needed extra courage because we all knew what happened if you didn't get your feet in. You could kill yourself if you landed flat. In fact, somebody had. He had been very fat, hadn't he? He had fallen forward from the high board, missed his footing and landed flat, front-first on the water. His stomach had split apart from neck to groin and all his guts had spilled out and he had died. They had to drain the pool, apparently.

This sort of stuff excited the troops. Would it hurt the soles of the feet? What if I went down too far? Even when you had finally summoned the will, some stupid, slow-moving breast-stroker would drift across the pool. 'Go on! Go now. You'll miss her. Go to one side.'

'Don't push.'

I must have stood up there taking counsel and advice for ten minutes before I finally went off for the first time, in a sudden fit of bravado: still talking, without anybody having the chance to advise me, I stepped straight off the edge and fell . . . arrrgh: my internal organs apparently losing their adhesion to my lower abdomen.

I bobbed up quickly and swam frantically, over-energized, to the side and went straight back up. Apart from occasional rests, I unremittingly tossed myself off a high platform into the water for much of my adolescence. After about a week I joined the others, running as hard as we could from the very back and recklessly launching ourselves, sometimes in formation, out and down into the pool.

Today, the boards have gone. As I padded down the tiles and left my towel on the side, in that self-consciously naked state before the water covers you with a clothing of wet, it was the first thing I noticed. The second thing was that the pool was almost empty. There were some mothers and children in a new shallow pool at one end. That was different, too. It had been one long Olympic-sized facility, and now it was divided into two. Five people were splashing in the deep bit. There were several signs warning against any diving at all, and I sheepishly lowered myself into the water like a Continental invalid and swam to the other end.

Rebuilding the gantries in my imagination, I then crept around the marks in the tiles where the boards had been, then I swam my twenty lengths and got out. With the familiar blurred chlorine vision and red popping eyeballs, I walked over to the lifeguard, who seemed to be backing away – presumably from the nutcase who had been staring intently at the floor, muttering to himself, twenty minutes before.

He couldn't remember when the boards had all gone. 'Even the flumes were taken out about eight years ago.' He pointed through the far window, where several hundred feet of intestinal tubing were going green in the drizzle. I had seen them, but not realized that they were no longer attached to any water splash.

'There was a café up there.'

'I don't remember that.'

'And there were windows here.' I was only saying this for the sake of completeness. Shamefully, I was pulling old-hand rank.

'No, no, they've always been murals. I've seen the pictures.'

(Later, I saw the pictures too, downstairs in the lobby. He was quite right. They weren't windows, but they weren't badly executed murals of palm trees and lagoons either. They were plain, dignified slabs of tiles.) 'But it's quiet today,' I said, sidling after him.

'Well, it's Friday afternoon, and there aren't any schools in.'

'When I used to come here we all wore different-coloured rubber arm bands and they'd call your section out after an hour.'

'Yes.' He pointed up at a light and a phone arrangement. 'It's not been used for at least five years. We get a hundred and fifty on a busy Saturday, but that's about it.' He anticipated my next question, although he was still backing away. 'They get taught it at school, and the fitness centre has a better gym. They'll be closing this place soon.'

He didn't mean it rhetorically. They were closing the place. Harlow was moving on to a new leisure facility. This impressive, clean and modern amenity was as dead as Weston's sea pool, High Beach or my junior school swimming baths.

The lifeguard moved away to stand vacantly somewhere else.

But as I got my towel and went back to the footbath, he suddenly reappeared, as if he hadn't wanted to leave it at that. 'It will be one of those corrugated steel warehouse things,' he said. 'They'll never build a lovely pool hall like this again, even though they put it up the wrong way round.' He was momentarily passionate. 'Did you know it was supposed to have these windows facing down over the valley and they put it up back to front?'

But even back to front, it was a magnificent piece of sixties curvy-wurvy architecture. Presumably, it is best to get it pulled down now, fifty years after it was built, before it gets old and features on a television programme and the public clamours to save it and embarrasses the council.

Perhaps children do get swimming at school. Perhaps they

get all their thrills from computer games these days. Or is it just that they've taken all the jumping, running and diving excitement out of the place in the name of health and safety? With the money they save on the pool, they will pay for another couple of television adverts warning us all of the dangers of obesity.

5. What We Did on Our Holidays

We fussed about presents in our family. As a child I resented the palaver. Pocket money was two shillings a week, but we were expected to save it up and buy proper things for each other; not like my friend Fred down the bottom of the avenue who got away with a Crunchie Bar and a motto. It wasn't just the money, it was a reflection of our acquisitiveness. Autumn came and I felt permanently on my uppers. Mother in September, my brother in October, a respite for fireworks perhaps, but then the festive season gift budget imposed its demanding burden, and I never had anything spare for my poor, demanding self.

Elwyn was childish about it all. He would lobby for opening on Christmas Eve. He routinely bought presents for himself, wrapped them, with casual Sellotaping, exposing the underside of the paper and the inside of the gift, and stuck them under the Christmas tree labelled 'To Daddy from Father Christmas'. This ensured that he got the right drill or the correct shackle or the brass light fitting he craved.

My mother had to make do. Her 'big present', one year, was a paraffin heater for the boat. But she never complained. All the cupidity in my family was left to the boys. Aged nine or so, I bought her something that I thought was strikingly beautiful from a sweet shop. It was a single-stemmed, plastic yellow rose in a conical black metal holder with a wrought-iron bracket to fix it to the wall. And Mummy loved it. If she was only pretending to love it, then she didn't blink. She even had my father attach it to the wall in the dining room.

The only crack in the façade came when I went out and bought her an identical one a year later.

For her eightieth birthday I decided to get at the old films. I guessed they would be in a cardboard box above the garage, where I'd put the rest of the junk she gave me. When my father died in 1989 my mother had hung on in their house until my sister persuaded her it was too big and got her to move to a cottage near by. Then she started dumping things on us: wonky bits of navigation equipment, an old telescope and a slightly overbearing Welsh dresser, which the man in the antique shop in Woodbridge said had been made out of twentieth-century packing cases. Since she couldn't sell it, I had to 'inherit' it. But there were other boxes of stuff, like my father's squiggly cartoons: hundreds of the things. The subject matter was invariably some vaguely misogynist sailing incident, with my squiggly mother failing to pick up a buoy and my squiggly father making some comment in a squiggly speech balloon. Did he have fantasies of publication? In another box there was a detailed breakdown of the plots and casts of a long-cherished project: the sailing club sit-com. ('It's got all the characters, just like *Dad's Army*.') He had grown bored with his work. He told me so. His retirement was full of his self-absorbed private projects, but only for a year or two. He barely made seventy-two.

Birds had got up into the garage attic because it wasn't a closed room, just a large shelf open at the eaves to the roof, and there were trails of half-built martin's nests and a bundle of feathers and spatterings in the darker corner. Two other boxes had photographs and documents; ration books and swimming certificates. One held my mother's own clipping service, an incomplete and sometimes wholly unflattering selection of articles or reviews about 'the Suffolk comedian' (*East Anglian Daily Times*). A mouse had got in and had begun to make a nest out of them; geometrically cut as if by a miniature shredder. I saw no reason to prevent this creditable recycling. And finally I found the films: some small reels in original Kodak yellow boxes (the yellow of road warnings) and another, in a grey-and-black, specially purchased, plastic box. It must be the long version. My father had spent hours editing these things together.

I was once close to an old actor. He had been very successful, a leading player in American movies as well as British ones, with an astrakhan-collared coat and a fifties Rolls Royce in the garage. I was talking about old photos with his wife. She looked away. 'Oh no,' she said, 'we can't look at old photos . . . no . . . it's too upsetting.'

Upsetting? I changed the subject. Frightened of intimacy, I assumed something externally disturbing about them. I had read the biography. I had seen a picture of them in California by the pool: him, tanned and debonair and dashingly handsome, leaning into the camera with his arms around his boys and a confident smile on his face. Had there been a scandal, some deep rift that photographs would revive?

I have since sat with my own photograph album. I know what she meant. There is such a thing as too much lost fun. There are the children as they were. Me as I was too, but pretty much as I am now; fatter, thinner, different hair cut, dreadful clothes, mistaken moustache, but my daughter Catherine is minute, then cute, then at her most dependent, then funny, but always different. The images are of time irretrievably lost. That holiday in Maine, the working trip to Australia, the walk along that grey beach: George, my son, running on ahead with that stick. But look, his very dimensions mock you ('My, how you've grown'). When did this happen? All that time we were afloat on a river being rushed downstream and we never even noticed.

For the cost of a small cinema, I got my father's films transferred to DVD. I remember that we used to watch them now and again, as a family; the projector whirring with that soothing, repetitive chatter, perhaps at Christmases. But that was years ago. I could barely remember the content. Now it was almost too easy. I just had to stick the disc in the DVD player and press a button. However, it is not possible to look at home-made films without an element of bullying. I gathered up the children and their cousins, promising entertainment, as if the whole thing was for their benefit. 'You wait till you see this. This is your mother at your age.' They watched and they dutifully sniggered. But it was the adults who sat quietly and stared.

The film had a pale, washed look, with none of the sudden flares of high colour or pixellated fuzz that you get on video. Sometimes the print was crazed with black cobwebby lines. There was no sound. The figures rushed about as if hidden behind a glass wall.

The first reel showed a long, developing shot of Gorran Haven in Cornwall, then a street. First my brother and I appeared in matching red tartan trousers and red sweaters clutching buckets and spades. We jeered. Then my sister sat playing on the beach. We 'ahhed'. There was my mother in slacks, then in a big print dress, throwing a ball for the dog. 'I remember those red cushions,' said my sister, and we all remembered the cushions from the Morris Traveller.

'How many holidays did we have in Gorran Haven?' I asked.

'Only two,' my mother said briskly. 'Then he got a boat. We had two more holidays in "a sailing hotel" in Dartford where you fell out of a window and had your arm in a sling. And then we spent every single holiday sailing.'

The children were already bored. But we adults were

watching with cold attentive eyes, not recognizing ourselves: the pot-bellied infants with the flat hair and scrunched-up eyes in the flabby high-waisted swimming trunks. We were greedily searching for images that would connect us to the reality of our own memories: the harbour wall, the steps down from the house.

And there was my mother, in black slacks, with her long dark hair up in a bun, throwing a ball for Bella the dog, or lying against rocks on the beach with Aunty Gwen reading the papers. They looked a glamorous pair.

We were all watching for that sort of thing, really, waiting to get a hit of direct sensual memory, something that our children couldn't share at all. And then, towards the end of this short film, there was a fluttering of black, one of those moments where a white line passes shakily across a blank frame and some numbers flicker up and for five seconds my father passed through the film, in a grey suit with carefully brushed hair. His round face was serious. Some colleague had taken this, as an experiment to check how the camera worked. He was slightly off guard. I recognized the look. 'Be careful with that camera now. Are you sure you know how to use it?' And then he was gone.

We sat forward and stopped the DVD. We rewound and watched it again. We watched the tiny extract five or six times in a row. We froze it, paused it and stepped it forward. This was the only moment, fleetingly, when a real ghost stepped out of the past.

Why was *that* my father so particularly? There were plenty of other photographs, films and videos of him: in the next film, twenty years later, but looking ten years younger, with side-boards, longish hair and stubble, and that louche look that everybody, even Ted Heath, adopted in the seventies and now means the sort of bloke who moves his caravan into your garden. I have a later photo of him swimming across a pool in St Lucia in pursuit of a plastic duck, with his daddy swimming shorts and thin, not thinning, hair in a tuft, delicately paddling on, his legs splayed like a pale frog. This was soon after he had been diagnosed with cancer. But that earlier flickering serious man held us all, because it was my father with all his ambition and purposefulness still in him, caught inside the institution at the age of thirty-six.

We stayed glued for the second film. It was the *Xara* film. This was what we really did on our holidays. (There must be one missing still, the *Windsong* film, although both are remarkably similar: it's just the boats that differ.)

It started with the waterside: West Mersea, in this case, an island at the mouth of the Blackwater estuary. Here we were pulling the dinghy on a trailer. Here was the long jetty.

Then came a shot taken from the dinghy, a remarkably steady tracking shot, as the little tender, powered by a miniature Seagull engine, slipped through the other boats lucky enough to be moored closer to the shore.

'It was a long way,' my mother commented.

'We rowed it for years,' I added. The dinghy was a wooden 'pram' with a snubbed end. It manoeuvred beautifully. I loved the way it sat like a bowl on the water, and could be turned in a full circle directly on itself with a twist of the wrist, or sculled with one oar on the half-cup hole in the back, a skill I tried and finally mastered. Sometimes if we anchored I would just get in the boat and row around.

'And you know why I did that?' I said. 'Because I was bored. There was nothing else to do.'

'How long did we go for?' asked my sister wearily.

'Weeks.'

'Oh, he liked to spend at least half the summer on the boat,' my mother chiming in now, with that slight sing-song of complaint. 'He'd save up his leave, and take four weeks in one go every year.'

Now the film showed us leaving the harbour, threading through the other yachts to deeper water: the impossibly glamorous, much bigger, comfortable boats like the Twisters and Holmans. The camera lingered on them for far too long, in a fit of boat-envy. They were sleek racing vessels, owned by members of the club who somehow managed to keep a boat, a nice car *and* a sense of proportion about the activity.

'I used to beg him to let us take a proper holiday,' my mother said with a slightly wheezy chuckle. 'No, no, every year, without fail we had to get on that ruddy boat.'

Now we were charging along, up the coast, to Suffolk. The camera was bounding. There were shots of other boats, particularly admired older, wooden boats sailing near by. There were shots of the boat becalmed. The boat at anchor. The boat motoring. The boat sailing. The boat tied to a quay. The boat motoring. The boat with just one sail up. The boat with all its sails up.

'Who are they?' asked one of the children.

Another boat had passed into view with people on it. They were becalmed and were smiling and waving.

'No idea.'

'Didn't you know them?'

'It would have been most unlikely. Your grandfather's idea of a holiday was to get as far from the rest of humanity as possible up a dismal wet creek and sit there.'

'Making one of those disgusting meals: a tin of spaghetti, a tin of chopped up spam, and a tin of tomatoes, on the one burner.' He did love the rituals of all that. He loved the primus. You had to burn the blue meths to make the paraffin turn to gas. He liked oil lamps and trimming wicks.

In the film my sister emerged through a forward hatch and turned away from the camera. I pulled on some clothes and glowered.

'But it wasn't just the holidays. It was the weekends too.'

We sat there, mordantly remembering. It had been the boat every weekend, if he could manage it. In the winter we varnished it. That damn wooden pram dinghy with the stringers.

'Well of course, *Xara* was varnished,' said my mother. 'She was a lot of work.'

She was. On a varnished boat, every stained scratch shows through, every nail hole where the water has penetrated goes black if you don't maintain her carefully enough and probably even if you do. So *Xara* had to be rubbed down and recoated with varnish, as did the dinghy, and the oars and the mast, and the tiller handle and the rudder, and the top sides and the cleats (fiddly), and the grab rails, thwarts, coamings, doors and separate planks of her clinker-built hull, twice – two coats every year. 'So we went to West Mersea on cold days throughout the winter too and rubbed and sanded and scrubbed.'

'What we put up with,' said my sister feelingly.

In the summer, though, we made our own entertainments. If I was ever in West Mersea when the tide was in I don't remember it. The water was usually a hundred yards off, down a slimy jetty, wide enough to take a single trailered dinghy, and dipping slowly down to meet the creek at a six-foot-square platform of green planks.

Everybody swarmed over this to get into their tenders to take them out to their boats. And that was where we stationed ourselves to catch crabs.

First we got string. Then we searched amongst the stones at the top of the harbour beyond the dinghy park for an abandoned rusty bolt or a stone with a hole in it, big enough to sink. Then we got meat. Bacon was best because we could poke a hole though the fat and tie it on the string.

There wasn't much point in sticking to one line, because you had to let it sink and lie. So we had six or seven lines strategically dangled into the murk close to the posts where the crabs lived. A bucket, half full of water, was kept standing by, but it had to be moved out of the way of fat men in blazers complaining and slipping on the ooze, or pale-faced women fussing as their husband's outboard motors passed over our heads and tripping over us anyway as we lay flat out on the jetty.

The trick was to pull up slowly. With their one free claw waving about like maddened mini-pliers, we had to flick the crabs off the bacon and into the bucket. None of them were huge. They could be anything from three inches across down to house spider size and green (though the bigger ones sometimes had a tinge of red around the claws and were especially prized because they looked more like proper crabs from a fishmonger) but all of them could pinch hard. The tenacious ones could only be induced to let go by crab-wrangling – grasping with a thumb and forefinger just behind the big front claws, where the edges of the shell have armoured sharp points. If we missed and it fell on the jetty, the angered crab scurried off backwards with both pincers raised, and we had to show off to any girl spectators standing by and squealing with awe.

By half tide, six or seven kids with six or seven lines each, several buckets seething with catch (which might also be tipped half over so that little girls could squeal some more at the crustacean mat), orders being shouted and boys lurching to get hold of the biggies comprehensively occupied the entire jetty and constituted a constant and efficient public nuisance. The day was rounded off by ceremoniously up-ending the bucket over the quay and admiring the particularly big ones running off for home, sometimes with the front legs of one of their neighbours clutched in their claw.

But all this had to be fitted in between the real business of being at the boat. My father's second joke went like this. 'Saintly Dai arrives in Hell.' (They were all dredged from some folk memory of a Cardiff swamp.) 'What are you doing here, Dai?' asks Pugh. 'Didn't you go to heaven?'

'Oh yes. And there's lovely heaven was: all fluffy clouds and blue skies. And I go to St Peter. I say, "What shall we do today?" And St Peter says, "Well, Dai, I thought we'd do a little harping." So I play the harp all day. And the next day I go to St Peter and I say, "That was lovely. What shall we do today, then?" And St Peter says, "Well, Dai, today, I thought we'd do a little harping." So I picked up my harp and played it all day. And the next day, I went to St Peter. I said, "What shall we do today?" He said, "Well, Dai, today, I thought (pause for effect) . . . we'd do a little harping." I said, "To hell with harping, and here I am."'

'What shall we do today, Daddy?'

Daddy, with a little smile, pulling up the sails on his boat: 'I thought we'd better do a little harping.'

'Wouldn't it be nice, if just for a change, we spent the day on the beach?'

My father, reaching for a halyard, 'Don't be silly. This is great sailing weather.' Or, 'We have to press on.' Or, 'We have to make the tide by five o'clock.' Or, 'It's bound to improve by the afternoon.' Or, 'Let's stick the sails up and see what happens.' Or, 'We don't want to sit here in this noisy harbour all day.' Or, 'You went ashore last week.'

So we went sailing. The implication was that, somehow, it was the boat itself that would mope if we didn't.

Very occasionally, if a torrential downpour combined with a freak Essex tornado and if the boat were in some very safe harbour ('You cannot leave it unattended at anchor in this weather!') my father could be constrained to take a day off from harping. Even then, he would linger on the slippery quay to gaze longingly back at her, while the rest of us charged hurriedly out through the rain to take the bus to nearby Ipswich. Here he retained his full coxswain's outfit: sea boots, Breton fisherman's cap and barnacle-encrusted oyster-dredger's smock. Wrapped in a capacious yellow 'oily', he shuffled through shopping centres, periodically holding up a wetted finger as if he half-expected a flare to bang above Dorothy Perkins and summon him back to the vessel. We hid in shop doors to disassociate ourselves from him.

I can measure the progress of my adolescent life by my father's boats. Where other suburban dads might have fulfilled their status anxieties with bigger, newer, shinier, faster cars, Elwyn went for ever-larger, dumpier, more impractical barques.

They were hardly yachts. The home-made Enterprise dinghy was abandoned in Itchenor and replaced by a 'Yachting Monthly Senior' called *Dunlin*, after the dull bird that sits on the mud. It had a pale-blue hull, retro portholes and a cabin, which was quite an achievement in a boat which wasn't much longer than an open dinghy. You opened the doors, pushed back the hatch, and, like some floating pup tent, there were two berths slap on the floor, separated only by the wooden slab of the centreboard case. Being nine, I could just about stand up in the well. Adults crouched and cursed. There was enough room for my mother to squat, giggling, over a bucket.

Oh dear. To a sensitive Epping boy, unwonted glimpses of the white pudding of his mother's bottom, wedged on a plastic bucket, were the stuff of nightmares. My father, in particular, seemed to delight in inflicting his morning 'ablutions' on us. The boats did get bigger. The groins, pumps, cocks and gurgling mechanisms got more Heath-Robinson-esque. But fifteen feet, twenty-four feet or twenty-nine feet – what did it matter anyway? There was nowhere to run to. My parent's carefree, hospital-trained frankness was met with concentrated adolescent disgust. We bonded as a family, in the most intimate, revolting way conceivable to an adolescent. Sometimes I had to wait days to get the boat to myself for a crap. And did they care? They laughed.

He kept *Dunlin* off the Harlow Sailing Club, which owned a patch of agricultural land by a creek in Maylandsea. It took an hour chugging across John Betjeman's favourite county to get to this outpost. Even when we were 'nearly there yet', we still seemingly had miles of bleak flat-lands to cross before the car pulled off the main road and lolloped down the track to the water's edge. Not that the water was often around. The sea struggled to reach this far.

My father would match his screeching to the car's as it scraped its sump across the potholed track. Harlow Sailing Club itself was no more finished than the rest of Maylandsea: one of those small-holder plot-lands, linked by unmade roads and then abandoned to the whims of the owners. Caravans, black sheds and Californian ranch bungalows were haphazardly jostled together. We left scrupulously planned Harlow to come to desperately unplanned Maylandsea.

At the age of eight I sat in the car eating egg sandwiches, while my father helped manoeuvre massive tubes of concrete into muddy holes to build the clubhouse. We played rolling games on the sea wall when they went to dig moorings. Three or four men pushed a boat out across the mud, holding on to the sides to stop themselves sliding under, and sprayed filth everywhere, trying to get a three-foot-diameter concrete pill with a chain on the end of it dug into the bottom. *Dunlin* was anchored to one of those.

Once he had done his bit, my father never really went near the place again. 'They're only interested in dinghy racing,' he said dismissively. He wanted to go harping. We used the little boat to go off to explore the mud and slept in a caravan he had bought, in a field near by.

Opposite the end of the two-mile creek was Osea Island. It had been a refuge for alcoholics. To begin with we rarely went further than its steep shingle beaches overlooked by massive elms topped with heron's nests, from where you could look across at what we were reliably informed was Anthony Wedgwood Benn's country estate.

We always seemed to be coming back late on the ebb tide, probably leaving it until the last possible moment. Even the tiny *Dunlin* had to feel its way up the gut. It was powered by a hot and dangerous-looking Seagull outboard engine, with its unprotected flywheel and a battered fuel tank. This latter was decorated with a picture of a jaunty yachtsman in a striped shirt. He had the whole engine lifted on to his broad shoulders and with his knotted scarf and a pipe, looked as if it brought him nothing but joy.

As likely as not, our own Seagull would fail at a critical moment. Time was short, the tide was in danger of leaving our mooring dry and the thing would sputter to a halt. The boat would continue to sweep serenely forward, but the extreme silence following the raucous clatter was broken by the natural sounds of the gurgling water, the swishing of a bow wave and the hysterical shouting of my father.

'Take the helm! Take the helm. Keep her heading upstream. Don't let the tide drag you down on the other boats. Keep the bow up!!'

Being close to our own buoy (that's why we were motoring not sailing), we were amongst other sleek vessels whose expensively painted hulls slithered past on either side. My mother would put on a look of determination and grasp the tiller with white knuckles, not something she was ever encouraged to do except in cases of the direst emergency. We knew better than to chatter or play or make smart remarks. And my father, with the urgency of a landing boat commander on D-day, frenziedly wound a knotted cord around a metal spindle on the top of his engine and repeatedly yanked at it. Sometimes the rope whipped up and caught him on the face. Sometimes the engine harrumphed and made wheezy choking noises but inevitably it failed to ignite.

'It's the plugs. They've oiled up again. Keep the bow ahead, ahead!'

The boat would gradually lose momentum. My mother, completely unscientific about the process of steering, would grip the tiller harder and look about her anxiously, while my father leaned over the red-hot casing and fiddled with a spark plug, his shirt bunched, his face streaked with oil (no pipe, no knotted scarf and definitely no joy), anxiously stealing looks to see whether the boat was going to prang itself on some trim racing vessel.

'Boat hook! Get a boat hook.' My mother would teeter outboard and try to hook on to another boat with the end of a pole.

'Hold on to a stanchion!' He knew that other boats' fancy wires and silvery metal protrusions might easily ping off, or crumple like silver paper. On several occasions, they did. Then my father would hold his head in his hands and give way to gloomy prognostications about insurance premiums. But mostly, after a few moments, the tide would win, the boat hook would slip out of my mother's grasp, and my father would throw himself into a panic; trying to get some sails hoisted or the lifting keel up, while the stricken vessel drifted quietly and, indeed, imperceptibly on to the mud.

Nonetheless, we went exploring further out on to the broad estuary itself, bounded by land so flat that all harbours were a surprise (at least to us) and dominated by the twin blocks of the Bradwell nuclear power station. Opposite them, during depressions, shipping companies would anchor redundant ocean-going freighters or tankers, but most of the miles of open water were shallow. It was possible when the evening was still and the winds were light to spend a good minute gummed to the bottom before anyone noticed that you had touched.

'We're aground!' he would suddenly bellow at the top of his voice.

'Are you sure?' my mother might venture, helpfully, looking about her.

'Get the plate up!!'

He would lumber forward, with the energy only granted to overweight doctors at times of imagined distress, to heave at a gnarled nylon rope around a pulley system and try to wrest the lifting keel from the abominable suction.

Usually it took several others heaving too. And the mud was not the problem. The pulley system was. When it finally gave way with its usual lurch, the team fell backwards into the cockpit, the unattended tiller yawed round, and the boat, now floating again, generally looked after itself.

Imagine, if you will, a wooden box: twenty foot long by about four foot high, narrowing at both ends. It contains five people, my family, like transported slaves, lying head to foot, on narrow bunks. My head is three or four inches from a gently perspiring ceiling. My father's legs are ingeniously slotted into a little opening immediately beneath my head.

My mother is on the other side of a small companionway. My sister lies stretched out forward of her in a separate box, separated by an eighth-of-an-inch plyboard panel and a curtain. My older brother is wedged into the pointed bit, between canvas sacks full of sails and a length of anchor chain. It is nearly one in the morning. We have lain in this way for about an hour, ever since the late-night shipping forecast came to an end. It is dark. Not a twinkle of light pierces the enclosure. We are peering into the blackness and waiting, and we are on holiday in our second boat – *Xara*.

The boat is floating in a narrow channel in a gut, in a slick of mud in the middle of saltings some two or three miles from the nearest habitation. Outside there are trickling sounds and a universal, low oozing and plopping. A sea bird mews. Inside there is only the sound of breathing and the occasional rustle of nylon sleeping bag.

Now, in the infinite blackness, my father starts breathing heavily. Like the steady and remorseless sloughing of a long surf on a gravel beach, a slow in-drawing of breath, followed, one would think almost deliberately, by a hesitant pause.

It reminds us we are in a box, the reverberative sonority of which Mr Wharfedale would have appreciated.

Suddenly we are transported into an episode of *Doomwatch*. We would have clapped our hands to our ears and creased to our knees like Robert Powell, if we weren't stuck full length in our bunks. A resonating, booming bass note starts somewhere deep in the back of my father's throat, gargles up through his oesophagus and emerges, half from his mouth and half from his capacious and hairy nostrils. What had been up until that moment a fitful and disturbed attempt at sleep in a damp and unconducive environment is about to become hell in the dark. That first, mucousy gelatinous rattle means my father is about to start snoring.

At the start of the holiday, we snorted back, coughed or finally lost patience and shouted 'Please!' into the darkness. But this was always met with a startled croak as he struggled up from the bottom of some deep well to break the surface.

'What?'

'You're snoring.'

He would smack some moisture into his mouth. Breathe more insistently, normally and tut.

'Oh.' And then, after a rueful pause, 'How can I be snoring? I wasn't even asleep.'

'Well, you were.'

The response was a disappointed sigh and a rustle of his bed nylon. Now we were all awake, lying damp and uncomfortable, the night stretched ahead like an endless sentence and nocturnal birds mocked our imprisonment by wading in the shallows and softly cooing to each other.

So, after a few days on holiday, we usually let him be. Eventually you fall asleep. And anyway, by the time I was twelve, my brother, three years older than me and destined to grow big and bearded, had already begun to rival my father in the glottal drain-clearing, snot-shovelling, nocturnal trumpeting division. No noise could equal the disgusting broken wheezing of their accursed duet. And yet we seem, eventually, to have slept through it. How, I have no idea.

Inevitably it became time to venture out on the sea. We had explored Mersea, Goldhanger and Tollesbury and had got as far as Brightlingsea at the mouth of the river. The first time we ventured up the coast, my mother was sent on ahead by car. She diligently drove to the end of every pier and headland and could be seen waving a handkerchief as the little boat slowly ground its way north. Eventually the Suffolk river system opened up ahead, and, exhausted by our mammoth journey, we put into Harwich. This was an error. Harwich was built to take ocean-going cargo ships and cross-channel ferries. We tied up out of the way in Bathgate Bay and tried to get ashore using a teetering vertical ladder covered with green slime that looked about a hundred feet high.

Having done it once, we did it every year, admittedly in bigger boats. *Xara* was big enough for all of us to sleep on, as long as my brother didn't come, which rather suited my brother. He went sailing properly with the Ocean Youth Club instead, and we went exploring the Stour, Orwell, Deben and Alde, much prettier estuaries than the Blackwater, with swelling banks and narrower channels leading to sleepy, appealingly dead towns like Aldeburgh and Woodbridge.

They were still tidal rivers. Even at famous beauty spots like Pin Mill at low tide, there could be a few feet to nego-tiate before you got to the hard. The dinghy would have to be rowed as fast as possible for the last few feet, with the oars digging in, bodily pushing the little boat and its passen-gers up and on to the ooze. Already the mud, like crawling paint, would have worked its way past the hafts of the oars and gobs of the stuff would be flying up and spattering us. And we would arrive at the famous beautiful pub covered from head to foot in stinking goo. Perhaps it wasn't that deep after all, but nobody ever tested it out. I only discovered you could walk on it by accident when I was sixteen.

Under the influence of the Incredible String Band my mates and I decided that it was spring and we wanted to spend Easter amongst the flowers. It was early March. The Romantics were wrong. It was freezing. Never mind the blackbird singing in the tall larch, we stayed in the green caravan filled with old Micky Spillane thrillers my father had bought to stay in when the boat had been too small. It sat in a caravan park just below a high sea wall in Maylandsea. There was nothing to do but go for a walk and look at the caravan park from a distance. Eventually we started jumping across the saltings. We discovered that, if you ran at the mud in the shallow areas and kept moving, you didn't sink. Gradually, we became bolder. We took longer excursions out across the sticky surface. If you stopped, even for a second, you started to go under, but if you ran, you flew, leaving a great trail of putrid black foot steps behind you. It was like discovering flight, or that you could walk on water. What had been terra infirma became, intriguingly, ours. There was nothing to be gained. Even if you got somewhere (to the water's edge, across to a mooring or over to a boat) you couldn't stop. You would slide beneath the ooze. It was just the thrill of riding on a deadly crust singing, 'Hunting gibbons out in India!' – a Bonzo Dog Dooh Dah Band track – 'Hunting gibbons, out in May-land-sea. Out, in, out, in, out in May-land-sea.'

In the 1990s, I was in my own small boat in a similar Suffolk gut, only we'd left it far too late to get back to the mooring. We were doing an east-coast creep, sneaking up a channel with the water rushing out like an emptying bath, touching the bottom, pushing off with an oar, feeling the way up until we stuck and realized that we weren't going to get there. 'It doesn't matter,' I said and threw an anchor over the side. 'The boat will just sit here until the next tide.'

'What about us?' someone asked.

There were three of us. Two writers had come up from London and 'quite fancied a boat trip'. Even as we anchored, the rest of the water sluiced out. We were sitting in the familiar sea of mud. The shore was fifty yards away. 'You can run across it,' I said, 'as long as you keep moving. Watch.' I lowered myself over the side. It was years since I'd done it.

I ran. Gouts of liquid mud flew up as I slapped away, but I stayed up. I reached the sea wall, shouted deliriously and ran back to the boat for good measure. 'See!' I said breathlessly, gripping the side to prevent myself being sucked under.

Andy smiled. 'OK.' He stepped over and ran. Splat, splat, splat, splat and he got to the wall. 'Yes!'

Henry came next. He was bigger than Andy. Henry was over six foot. It was difficult for him to get out easily and prepare himself, because somehow he was just too gangly. The sides of the boat were too low. Perhaps he was worried about his Musto jacket and new jeans, but he just didn't seem to overcome the viscosity in the same way that short people did.

Pretty quickly we could see that Henry wasn't quite gliding. He wasn't even slapping. Like some giant panic-stricken frog, with each twitch his feet were plunging further into the ooze. So he worked his legs faster. Up and down went his thighs like pistons. Faster and faster went his feet, huger and huger rose the fountain of black sticky mud. Now, like some mad engine, he frenziedly gyrated his limbs until all we could see from the shore was a berserk, thrashing whirlwind of flying black slop which, to our amazement, like something out of Ali Baba, gradually started to move towards us. He made the shore, a slimy zombie, and staggered across the grass. He opened two black and white minstrel eyes. 'That was quite fun,' he said.

6. The Back Route

'Where are we going now?'

'We're going to go on to Brentwood, the back way,' I told my mother, driving on up towards Stonnard's Hill playing field, half-way out of Epping.

Having the others in the car was just an excuse. I should have walked up the hill, just as I had . . . how many times? Senior school is a demanding lump of our lives: seven years; three hundred and sixty odd weeks; six days a week. (Leave out the holidays, of course. You can do the maths. It was never my strongest subject.) Yes, six days a week. The blasted school had boarders, so the rest of us had to turn out on a Saturday for their convenience. The school didn't want the inmates loose in the town at the weekend.

'They wanted you to board originally,' said my mother.

'They didn't?'

'Oh yes. But you wouldn't have it. So we settled on a year. You were going to be a year as a day boy and then go boarding.'

This was a fine time to be telling me this. 'I've never heard this before.'

It wasn't because the school wanted to clap me to its echoing and smelly bosom. It was because of the distance. Brentwood is twelve miles from Epping. I was well outside the school's natural catchment area for day boys.

'Well, that's what they wanted, but you started and they never mentioned it again.'

Bancroft's in Woodford, which also seemed miles away at

the time, was probably first choice, but I must have flunked the exam. There was talk of Chigwell Grammar or Merchant Taylors or Haberdashers Aske's (maybe that was a department store). Most of these 'good' suburban grammar schools were founded by City Guilds or self-aggrandizing potentates in the Tudor age, to take the place of the monks seen off by the Reformation. They served the same purpose: churning out well-mannered bureaucrats. Sparsely dotted around the green belt, in the late 1960s they encircled London with good A-level prospects. I didn't know then that many of my future adult friends, like Clive Anderson and Geoffrey Perkins, were banged up in similar establishments further on around what is now the M25 in suburbs like Stanmore. My wife was at a place in Ealing. This was the 'direct grant grammar school' era.

I don't believe that my father ever seriously considered any sort of public school. He was from Welsh high-academic-performance state-school stock himself. So I went for an exam in the Bean Library and an interview with the chiselled Mr Tarrant, a Mount Rushmore of a geography teacher, and I was admitted to the imposing place with 'the old red wall'. It would take fifty-five minutes to get home by bus every afternoon, but I got a lift in the morning from Robert Dickenson's father, who worked in the labs at Ilford Films.

He would pick me up opposite a big housing estate of mock-Georgian terraces, built in the grounds of what must have been some important suburban mansion.

'I don't recognize any of this.'

'Yes, you do. We came this way thousands of times. It was the way we came to avoid the main roads.'

'Not this way.'

'Yes! This way! It was this way.'

How many times, then? Of course, I have to leave out

the Saturdays, because Mr Dickenson didn't work Saturdays, so I had to get the bus. And holidays. So five days a week, forty weeks a year for six years. Leaving out sick days and other arrangements, I must have made this journey at least a thousand times.

I got us lost almost immediately, but in peaceful country-side: copses, river valleys and high hedges, less manicured than its equivalent in Surrey. I had never noticed it all before. I was too busy wittering on at Mr Dickenson, a nice, quiet man with glasses, about why cars should be designed more racily and what was happening in last night's episode of *Ironside*, the show with the disabled detective.

My mother and I gawped at the route now, as if for the first time.

'We used to go through Ongar.'

'No, we didn't. You must remember; there was terrible fog sometimes.'

'Oh, I remember the fog. We once had to ring the head-master, because we couldn't get through to pick you up after a play rehearsal and he had to put you up. He wasn't happy about that.'

Wasn't he? I remembered only the amused condescension. It had seemed a huge joke to him and an awful disaster to me. But then we boys always seemed funny to Mr Sale. With his hooded eyes and wispy smile he came across like Dennis Price after a particularly ingenious murder. All headmasters have an act. His was very successful, if a little cold. I remember my uneasy sense of intrusion that night when Sale, who never seemed to stoop for anything, stalked into the rehearsal and led me off to his very own house. It was over on the other side of the school where we day-boys never went; a large Georgian pile, fronting on the green. His wife was Italian, but I had never met her before either. None of the parties seemed that keen to associate off duty. He marched me up to the top of the house, through upper corridors of sharp-green lino, to a cold bed. I can still hear the ghastly, ancient plumbing in the frozen lavatory. Still feel the horrible sense of breaking all the rules. In the morning, I was dispatched to the dining hall to eat a breakfast of squishy tomatoes and paper bacon with the boarders. What on earth was my mother doing, presuming on the headmaster, as if he were just an ordinary human being? I would rather have walked the fifteen miles home in the darkness through the fog, pushing the car.

It was later made clear that overnight accommodation was not part of the service. When, the following year, I was given a bigger role in the school play, as Lady Macbeth, a coded message must have been passed to Mr Baron, the head of English. In mid-rehearsal, I was suddenly demoted to third witch. That twelve-mile journey was the beginning of the end of my school theatrical career.

'I never intended to be an actor anyway.'

This wasn't strictly true. I certainly intended to be an actor at the age of six, when I wrote in my big, childish hand (which, rather irritatingly, I still have) that I would like to grow up to be Charlie Drake. This was after a Christmas trip to the Palladium to see him say 'Hello, my darlings' to a row of dancing green monsters from Mars. To be honest I would have been perfectly interested in being one of the dancing green monsters too.

Kenneth Tynan observed that, in his experience, far from coming from harsh backgrounds, actors generally had supportive, applauding families and were 'brought up to be the centre of attention'. Geraldine James, who is a proper actor, disputed this. She told me that she had become an actor to hide. Suddenly she was given the right words to say.

She was able to disappear and become someone else. That's why Geraldine is such a wonderful actor. Me, I'm one of Tynan's babies. I just liked showing off. I was just as pleased to win the junior elocution prize (well, it was Essex) or tell elephant jokes to some old ladies' club ('How many elephants can you get in a mini?') as to gurn and gibber as Scrooge in Mrs Wiltshire's lavish production of *A Christmas Carol* at Epping Junior School. (I had to fall asleep convincingly, have my dreams and wear a funny hat.)

From an early age, I had decided it would be fun to be a famous actor. I liked the frisson that ran through Hartland Road when we discovered that the people up the end had an uncle who was the man who was Maigret on the telly: Rupert Davies. The grown-ups earnestly discussed his career dilemmas. 'He had become so famous for that role that he was "type-cast",' they said knowingly. They certainly never talked about Harry Kopelman, my father's colleague at the hospital, like that.

I equated acting with riches, prestige and esteem. My father watched Roger Moore on the telly and told me that if I wanted to be a proper actor I would have to be able to raise one eyebrow, so I went back to the bathroom mirror and, by physically holding down one half of my face, perfected the trick of letting the other half rise in an all-purpose, querulous tic of mystery. I can still do it, even though I probably shouldn't.

But unlike today's proper actor friends, who joined amateur troupes and were taken frequently to the theatre, the Rhys Joneses were not a cultural family. We had our own children's books, but my father was a typical doctor. He read his BMJ journal and his boating magazines and kept vast hoards of both stashed about the house. He had a shelf of medical text books, but they weren't much help, although there was one dusty volume that my friends and I discovered in the garage: *An Introduction to Forensic Science*. The local gangs used to make appointments to open the book at a black and white photograph of 'the baby half-eaten by rats'.

I read everything knocking about, including a complete set of Arthur Mee's *Children's Encyclopaedia*, with its coloured plates of the flags of all nations, and its 'Ten Small Tales to Treasure', and its grainy photographs of statues of worthy exemplars, like Nurse Cavell. Having gobbled up my own approved literature (C. S. Lewis and Arthur Ransome), I was even discovered by my father, one rainy afternoon, leafing through our *Complete Works of Shakespeare*. What pater's heart would not lift with pride? I apparently ruined it for him when he found me on the same rug the following day stuck into *The Green Lantern*. I read to combat tedium.

Alice Thomas Ellis pointed out that childhood is full of long periods of utter boredom. But that was then. Not any more. My own children were bombarded with more visual spew in the first three years of their existence than we had experienced by the time we were twenty.

Television was a novelty for us. It arrived in our house as a flickering fuzz the size of a paperback, and must have taken at least five minutes to dominate our lives. But we were only ever allowed to watch the BBC, and the BBC, of course, had only one channel. Even then, the class-based quarantine was extended to certain specific programmes. My father refused to allow us, under any circumstances, to watch the blameless *Dr Kildare*. He resented the way that his patients arrived suffering imaginary symptoms and demanding instant miracle cures.

Today, by jumping channels, any sentient nine-year-old can watch programmes deliberately aimed at their tastes from six in the morning until, well, six the following morning.

But in the early sixties, television went grown-up after *Muffin the Mule*, *Blue Peter* and *Doctor Who* (which was considered so complicated that the first episode had to be shown all over again the following week). If we wanted to stay up late, we had to watch *Panorama*. There was nothing else on. My kids just turn over and carry on watching more exciting adventures of real people being moronic. We only had one telly and no remote control, and usually a supervisor in the shape of my father snoring in 'his' chair, a brown-covered wing-arm chair, only otherwise allowed to be occupied by the dog, Harold.

By the age of eleven, however, I had an hour and a half's homework a night, which, if of a scientific nature, would take me three. I would sit scowling at equations, tormented by my father's gibbon-like laugh from below, as he howled at *Dad's Army* or *Steptoe* in the sitting room. I couldn't see him, nose up, his belly shaking, his head thrown back, but I could certainly hear him: a high, whistling 'hee-hee', followed by a prolonged, hooting whoop. Bah. Sometimes I would creep down to find out what had been so funny and hang about until I was told to get on with my homework again, and then his tormenting braying would start all over. He loved television comedy: Morecambe and Wise, Alf Garnett, Hancock, *The Frost Report*. Eventually we both sat down in front of *Monty Python*. He encouraged me to watch it, in fact. My mother resolutely refused to find it funny. It became a thing for us. Even if he never read the *TLS* my father had an intelligent bloke's judgement. How could the man who played the Dame in the hospital panto not have?

Cultural education was pretty much left to 'Aunty' Gwen Powell, my brisk, no-nonsense godmother and a friend of my parents from their early years. Or at least, she felt it was.

Poor Gwen, she was as concerned about the moral responsibilities of art as my father was indifferent to them.

The vicar at her funeral, where I embarrassed everyone
by sobbing in the pulpit when I was supposed to be reading the lesson, told me that, on Remembrance Day, all the
veterans in the village had been taken aback to see Gwen,
the fiery old lady from the old people's home, marching up
to the church gate, straight-backed and bearing the weight
of a massive display of medals on her bosom. Gwen had been
a matron on hospital ships in the Atlantic convoys. She was
a formidable woman.

She asked me in her slightly imperious way one evening,
as we left for dinner after I had been performing at the Lyric
Hammersmith, whether I was short of money.

'No, not particularly,' I replied.

'So you don't *have* to advertise cat food, then?'

As well as improving books on birthdays, she took me to
art galleries and to St Fagan's Museum near Cardiff, to
Cambridge (long before I understood the concept of going
to study there), to archaeological sites and to the theatre. We
went together to Stratford to see David Warner play Hamlet.
Gwen encouraged me to think I could be an actor.

David Harris had an indirect effect as well. David Harris
Senior was our dentist. David Harris Junior was my bicycling friend. They lived in a modern house like the ones
in American films, built in an immature wood near Harlow
and matching their American family structure with big plate-
glass windows and white sofas smelling like the surgery:
vaguely clean and antiseptic. They were a spare family too.
June, the mother, had a slightly vague, pop-eyed expression,
and her son shared it. Dad was equally reserved but more
direct. There was always a slight dour playfulness in his eyes,
as if the only proper reaction to young boys was one of

quizzical wariness. But then adults have to do something. Dr Kopelman was a barker – head back for pompous generalizing. Dr Hayden was a stooper – cautiously playful and one of the boys. I am abrupt, brook-no-nonsense. I can't help it. Adult males struggle to retain control with adolescents. We all do it. But Mr Harris was 'Go on, impress me, you garrulous twerp,' though he would never have said anything as coherent. Most of the time, he seemed to tick along slowly, as if his whole metabolism had been slowed down by the frozen process of dentistry.

He was one of our family's new friends when we first got to Harlow, a fellow health professional. On one visit, in my early teens, after he had counted off the teeth and poked around with a broad, flat-ended finger in his American-looking surgery, in what must have been a specially planned, dental surgery zone of Harlow New Town, he summoned my mother to take a look. I had a crowded mouth, he explained, in his slow non-committal manner. He pointed to my canines, two sharp teeth. They had detached themselves from the top row and wandered off to some higher point on my gums, one on either side. I also had an under-hung jaw, inherited from her, apparently. The combination of the two meant I looked like a Cro-Magnon Dracula. I rather liked it, but it was decided that I should have orthodontic treatment to fix my bite.

This had its plusses. Every three months I would take an afternoon off from my big school. My mother would accompany me on the Central Line tube: Epping, Theydon Bois, Debden (where they made the banknotes) Loughton, Woodford, South Woodford. I have to stop there. Once I could do the lot – at least as far as Oxford Circus, including Leytonstone, Snaresbrook, Stratford, Liverpool Street and Tottenham Court Road. If there were singularities connected with any of these places I never knew them. They were just stops along the jiggling way, through the immense outskirts of London – miles of flat-backed yellow houses, linked by the skein of pipes that runs alongside the track on posts, until Stratford. Then the Underground finally lived up to its name and plunged into the darkness, and the pipes looped and soared alongside in the dirty tunnel, sometimes up six feet, sometimes dropping down to run alongside the windows – always snake-like and always caked with what must surely be 'grime'.

For a twelve-year-old, central London meant the fixed determination of the anonymous crowd, bustling off the carriage with practised purposefulness, knowing which exit to take, which side of the escalator to stand, where to stick their ticket, when to get up for the stop. Even then, I could sense the collective pride in being a skilled native Underground traveller and I sought to emulate it. After the long, boring ride through the deserted midday platforms, the stations in the black heart of the city were always exciting warrens of expectation. The platforms had sudden gusts of hot wind blowing up them in front of hidden trains. There were thrilling advertisements for corsets and brassières all up the escalators and brightly lit heel and key bars in the concourses. All of them seemed to be comprehensively ignored by the passengers hurrying up to the light. London was far from being a meaningless jumble. We very rarely went there by any means other than the tube, and its uniform, slightly out-of-date spirit linked everything. London *was* the clanking mahogany doors of the lift, the big red sixpence signs on the blue ticket machines, the tiled octagonal ticket spaces, the wrought-iron bridges and white on dark blue station names, whether we were emerging in Westbourne Grove for skating at the Queens Ice Rink or in South

Kensington for the museums or Holborn for the Eastman Dental Hospital.

My teeth were fixed up in this giant shop-floor of dentistry on the Gray's Inn Road off to the north of High Holborn. Dozens of dental chairs were arranged in ranks. It seemed a factory of pain. The pinkish consultant came and played around with a plaster cast of my gnashers, before leading the inspection of the real thing. It was a status deformity. All these people may have been focused on my teeth, but I was definitely the centre of attention. They had clearly never seen anything like it. Then the consultant paraded on, and my jaws were left in the hands of supernumeraries.

Orthodontic treatment seemed to be based on the most rudimentary of medical principles. Since my teeth were crooked they would be yanked into line. To make room, a couple of back teeth would be heaved out first. The straight-forward physical effect was achieved through the most complex of in-mouth engineering. The remaining teeth were encased in sheaths of metal and fixed up with hooks and wires. I wore a plate, made of the same startling shiny pink plastic as my grandfather's dentures, which slotted around my upper teeth and rested up against my palate, where it collected a gooey mat of whatever I ate. After meals I was supposed to take it out and wash it, but I was twelve. If I could be bothered, or if the food was particularly suety or even tasty, I would lever the thing off the roof of my mouth and suck the residue off. Otherwise, it stayed in and hurt. It hurt because it was designed to force my teeth into new positions. I was given plastic bags of minute elastic bands. One end of the rubber was attached to a hook on the back of my plate and the other around a projection sticking out of the front of my teeth. These projections sometimes caught in the inner flesh of my cheeks, but were supposed to act as a grappling hook for a steady, medieval, rack-like torture of the elastic, pulling the teeth into a new angle in their sockets.

Every three months I got another morning off school and paid another visit to the tooth factory, and out would come a selection of ingenious miniature pliers and spanners. The dentists would tighten up their diabolical machinery, and I would fail to sleep for a few nights, groaning under the relentless stretching of my gums. Finally, even this was not enough, and a scold's bridle was constructed from black garter elastic and wire. It had two loops on projecting prongs at the front. I had to wear it at night. The loops went over two minute hooks attached permanently to my upper teeth, the elastic went around the back of my head and all night long it pulled agonizingly hard. Sorry for me yet? I was a boy, so I had no particular vanity, but apart from Nichols I seemed to be the only one in my year put through this torture. Every American kid in every TV series or Hollywood film appeared to be similarly afflicted so I didn't have to explain to anyone why I had a mouth like the inside of a clock, but my school mates all grew up buck-toothed and proud of it. Nichols, despite wearing short trousers and polishing his shoes, took his plate out and stuck it in his pocket as soon as he got to school. He eventually resorted to accidentally treading on it. His treatment was abandoned – a hopeless dental recidivist – but I was an obedient child. When it came to professional medical advice I had to be. There were too many adults prepared to gang up on me, including Mr Harris.

After eighteen months the consultant returned. He fiddled with my plaster casts, peered into my mouth and told the assembled experts that the problem was hereditary. Tenderly chucking me beneath my prognathous hamster cheeks, he explained that they had been wasting their time. The only recourse was surgery. He offered to cut out a section of my jawbone on either side of my mouth and set the whole thing back a couple of inches. This way I would have a perfect bite. I would also look like a selectively inbred Hapsburg with an Adam's apple bigger than my chin. He added, idly, that the operation was tricky (a lot a nerves and blood vessels to negotiate) but I would boast a standard chomp, so the dentally critical would be satisfied.

I was relieved that they didn't take advantage of me there and then with their miniature buzz saws. This was before *All New Cosmetic Surgery Live* became a mid-evening television favourite. People are made of sterner stuff now. Then, it seemed a bit radical, and I backed off down the corridor clutching my mummy's hand and making her promise that I wouldn't have to have it done.

She would have taken me to Gamages as a treat. Somewhere in High Holborn, not far from the bright-red castellated Flemish fortress that belonged to Prudential Insurance, was a department store with a similar rambling, gothic provenance. It was a country-house emporium, with echoing back staircases and hidden annexes up in the attics, which is where I went, to the make-up department. I don't know how I found it. Perhaps my mother took me there to look at toys. I think it was just beyond and behind the toy department, but it sold proper, Leichner, theatrical make-up. I developed a fascination with the stuff which would have frightened Michael MacLiammoir. I still have some of the sticks of greasepaint I bought then because as far as I can tell you can never use up a stick of carmine.

I can remember the long, slimy bars of colour, like lipstick, wrapped in gold paper with black printing. I must have had an instruction book too, because I knew that you had to smear the lot over the face, then paint wrinkles, moles and shadows to mould a new you – dab a tiny dot inside the corner of the eye, to make the whites shine brightly, add a half black line under the eyelashes for a bloke, a full line for a woman and finally add loads of powder to 'hold' everything in place. When did I do this? What for? Who did I show? I must have gone downstairs eliciting approval, and I think the intention was to create something ghoulish rather than camp. I bought long pigtails of crêpe hair and glue. I had both grey and black woven into ropes. I pulled out a lump for use, but I never steamed it to get it straight. So I bought some complete false moustaches instead. At one stage, I had a stick of nose putty which required endless kneading to make pliable and I made myself a false nose, added pirate whiskers, blackened my teeth and stuck some convincing warts on my still protruding chin. But the biggest hit was the packet of blood capsules. These were lozenges made of clear plastic which contained some sort of red sherbet and when chewed frothed and bubbled with a convincing approximation of a tubercular haemorrhage, particularly effective in the middle of Brentwood High Street on a dull Wednesday afternoon. At some point I got hold of a convincing severed thumb as well, but I'm not sure if that came from Gamages. It was just normal, healthy, attention-seeking exhibitionism. I was quite convinced I would become an actor.

As soon as I arrived at senior school, I decided I wanted to be in plays. Mr Baron was in charge. He organized his 'Winter Theatricals' on a model seemingly derived from mid-period Tyrone Guthrie, with a bit of Donald Wolfit thrown in on the side. He had no truck with modish 'ideas'. Only Shakespeare was ever performed – in period costume, with sets derived from page six of his Penguin copy. Executed by Mr Featherstone, the head of the school art department and a fencing-champion enthusiast for heraldry, but not, thank goodness, for modish ideas, they consisted of painted flats depicting battlements, towers and gothic entrances of a flexible, not to say wobbly, nature.

Mr Baron jealously guarded his dominance of school theatricals. In my second year, for example, almost every boy who could stand up was dragooned into the junior school play: Christopher Fry's *The Boy with the Cart*. It was an excruciating Christian parable, delivered in blank verse with uplifting songs ('Boy with the Cart, where are you going to, Boy with the Cart, where have you come *from*?'). Even we tiny ones sensed that the sophisticated French master (who wore a bowler hat like Jeremy Thorpe and could sometimes be spotted sneaking into school from the direction of the station, looking a little rough, at one minute to nine) was a director rather given to modish ideas. He wanted energy ('lots of energy, boys!'). He wanted light ('more light!'), and he wanted big white blocks as a set. 'Spud' Baron was not impressed. He called it 'Boy with the Fart'.

For Spud, it was acting that was paramount – his acting, mainly. He never indulged in such frippery as improvisation, he simply showed us how to do it. The rehearsal was an opportunity for him to perform the entire play himself. In order to demonstrate how Ariel might attend on Prospero, Mr Baron would kick off his shoes and pirouette on points across the Memorial Hall stage. We sniggered at his claims that he had 'trained as an actor, my dear' but he was quite shameless, delivering speeches in floods of tears, or charging across the stage with startling shouts, or draping his jacket over his head and mincing about as Miranda. Given that he was so small and so round and so bald and so potentially foolish, what he really taught us was fearlessness.

Once the production was up, once the huge wicker baskets of period costumes had arrived from Bermans, and been plundered by us, he was everywhere: in the classroom dressing rooms, skittishly arranging a veil, or bellowing about jock straps from the back of the hall, or supervising make-up, which he applied freely, with outlandish streaks of carmine greasepaint. During an electrical blackout, he sat in the dark at the piano and tried to calm us all by playing Rachmaninov.

As for me, I started as one of the little boys playing women. My first role was Ceres, goddess of plenty. I had to emerge from a back-lit cardboard cavern dressed in diaphanous robes, hung about with plastic autumnal leaves and sporting a full length wig. I got a big laugh. This was not what was expected, but I liked it. One of the older boys stood in front of me while I applied my slap, looked me up and down and pronounced, 'God, Rhys Jones, you make a very ugly woman.'

And then the next year I was third witch. It was a serious demotion, after I had originally been asked to give my Lady Macbeth and I took it badly but probably had a better time. Fischl, Gotley and I danced and hooted, cackling and gurning, around a proper black witch's cauldron (a typical Baron literal prop this) with a hidden electric kettle steaming inside it.

Gotley was a close friend and a bad influence. He never seemed to take what he did entirely seriously. He and Fischl whispered obscenities under their breath during anybody else's lines.

By the fifth form, too ugly for women altogether, I had become part of the crowd in *Julius Caesar*, shouting 'Ave, ave' at Douglas Adams, the future author of *The Hitch Hiker's Guide to the Galaxy*, as he strutted about with a double bedsheet over his shoulder and his huge conk in the air. I was Rosencrantz in *Hamlet* and in my last year managed no better than the pitiful Aumerle in *Richard II*.

Backstage visitors, even as a boy, could be difficult, though.

The plays were one of the few occasions when the hier-archies of the school broke down.

In one junior production we fell under the spell of Skinner. He was crop-headed and foul-mouthed and a year older than us. He was probably playing a fairy too. He already had collections of *IT* and *Private Eye* and could tell an endless succession of filthy jokes. So we worshipped him. Then on the last night, the Saturday, my parents came to see the play. And, foolishly, they wandered back to the classrooms to pick me up. Why did they do that? They were just being parents, thinking they could go anywhere, barge into any room. Why the hell couldn't they wait in the car, or somewhere in the dark outside, like a sensible relative?

My father was wearing a flat cap and his buttoned-up mac, my mother was fussing behind him. I was up at the back of the room, getting make-up off, standing by Skinner. He began shaking and tears appeared in his eyes. He raised a quivering digit, pointed and collapsed in howls of laugh-ter. Look at that! What the hell were they? How did they get loose? And all the others laughed too. They held each other up. They gasped for breath. They sniggered and guffawed. And then my father spotted me. 'Griffith!' he called.

'Griffith!' This was too much for Skinner. He was pole-axed. He brought his cream-covered face right up to mine, almost unable to speak. 'They ... they ... they're your *parents*!'

I nodded helplessly.

'Har har har har har.'

Skinner collapsed on the floor and crawled away under the desks. And I was left alone to greet my mummy and daddy (at least I hadn't called them *that* in public). To their puzzlement, I hurried them out of the room, foully betrayed, hating them and hating Skinner and hating myself for not knowing what to do or who to blame.

7. The Three Three Nine

I rather fancied taking the 339 bus from Brentwood back to Epping. Half my adolescent life had been lost lurching around upstairs in that double-decker bus. And I was astounded to discover that, after forty years, the thing still ran. It followed the same route. It still went all the way from Brentwood to Harlow, passing through Epping — just as it had when it wallowed me homewards every afternoon. Disappointingly it had changed its number. It was now the 501. Worse, it didn't come from Warley any more. It began its trans-Essex marathon from some other meaningless suburban outpost. These were small changes, perhaps, but of arcane regret. The number 39 and the name of the village of Warley had had a cabalistic significance when I was twelve.

We were initiated into all this at the beginning of our first English lesson by a bald, fervently twitchy house master known as Daddy Brooks. He swept in, threw his gown into his seat, flung his books on the desk with a frightening bang and told us that he had some serious matters to establish. He leaned forward and spoke emphatically. First, there were to be no sniggers at the mention of the number thirty-nine. Any foolishness of this kind would be *severely* punished. Nobody was to stroke his chin, thus, or mention Warley. Nobody was to say 'aww ginn', or speak of Percy. 'Now, I will never mention this again. Open your Ridout on page seven.'

Crikey. What was he talking about? We found out quickly enough. The name Warley and the number thirty-nine were both associated with one master: 'Bilge', otherwise known as Mr Gilbert, otherwise identified by the number thirty-nine in the 'Blue Book'.

Mr Gilbert was a master of staggeringly sadistical demeanour, who taught science with astonishing incompetence. He was what only a schoolteacher can be – at once terrifying and ludicrous.

'Bilge' had a length of pink rubber Bunsen-burner piping in his pocket. With no apparent irony, he called it 'Percy'. If not close enough to hit a boy with the palm of his hand around the ear, or tear the hair upwards on the temple, he would happily beat him with Percy. Or he would wait, smelly, blubbering spittle over you, leaning against your desk and rubbing himself against it, so close that you could smell his beery breath and see the underpants sticking up beyond his waistband with his shirt stuffed inside them. After three weeks he would come in and begin the first lesson all over again. It was a brave pupil who raised his hand and said, 'Sir, I think we've done this already.'

'Aww ginn' was the noise that Mr Gilbert made when 'thinking'. It could be reduced to a simple 'awwww', delivered under the breath, faintly, imperceptibly, to begin with, but growing in intensity with repetition. Any mention of any of the key words might start a sudden rustle. Should the ignorant teacher taking morning assembly be unlucky enough to have to use the number thirty-nine, or mention an Earl of England called Percy, or have to refer in some way to the nearby suburb of Warley (where it was widely bruited Mr Gilbert had been incarcerated in a mental hospital for some of his adult life), a noise like unto a gathering wind would pass through the inmates of Mr Dotheboy's prison camp.

'Awwwww . . .' it would start, very softly. Nobody could

be fingered. It was impossible to apportion blame. 'Awwwwww . . .' the sound would get louder. The school-master would adjust his spectacles. His myrmidons, the house praeposters, over from the senior school, some of whom *could already be seen smirking*, would start pacing the butts, trying to identify the offenders, but with straight faces, the noise would continue rising in volume, a nasal, flat Essex drawl, 'awwwwwwww . . .'

'Silence! I will have quiet! I promise you, you will all be facing detention if you do not stop this instantly . . .'

And it would fade, as if by secret signal. Though a bolder boy might just pretend to sneeze 'ginn!', and the hall would erupt.

'Silence!'

It was the great divide. Like a Spanish tyrant in Sicily, the governance of the school refused to even acknowledge the injustices of one of its satraps. It pretended that everything about Mr Gilbert was normal. It was we who were mad, and so two hundred little boys registered their protest through acts of dangerous absurdity. They must have cursed the number thirty-nine.

Every boy, on his arrival at Brentwood School, had to learn the details of the 'Blue Book'. It was a natty, bound volume, similar to Chairman Mao's *Little Red Book* though without the plastic cover. (Actually, Tompsett once wrote to the Chinese Embassy and claimed to have converted a factory to Communism. 'Would it be possible,' he inquired, 'to supply us with a number of Little Red Books for our revolution-ary studies?' The Chinese Embassy provided eight books and a poster. We were impressed. The rest of us sent letters too. Eventually the embassy ran out of books, or perhaps they worked out that all this Maoist fervour was really sixth-form Cultural Revolutionary kitsch.)

They never ran out of the Blue Book. It was a detailed repository of all the rituals and laws of our school. The prefects were called 'praeposters'. Their ranks and powers were listed in the Blue Book. Where boys were allowed or not allowed to walk, the size and names of the boarding houses, the whereabouts of the Chase, the Old Big School and Houghs were all laid down in the Blue Book, as were all twelve verses of the school song, a doggerel guide to the origins of the institution.

> They bound a lad to a green elm tree,
> And they burned him there for the folks to see.
> And in shame for his brothers and sisters all,
> They built them a school with a new red wall.

There weren't in fact any shameful sisters at Brentwood while I was there. There are now. I came back to sign television spin-off books at Burgess's book shop in the eighties and found it full of girls in uniform – military uniform. The boys had turned their back on the Army Corps when it became voluntary, but the girls had keenly adapted to it and become a rather distracting presence.

The school army play-acting never drove me to anguished despair like some of the more morally acute members of my sixth form set. Public-school ritual is a perfectly rational way of running any institution: regiment, fire service or prisoner-of-war camp. The gang mentality works particularly on little boys, who would happily choose cruel temporary leaders, curious nicknames and colourful uniforms if left to their own devices. It could even provide a lump in the throat if you let it, and there are few things more enjoyable than a lump in the throat.

House loyalties worked for me. We used to have a house

music competition. The bigger boys were left to train the trebles and, for once in this world of thick-headed junior pomposity, the fey musical types were put in charge. I can still sing bits of 'The Ash Tree' or 'They Told Me Heraclitus'. Each house had to massacre the same part song, but they were left free to work up a 'unison song'. (I can also get through the 'Pirates' Chorus' from *HMS Pinafore*.) But East House's musical leader was the son of an ambassador, so he taught us 'The East Is Red' in the original Chinese.

'Dong fang hung, chai yang sen, chung qui choo liaou ke Mao Tse Tung.' It was a belter.

Did we win? I don't recall. But I can remember that first verse of the song, and I can remember at the age of thirteen the excitement of the night – the school hall crammed, the deafening cheers, the bright-eyed commitment and the rivalry. It was the sort of occasion that P. G. Wodehouse yearned for all through his adult life. We only got a taste of it from time to time. Perhaps any school which was largely a day school had difficulty working up that sort of thing on a regular basis.

For our part, as absolute beginners, we were glad that some of the traditions were falling away. The year before I arrived they had finally abandoned summer boaters, so we stood a little less chance of getting beaten up. But we stuck out like sore and slightly furry thumbs anyway because until the sixth form we wore grey flannel suits – quite enough, we felt, to make us conspicuous on the bus.

'We may ride by land, we may ride by sea', but there are few places more deserted than the outskirts of a suburban town in the middle of the day. In Brentwood in 2005, I stepped out into another empty dreamscape, with a solitary window cleaner walking by carrying a ladder and whistling, like a fake extra. We used to get on my bus here, by the station. Originally, we waited in the middle of the town, but it got too busy, so we walked the extra distance down the hill, often following a couple of hairy blokes in the year above us who wore exceptionally pointed Chelsea boots with the heels worn down so that they loped like Mexican cowboys.

The stop was still there, in front of that deserted parade of shops, opposite the Essex Arms. Five minutes, ten minutes a day, ten thousand minutes – a hundred and sixty-seven hours of my life spent waiting for a daily bus, and the only specific incident I recall was the day that Jimi Hendrix died.

It was on the front of a copy of the *Evening Standard*. We leaned down to peer up at the headlines, until, irritated, the man in front of us in the queue lent us the front page.

Hendrix dead! And we had never even seen him 'live'. Jimpson was particularly upset. He had adapted like the rest of us into a cool sixth-former schoolboy, with dog-fringe hair, but, like the rest of us, hung on to his fourteen-year-old obsessive collecting habits. In the sixth form it was live performances. It was why rock festivals were so popular. You could knock off nine or ten international guitar heroes on one ticket. It would have always been Graham Jimpson and me at the bus stop. We took the 339 home together every day for six years.

My old bus no longer ran from the station, so I walked up the hill through the quiet town towards the school, past the Ursuline Convent, presumably still a hotbed of what we thought of as the naughtier gels, and stood finally in front of the main red-brick block and clock tower. There was not much visibly stirring at my school either. The front – the imposing main entrance under the tower – was never used by anyone except passing members of Royalty. It was half past ten. I felt like a voyeur on my own life. The dense red brick walls revived only a slight anxiety: the trepidation of dreams about abandonment and inadequacy.

I didn't have to go in. I could easily revisit the place as if in one of those dreams. I can trace the topography like a half-complete computer-game. Drifting in by the side gate, past the crumbling Essex red-brick walls, facing straight on to the fat, flat end of the old junior gym (the one run by Mr Odell, the trim and moderately sane old boy instructor, who wore a pair of tightly drawn up white trousers and a singlet), I can easily walk down that alley in my imagination, leaving the bicycle shed to my right, cross the playground asphalt and enter the junior school, Lawrence House.

It had a flecked concrete floor. There were steps up into an assembly hall. Nothing ever seemed to happen in that room except morning assemblies, presided over by Mr Taylor, a French teacher and the head of the junior school, who had a demeanour of weary concentration. I can clearly remember his fishy eye and his seeming lack of direct contact, a good protective amphibious skin. You never cheeked mystery in the junior school.

I could slow down now for a few seconds. There were two scuffed and battered double doors on either side of this assembly hall. The left-hand side was my staircase. I spent the first year at the top of it in Middle Two, at a desk half-way back in the middle of the second row away from the window.

I had a briefcase. That was important for some reason. It might have been bought to calm my nerves about the frightening, new, big school, because I remember the ritual of it and the slight foreboding I associated with these new plasticky, smelly things: the tubular pencil case with a zip around the top and the Perspex protractor and the silver metal pencil sharpener fitted under an elastic retaining strap.

We did the 'new maths', so soon I had a slide-rule too, in a grey plastic slotted case – nice but never quite the best. Some boys had very swish ones. But I feared slide-rules anyway because they were to do with maths and I found maths – new, old or ancient – perplexing and time-consuming.

I recall that even the blackboards in my new classroom were different from St John's Junior. They seemed to be a deep, deep green, not black at all, and they slid sideways. The masters wrote on them furiously, urging us to 'get this down', with lumps of chalk breaking off and flying across the room in their haste to impart all the necessary instruction. The mummying had gone. I wasn't the top of the form at this school. I was struggling to keep up.

It was here, on this first floor, that I wandered up one lunchtime when I should properly have been outside and heard a painful, breathy sobbing. I glimpsed, in the further classroom, a boy darting about. I can't recall his name, but I knew that he was soppy and a pain, not a friend of mine, but one of those boys who gradually and effectively alienate the masters, because they never do exactly what they're told, or look wrong or talk funny or just fail.

He was running around the desks that lunchtime, refusing to do what he was told again, with a master, one of the younger, tougher, geography teachers, in pursuit, holding a gym shoe in his hand, trying to get him to stay still long enough to be beaten. Both were pleading, the one with the other. The master with the boy, to try and make him accept the inevitable, and the boy with the master, refusing, crying and running around the room, pushing desks in front of him.

I had to press myself back against the wall, in case either saw me there: a voyeur, witnessing something that I certainly didn't want to see. I didn't want to experience it either. Somewhere in this school there were canes, and boys were severely beaten. The theory was that once you'd had it, you could take it again, but I never wanted to have it. Most of all I was scared that I would be like the crying boy, unable to face the ordeal itself.

Moving back, back down the stairs, there would have been that room where we sat for a year in Upper Three, quite a small class. Mr Rance (with his red face and hunched body) taught us history in that lower room. We liked him because he had been a wing commander in the war and at least he could be diverted off any subject with astounding ease. 'Please sir, please sir, are these Huguenots a bit like German pilots, sir?'

'What do you mean, Phillips?'

'Well, sir, didn't they defend themselves with cunning and guile too?'

'Yes, yes, I suppose . . .'

'What was it like, though, sir, when the Germans attacked?'

'They came with very little warning. One minute it was a blue sky up ahead and the next you saw them . . . ah, Phillips, are you trying to distract me from the lesson?'

'No, sir, but did you fire straight away?'

'No. You see, we only had a limited amount of ammunition . . .'

If I walk out of the back of the building and turn left there was a metal door down there in the back of the swimming pool which we only penetrated later because it led to the rifle range. When I was in the Corps I had a go at shooting two-twos and I like the fact that when I am caught in a log cabin and the red Indians are rushing round outside and the women are loading rifles over on the table I can be at the loophole with my jacket off, the ineffectual schoolteacher figure in glasses, but nonetheless a pretty decent shot.

And beyond that there were some corrugated iron huts, weren't there, edging down the side of the lawn in front of Otway under the beech trees?

The junior library was over that way too, in one of the corrugated huts where we flipped though *Amateur Photographer* and sometimes, amongst the studies of birch trees on a hillside and northern streetscapes with big shadows, we found a gloomily lit nude. One little spiv, a dealer in smut and poker dice and American comics, who often managed to find dirty books or pornographic playing cards (he must have had older brothers), once proudly showed us a hugely blown-up photograph of a crotch – I assume from one of these *Amateur Photographers*. It was utterly unfathomable – a few darker smudges on a dark smudge. Even after his lurid explanations, there was almost nothing to decipher, but we were happy to peer and to speculate.

But that's what boys did. They offered up things in the playground: a card trick, or a joke, or a look at some magazine, or a pair of shoes with a compass in the heel and the tracks of various animals in the sole. It was a way of doing business. We had little else to offer each other but we were shamelessly open. We wanted to play.

Walking on into Brentwood High Street in 2005 I passed a poster advertising the return of *'Allo 'Allo*. The town was struggling to adapt to the twenty-first century as much I was. And when the bus finally came I was disappointed. The top deck had gone. We school kids used to push up the Routemaster spiral staircase to get to the six good seats: two at the back, immediately behind the top of the stairs, and slightly raised up, and four across the front with the winders on the windows and the extra leg room. Housewives and OAPs wisely stayed below.

Now, I got as high as I could by sitting on the seat above the wheel arch. There weren't any children going home today, but the bus followed the same pattern, nosing its way painfully slowly along the A128, out of the town, past a sign for

'Heritage of Brentwood' (it was a used-car lot) and on through retail pun country: 'Crafty Arty' and 'Rosie's Posies' and 'Time 4 Pets' and, just like the 4.15 I used to take, the bus virtually emptied before it reached Bentley and the beginning of the countryside.

Jimpson and I and a couple of others were the only ones who stayed the distance, probably doing our homework by the time we reached Blackmore. ('What is this supposed to be?' 'Sorry sir, I wrote the essay on the bus.') Or I would have to listen to Jimpson recite the entire First Division league tables and the name of each player on every team from memory. He made me test him. God, I hated football, and we were a football school. I had never played football properly before I arrived at Brentwood and my mother, stunned by the cost of the plastic-studded slinky black plimsolls that I craved in the school shop, provided me instead with my father's old rugby boots, and huge lengths of laces that had to go right around the back and twice under the instep. The boots curved upwards, like canal-fished boots, and had great bulbous toe caps. Once we had all got over the initial worry of abandoning our pants under our shorts (something the gym masters seemed obsessively concerned about) I was singled out as a collective object of derision thanks to my bloody boots. My rounded toe caps were routinely blamed for sky-ing the ball. Jimpson called them my Dixie Deans, after some pre-war centre forward. Dean became my nickname until Stub or Stub-man or Stubbers or the Stub or the Stub Person or other variations on the theme of my supposed resemblance to the end of a pencil took over.

In 2005 the countryside was still surprisingly undeveloped this close to London, with long vistas across undulating autumn-jaundiced fields. A series of huge brown signs ironically advertised the location of a secret nuclear bunker. They annoyed me with their pointless intrusion (at least the bunker had been purposefully hidden) but otherwise I felt calm, perfectly content to be jolting through this unconsidered Essex countryside. It was a sentimental journey, and, as such, quietly joyous.

It was a lasting friendship with Jimpson. We were bracketed together for most of the middle school, sat opposite each other at lunch and got picked out to be servers at the master's table. I went to visit his house sometimes in the holidays, which showed a dangerous intimacy in boy's school terms. He wore glasses held together with Sellotape and adopted an air of geekish defeatism, wearily accepting his painful lot as the butt of imagined tragic occurrences, but it stood us in little stead in the sandpit up behind his house when we met two Ongar boys who wanted to play fighting. We didn't want to play. As we inwardly predicted, they really wanted to fight properly. Graham was suddenly thrashing around in the sand, beating off this bloke, while the other one held me back. They drew blood, smashed his glasses and taunted us. But we were grammar school boys. All the fighting in our playgrounds was mock wrestling matches, 'no fists'. The only injuries were to the precious school suits and someone's pride. The groping, grappling, gouging earnestness of Graham Jimpson's struggle with a complete stranger, who wanted a proper fight for fun, was scary. We didn't have the guts to try to hurt someone by any means other than verbal assault, even then, at the age of twelve.

Early school itself was a bit like a bus ride. We moved further up the deck, played games, and worked as it rattled along but I don't think we ever looked up to examine the scenery or think where it was going. We hardly marked off years except as a progression of term beginnings and endings. There were occasional bus stops: like birthdays, or the fifth of November, which rose out of a flat landscape, but were themselves utterly routine, even if invested with a manic anticipation.

I kept my fireworks in a box in the cupboard in the back cloakroom. Somewhere around the middle of October I used to go to the newsagent at the far end of Epping High Street. It had the biggest selection in town, in a glass-fronted counter; down a couple of steps, as I remember. Up one end of the vitrine were the hat-box sized mines of serpents, or triple roman candles on wooden spatulas, linked by gunpowder tubes and sealed together with different-coloured tape. They were generally far beyond my means; I sometimes pooled everything, or badgered my mother, and got one, just one, and it became the star of the collection, to be minutely examined on a nightly basis. I collected nothing else quite as mysteriously fragile as fireworks. The best ones rattled. The really big rockets had a tube and then a bulging bit. They were straight where it ran alongside the squared-off stick, but they jutted out and widened towards the top. You could even see where they had been glued together. Sometimes the cone was stuck on slightly wonkily. It added to their individual character. I quite liked just the sticks themselves. As soon as I got in from school I would get down the box and pore over the reds and blues of the wrappers, covered with magic signs of stars or Romany zig-zags, the instructions that promised a rain of fire or a golden fountain of flames and the indigo blue slightly transparent touch paper which emerged so delicately from the tubular cover. Even today I would happily paper a room with some of the Brock's glamorous firework paper designs. The smell of the cordite was the essence, like something powerful, strong and heady. I would arrange them in ranks, imagining their power, sniffing each one and organizing them around a particularly potent long, thin candle with the little cardboard indent at the bottom and the twist at the top. It would have blown a Freudian analyst's head off.

It was hardly surprising that the actual day was always a bit of a let-down. My father took control. People were burned, maimed and disfigured for life by playing with fireworks. They were not toys! As soon as it was dark enough we would get him outside, usually in company with friends who had brought their boxes too, and the dads would wobble to and fro in the dark, lining them up and setting them off on the walls of the rose beds while we huddled by the kitchen door and I tried to identify which disappointing squib corresponded to which luridly packaged fetish object from my collection. 'Was that the Cracker Pot?' That one piff and fizz can't have been the huge one with the special red plastic spike in which I had invested so much hope. I spent more time peering in the box trying to orchestrate the display than I did watching them go off. I always saved the biggest for a finale, like the really huge Catherine Wheel, arranged like three bombs on a wooden hub cap, with its own six-inch nail Sellotaped across the centre. It usually failed to go. My father would scurry away. There was a tiny glow worm in the dark. 'It's gone out.'

'No, just wait.' And then, after waiting for ever, he would take a lot of persuading to go back, shine the torch on it and try again, until when it finally did cough out a lot of sparks he sometimes broke all his own rules and bravely stuck his hand in to give it a push. Usually it shot off for a disappointing thirty seconds of whizzing light. But the aggrandisement of the collection was the main thing. Even ponderously setting them off one by one my mighty box burned up in half an hour flat.

The following day we would search around in the wet,

collecting the flaky, charred remains, the stubs of cardboard and sodden rocket sticks, as if trying to rescue some of the their former true magnificence. But they only made our fingers black.

Jimpson used to slump off the bus in Ongar. I would watch him trail off across the road, lugging a briefcase full of books, his head bowed, a finger habitually poking at the bridge of his glasses while he blinked myopically at the pavement. He was the last of the school commuters to alight, just opposite the tube station, except for me. By then I was only half-way home and had the top deck to myself.

The adult me was happy to be on the bus again, but I would have been nervous to breach the school itself. For years I had avoided all the 'Old Brentwoodian' stuff and finally only gone back in the early nineties to give out some prizes.

I was greeted in the headmaster's sitting room. I had only ever been there once before, for a reading of Tennessee Williams, so I was unprepared for the shock. They walked me across to the new sports hall where I was going to pretend to be a retired colonel, and as we banged through the swing doors, I tottered. 'Stop. Stop,' I said.

It was uncanny. I had expected the classrooms to be vaguely the same, but they were precisely the same. There was the tiling half-way up the walls. There were the boards, the parquet floor, the room divider in Upper Four through which we used to listen to the Remove baiting 'Zip', the physics master. The desks must have been replacements, but they were battered just like ours. But there was more than that. It was the smell. I had completely erased the stench of floor polish mixed with sweat, and now it hit me like a chloroform gas attack. The teachers, the new teachers, stood looking bemused. They wanted to hurry me on. But I wanted to just sit there, in the classrooms, even though the entire junior school and their parents were already rustling their order papers somewhere in some distant hall. This was like a youth drug. It was acutely, painfully evanescent, because it was nothing more tangible than an atmosphere, and I wanted to absorb it before it evaporated.

Everything else about school life has proved almost too fragile to retrieve. You can easily contact old friends, but standing under the oak trees by the science block listening to Gotley tell a dirty joke, or shouting above the noise of the dining hall, or sheltering in the junior library reading old *Punches* when it rained was a small proportion of school life. Most of the time was spent in a one-way relationship with a series of adult males; men like Mr Gilbert, Mr Baron, Mr Cluer and Mr Best. Nothing can get that back, certainly not meeting them 'in real life'. As they stood there, wittering on, to thirty or so boys for a year at a time, did they have any appreciation of the effect they had on us? Mr Ricketts, for example, was an intelligent teacher. We admired him. We were impressed that he went off to some American school for some reputedly huge salary, but what I remember most about him is that his trouser zip never did up at the top. We knew the three hairs on the mole on Mr Cluer's face far better than we knew the declension of any transitive verb. In the sixth form, we even encountered our teachers as independent adults. We were cloistered with them for longer and we assumed we got to understand them as men. But I wonder. Did we really just meet their theatrical, public selves?

Mr Baron we cruelly took to be absurdly childish, with his boasting of supposed wealth from his 'connections to the Pilkington family', his sudden absences 'to visit the headmaster' when he was probably popping out for a fag, even his claims to have worked for British Intelligence. But we also encountered an inspired teacher: hanging from the blackboard, waving with one hand to imitate the wind, bellowing lines to illustrate onomatopoeia: 'now . . . as the loud . . . winds howl . . . in my ear . . .' or teaching us to unpick a poem's internal structure with forensic glee. I learned more about the nature of practical criticism from Baron than my university lecturers, principally because it seemed to matter so fiercely to him. And if he was ineffably silly, then that meant we developed an attitude, perhaps even the strongest of affections. He became a surrogate daft uncle: unshameable, quite as happy to warn us against sitting on the radiators – 'because you'll get piles' – as he was to read Chaucer 'with the original Middle English pronunciation'. At the beginning of the sixth form he played us his 'readings' of *Paradise Lost*. He set up a little reel-to-reel tape recorder and announced that he had originally performed them for the Third Programme. Cruel observers pointed out that these broadcast recordings had coughs and rustlings in the background. But I still found that, after one playing, I could recite most of the opening of Book Six from memory.

But would it be possible to meet them off duty? Ten years after I left the school, I appeared in a play in the West End. A stage doorman rang down to tell me that Jeffers, a school friend, had 'come round'. Jeffers came in and explained that he had been away, worked in the Far East and now, after some sort of failed marriage, had come back to England. He had been walking down Shaftesbury Avenue and seen my name up in lights. This was eerily 'Somerset Maugham'. We had hardly been close. And I behaved like most busy people in a short story confronted with a school chum. I fobbed him off by smiling weakly. He seemed content but, as he was leaving, told me he was thinking of looking up Jim Rennie, our economic history teacher.

Rennie had been an enigma. In our early years at the school he was best avoided, striding into assembly at speed and handing out punishments to anybody who caught his eye. ('Proverbs, chapter one, by tomorrow morning.')

Then he took me for history. I told Jeffers how I remembered I had been late for the first day of his first sixth-form set. When I apologized frantically Rennie laughed at me. 'We're in the sixth form now,' he said. 'We can behave like gentlemen, I think.' He explained that when he had first worked at the school some time in the 1920s, he couldn't keep discipline, so he had decided to spare no one below the age of fifteen, but for us, now we were in the sixth form we would be adults together.

Jeffers agreed. He had been tolerant, wise and funny. He made us write a list of useful sayings in the front of our folders. 'Life is real, life is earnest and the goal is not the grave,' and 'Me and my dog got lost in a fog.'

'Do you know where he lives?' I asked Jeffers. I began to see that he was a lot more interested in tracking down this surrogate father figure than he was in meeting me.

'No, but it must be up near Penrith. I can ask at the school.'

Rennie had come from Cumbria. He had dressed in what I now realize were rather beautiful tweed suits, like a Penrith solicitor. Penrith had been the source of all wisdom, and it made sense that he would have gone back there. I wished Jeffers luck, told him to call again if he wanted to get back together.

I didn't see Jeffers for another ten years. I was appearing at the Apollo in Oxford. The stage-door keeper called down again. In a few moments Jeffers was sitting in my dressing room. 'You remember when I saw you last,' he began. I nodded. I did. 'Well, I didn't get back in touch because I decided to go to France.' He paused and looked distant. 'But . . . well, things haven't worked out over there and I've just come back and I was in Oxford and I saw your name . . .'

It was up in lights again.

'You're still in the same line of business, then?'

We talked for a bit about mutual friends that neither of us had seen, and after a while he got up to leave. 'Oh, by the way,' he said in the doorway, 'I tracked down old Rennie. He was in Penrith. Rather lovely cottage. I went to his door and knocked. He was perfectly nice, but . . .' his brow darkened. I had never seen this before, but it was quite a neat trick. '. . . but . . . he didn't remember me.' Jeffers looked depressed.

'Well, I suppose he must have had hundreds of pupils in his time.'

'That's what he said, but I said to him, you know, I was in your set for two years. Two years, five times a week. He must have remembered me.'

Nothing I said convinced Jeffers that Jim Rennie wasn't engaging in some schoolmasterly subterfuge. He shook his head and went off into the night and for all I know to Zanzibar. I suppose I will meet him again in another ten years, backstage at the Oldham Coliseum when I'm touring *The Odd Couple*.

On the last day of school ever, some of us went for a lunchtime drink with Roger Perrin, who taught medieval history. He was another great teacher, who deported himself like a big-game hunter loping around after some comical prey. We were his first set. His lips would twitch with amusement at the experiments of Frederick II or the Chronicles of Geoffrey of Monmouth. It was rare at that stage to allow any intimacy. It was rare for teachers to even admit that they drank beer. But this was the end of the seventh form. We

were leaving with Oxbridge success. Just those few pints of
beer in the back room of a pub seemed the culmination
of a steady progression towards the outside world, like one
of those scenes from a madhouse movie where the inmate
is taken to a restaurant and shown a menu. 'Go on, you can
have anything you want.'

I kept in touch with Roger. He seemed an exception –
able to free himself from the conspiracy of 'them and us',
perhaps because he had been young himself when he taught
me. He laughed about Mr Gilbert. He told me that the headmaster, Sale, a man Roger admired, had tried repeatedly to
sack Bilge but he had been thwarted by the teacher's unions.
It was a telling moment, like being allowed a glimpse behind
the scenes.

Spud Baron sort of remembered me too. I had hoped he
would. Again, I was in a show, with my name up in hard-
board. The stage-door keeper rang me. 'Do you know a
Major Baron?'

I cringed slightly. This was too dad-like. I remembered
that he sometimes adopted his military rank at ticket offices
and in theatres.

But I braced myself for affection. We were off duty. I
assumed that he would greet me and reminisce fondly, that
he would drop his pretensions, have a laugh and we would
talk as veterans. I was making Jeffers' mistake. He never even
took his hat off. He sat with his coat on his lap and hit the
chair with commentary, analysing my performance in
perfectly complimentary tones, but remote and smiling, no
different in his manner from the classroom ten or so years
before. Can you believe that I wanted to take this short,
aged, pompous bachelor in my arms, acknowledge him on
behalf of us all as the figure that he had been to me and so
many of my friends in those years? I wanted, somehow, to

repay the affection that he seemed to have squandered on us.

I wish I had. As it was, I sat there with a helpless smile on my face, utterly unable to get a word in edgeways, shook his hand when he finished and let him bustle off. He's dead now.

That last day, though, had also been my last trip on the 339. There was a girl who had split up with her long-term boy friend some weeks before. She was gorgeous. She was intelligent. She was highly experienced. I had arranged to take her out in London. This was irresponsibly mature. I would have to talk to her all evening without other boys as props. But whatever happened I had to get back to Epping, get changed into my loon pants and tie-dye vest, back-comb my hair and then take the tube to meet her in Piccadilly. It was a three-hour commitment. I needed to be on the two-fifteen bus. So I had to swig down a last half pint and run for the damned 339, though even as I climbed aboard, I noticed that I wanted to pee.

By the time we got to North Weald on that trip – the last journey I was to take on this route before I sat on it now – I was the colour of a five-week-old corpse. Sweat was pouring down my brow. Alone on the top of the bus, I writhed in agony. By the time I got to Ongar, I had been in excruciating pain, my bladder begging for release. As we crept through the bare countryside I nearly fainted away. North Weald was as long as it is now; an endless parade of rubbishy villas and nondescript airforce houses. The bus had never lumbered so laboriously. It stopped at least four times. There was no way I could urinate out of the window. I couldn't surreptitiously piss down the central aisle. As the 339 swayed ponderously past the Battle of Britain airfield and approached the edge of Epping Forest I could stand it no longer. I was within ten minutes of home. I had waited for two years, pining after Helen. Here at last was a legitimate toehold on her favours. I was within shouting distance of a hand up her bra. But it was no good. I was going to die. I rang the request stop bell, leaped past the startled bus conductor and charged across the road into the forest of ancient oaks. I stood there swathed in clouds of steamy relief. I had had to go. That last journey had defeated me.

8. Weekend Hippy

My relief in Epping Forest left me in a state of ecstatic bliss. I was close enough to town to hitch in and get the Central Line to meet the lovely Helen too. But it didn't work out. It may have been my stream of offbeat chatter which became a fire hydrant and drowned her. It may have been the entertainment. Leafing through *Time Out*, I chose the most pretentious film I could find. (She was after all doing history and English A levels just like me.) *Time Out* failed to mention that *WR: The Mysteries of the Organism* was borderline pornography. As the lights went down, some respite from my jabber was provided by six naked people breaking eggs over their thighs in an Orgasmatron. She was mature enough to cope with it. I wasn't. What if she thought I had taken her to this deliberately? I started whispering my anguish from about five minutes in. (She may have wanted to continue the relationship. Who knows? I never gave her a chance to get a word in edgeways.)

Passion had surfaced with astonishing virulence around the age of fifteen. Girls, who had been avoided, swept into the schoolboy consciousness much like Airfix kits five years previously. One minute we had been happily indifferent to their existence and the next minute they were an all-consuming obsession.

At the beginning of the sixth form, newly kitted out in blazers and flannels to differentiate ourselves from the hairy-suited lower forms, divided into sets instead of classes and tentatively discovering each other's Christian name, a group gathered in 'six thirty-two' every lunchtime and break. The headmaster directly referred to the 'unpleasant sound of cliquish laughter emanating from one of the classrooms in the new block'. There were other sixth-form gangs: better-heeled smoothies who seemed to have money and the demeanour of a junior sales team, or geeky chaps who hung around the library to do crosswords, but we were the ones who felt most pleased with our own company. 'The Clique' – Gotley, Macey, Tompsett, Squire, Roberts, Holloway, Jimpson, Jaques and the rest – shared a considerable passion for 'progressive music', animated discussion about the existence of God (a number discovered Christ along with deodorants) and meeting girls. Tantalizingly, there were two girls' schools within a condom's throw of our school. And in the very earliest days of the term it was announced that there were going to be ballroom dancing classes.

The first lesson had an explosive erotic charge heightened by a strong smell of floor polish. A veritable rack of girls, in dark uniform short skirts, knees together, trembling with anticipation, were lined up in front of us in the Memorial Hall. The portraits of a dozen ex-headmasters looked on helplessly as 'madame' flounced down the centre of the Memorial Hall, clapped her hands and announced, 'Now, boys, step forward and choose a partner.'

There was an undignified scuttle towards Louise, who had the shortest skirt. 'Come on. Come on!' She clapped again. I offered a hand to my sixth-form feminine ideal. Janet was blonde, with a fringe and a snub nose. She was also an identical twin.

In the 1980s, when I directed a production of *Twelfth Night*, itself about identical twins, I felt I needed to get the cast to search out their memories of infatuated love. 'It's what this play is about,' I explained. 'You remember: sitting in class, unable to concentrate, mooning after that girl you took to the disco . . .'

Orsino, Viola and Olivia stared blankly at me.

'You know, you do . . . you must have done this: when you couldn't bring yourself to telephone; when you wrote her name in your exercise book. When you got like Donne, and you just glued eyes together.'

They exchanged looks. 'No,' said Viola. 'No, I've never felt anything like that.'

The others shrugged in agreement. (In the end, it wasn't a hugely successful production.) But I was mystified. I fell in love all over the shop in the lower sixth. We all did: silly schoolboy love, with yearning and sleepless nights and that fluttering feeling in the thorax when you're thinking about her in class.

'Are you with us, Rhys Jones?'

'Yes, sir. Sorry, sir.'

After the first few dances, treading on her toes enough to get myself noticed, and after a bit of pairing off with a few others, just to check them out, Janet and I became regular dance-partners. It was a particularly clammy-handed moment when the tables were turned. ('Now, girls! You choose.') But Janet walked across the parquet and asked me for the first foxtrot.

My friend Fischl took up with Janet's identical twin sister, Clare, which was handy, because I reckoned I might need someone to talk to. Clare looked startlingly similar to Janet. (They were both in school uniform, but even in the little details that girls fiddled with, such as the length of their skirts and the way they tied their ties, they were of a piece.)

I found myself wondering, was Clare perhaps the better-looking of the two? No, no, impossible. They both had rather, well, square faces and strong jaws, but Janet was divine. I was intoxicated. Not that we talked much. We weren't encouraged to talk. We had complicated steps to learn. Janet looked demurely down, and I loved that, though she was probably just keeping her feet out of my way. She was quite practically minded. I was full of admiration. Admiration and infatuation; this was perfect.

The waltz encouraged us to hold on tight because, as we gained confidence, we could sort of pull the girl, I mean Janet, up close and spin around to the twirly bits of music. This required us to be deliciously firm, though I suspect neither Fischl nor I was as strong as Janet and Clare. They were both stars of the high-school hockey team. Gotley said they looked a little stocky with it, but then what did he know?

I invited Janet to a party at Jaques' on a Saturday night. It was near by. After a day moping around I got into my pink shirt and blue hipster brushed denims and drank a half pint, hiding from schoolmasters in a local pub. I waited to ring the doorbell in Shenfield Road as close to the agreed time as I dared.

I stood breathing heavily, waiting in the yellow light from the pebbled hall window by the rose beds. There was bumping inside and the door opened. And there she was: my passion.

Or was it?

Was it her sister Clare? I quickly switched off the engine of ecstasy.

But no, hang on, it was Janet after all. She was dressed up and looked and smelled different. I switched it all back on. This was harder work than I had imagined.

We escorted Janet and Clare to the school disco in the pavilion. The school stage crew had hired in a lorryload of late-sixties disco lights. I found it swooningly hedonistic. I still associate colour-wheels, swirling psychedelic gloop, drifting around the walls in splodges of specimen-tray glamour with the promise of unparalleled decadence. Everything became fluidly groovy. Even the girl's short, polypropylene dresses seemed to pulsate with organic promise. But it was so dark and mysterious and loud that we had even more difficulty than usual telling our partners apart.

The music was stomach-wobbling. During 'Je t'aime', the panting Jane Birkin and Serge Gainsbourg hit, I took the opportunity to clasp Janet even tighter than in the waltz. I tried a kiss. There was a hiatus when our teeth clashed, but after that we rammed our mouths together until our lips grew sore. Over the next few weeks, I stayed hot, but Janet cooled. Was it because, away from the dance floor, we had nothing in common at all? Or was it because both Janet and Clare were determined to stick to kissing and used those strong hockey-player's arms to pinion wandering hands? Or was it because I still couldn't work out which one I was yearning for? They were quite serious really, like so many girls. We wanted to wag our tails and lick them and then run off back to the rest of the boys.

So then I was out of love. It was a bit of a relief really. Never mind the ballroom dancing, there was still the mixed folk club, and the joint historical society. We trotted off to those and met less sporty girls with glasses and funny hair-dos – more like ourselves in fact. And if the historical society seemed a bit heavy, then we organized a medieval banquet to lighten it up. Despite rather too many apples and a surfeit of cold chicken, the chair-girl from the high school wore such a low-cut gown that we elected to have another feast. Only this time it would be a Roman orgy. The girls thought this was a fantastic idea. Good girls. It was chicken in togas instead.

I liked being with girls, but I probably liked being with

blokes a bit more. Blokes were funnier and grubby for a laugh. 'Did you get a hand up her skirt? Cor.' We may have joined the film club and the debating society and talked about apartheid and Jean-Luc Godard, but we preferred Gotley enthusing about one-handed wrestling with a bra-hook.

Clearly, a steady relationship got in the way of real fun, and every Saturday night there was now a party in some blank bit of Essex hinterland. Romford had its brewery. Ilford its camera film. But Upminster was the quintessential suburban playground where all the parties happened. Somebody who knew somebody called John had definitely been invited. So we would gather in the late afternoon at a friend of a friend's to listen to most of 'Albatross' played badly on a cheap electric guitar and would then lope off into the indistinguishable streets to negotiate entry. That was the plan. Often the friend of a friend would have forgotten the exact number, or even the exact street, so we would cover Upminster, trudging up mock-Tudor avenues, keeping a careful look out for a tell-tale red light or a glimpse of pyramid hair or a reefer jacket in a porch.

'Martin!'

'That you, Graham?'

'Yeah. Is this the party?'

'Yes. Can you get us in? Have you got an invite?'

'Yeah, but I've got this lot with me already.'

I was a long way from home, a hanger-on. And Graham was undoubtedly only a peripheral member of the 'Upminster Fun Gang' anyway. If it all went to plan, then Martin saw Alison whose party it was and we pushed on in, past the blokes leaning with one foot up on the wall in the hallway who were knocking ornaments on to the floor with the back of their coats, on into the living room, where it would be dark except for a single lamp with a shawl thrown over it which was threatening to ignite. The smell of singeing was hidden by the joss-sticks, there to provide a whiff of Kathmandu. The radiogram was turned up so high that the plywood sides were rattling. Some girls had put on Tamla Motown and were dancing together. Later, some boys would put on Deep Purple and dance together too, fingers in belts, arms akimbo, swinging down towards each other's crotch in a way that might have impressed a Zulu but was steadfastly ignored by Upminster girls, who didn't really like heavy music anyway.

At some point there would be an argument, because Bez wanted to play some 'real music'. After Mike's precious Deep Purple had been scratched, they would reach a compromise and put on Pink Floyd and lie there in a drunken stupor on the floor until the room had emptied, apart from the two girls who had been sitting on the sofa against the wall all night waiting to go home. It was bliss.

I usually stayed in the kitchen. It was the only place you could see. It was the place where all the drink was deposited. The cheapest party-ticket, brandished at the door, was a bottle of Hirondelle, which cost under a quid – reputedly a mixture of Corsican wine and sulphuric acid – and it knocked you out.

We made occasional forays into squats, or parties in huge houses, like Wendy's at the end of the road in Epping, where the upper levels would be full of young men vaguely wobbling back-combed billows of hair to freaky music. I loved to go into these dark rooms, in search of the inner sanctum of hipness. It was quite possible in the late sixties and early seventies to grow a large head of hair, wear excessively wide flares and aspire to be more moody than any one else as a life-style option. 'Don't hassle me, man,' could be applied equally to domestic chores, moving one's legs out of the way or engaging in any form of discourse at all.

I remember one squalid homestead, where everybody was huddled in a corner of the basement room. What were we doing there? It was just another party. We went to sit ourselves down and do a bit of head-waggling of our own, but someone spoke up from the haze on the other side. 'Hey, man, careful over there. The water bed exploded.' We stepped gingerly over an enormous damp patch.

Or what about the visit to my brother in Colchester, where he was at the hippest of all universities – Essex, so freaky that Mrs Thatcher specifically singled it out for verbal assault. Here indeed was the epicentre of unstraightness. Imagine my excitement. The whole place was *en fête*. It was an enormous party of huge darkened rooms. In one, severely dressed, bearded men were dropping big pipes, just to hear the sound they made. It was a 'happening'. On the whole, little actually seemed to happen at the happenings I went to. They all demanded reserves of patience. There was an initial buzz. Gosh. This really is 'other', but when you got used to it, it became just a bit too extenuated and unimaginative, like a Hawkwind concert.

I suppose it was the drugs. Anybody seriously into drugs has to accept that life is mostly anticipation. All that waiting around, knowing that any minute or half-hour, or possibly sometime early the next day, someone 'holding' might bother to turn up. But we weren't a drug party scene. How could we be? There was scarcely enough to go around Kensington Market at the time let alone Upminster.

When the beer ran out we moved on to the cheap Riesling, and the herbaceous borders ran with puke. It was almost a ritual. The early part of the evening was spent commiserating with some poor girl whose friend had had to be helped into a quiet room. 'Don't go in there, Alison is lying down.' Alison, fourteen, had celebrated her first introduction to alcohol by drinking half a bottle of Stone's Ginger Wine and a pint of cider. 'She shouldn't mix. Take things easy, silly girl. No, don't ring her mother.' Wise words but later, the Party Seven gone, and, somebody having stubbed out their cigarettes in the half-finished cans of Guinness, we usually risked the rest of the ginger brew ourselves, on top of five pints of beer and the remains of that Blue Nun.

Sometimes, I woke up in the middle of playing fields, wondering what arrangements I might have made to stay the night. What time was it? Where was that party anyway? Wasn't I supposed to be staying there? I was miles from home.

It was then that the wastelands of outer London became their strangest; the houses with their black windows, under the constant yellow glow of the street lamps, looked false. I turned a corner once and found a whole cul-de-sac under six inches of water in the middle of the night, nobody around but me; the street a shallow canal reflecting the unearthly, inhuman dormitory glare.

Once, maybe twice, it was my turn. I brought the whole party back to Epping.

'We'll stay in the back room,' said my parents firmly.

'No, no. It would be much better if you went out.'

'This is my house. What is that you intend to do, that I can't be here?'

Well, of course, they wouldn't want to know. The boot was on the other foot in the door. What was I going to do to keep out those blokes who arrived and said, 'I'm a friend of John. John said I could come.' John was handy. There was always a John, somewhere. And it was those friends of the non-existent John who wrecked the place.

'I'm going to make them food.'

'No, no. They won't want food.'

'They must want to eat. If they eat it will stop people getting drunk.'

Dear God. They want to get drunk, that's the point. The more food provided the more they have to grind into the carpets. What does she think this is? A dinner party?

Sometimes entire houses were trashed. It was common for banisters to come loose, for fires to be started in the kitchen, for white carpets to be stained an indelible, purplish-red, for precious porcelain models of shepherdesses to be decapitated, for prize-winning gardens to be trampled and razed. In the worst cases, furniture was stolen and people were taken away in ambulances. It was not possible to explain what fun this was to an adult. Better, much better, for an interim period to elapse in which some restoration was accomplished.

How many times had I helped some panic-stricken school friend, standing pale and horribly wild-eyed after everyone had been kicked out and the lights turned back on to reveal the horror. 'Christ! My parents will be back in a few minutes. Help me get some of this sick off the carpet.' Usually, I was staying the night. I would be sleeping on the sofa. I would have to try to blend into the bamboo wallpaper while the leading member of the Upminster Fun Gang, a storm trooper of joint-trashing himself, cowered before sober reality.

'What on earth has been going on here?'

'It's just a little mess. We put salt on the worst of it.'

'We trusted you, and this is how you repay us.'

'There were some gate-crashers.'

'Did you call the police?'

Stupid men, fathers, sometimes. Somebody else, a neighbour probably, had called the police, yes. But they were long gone. Often, it was only my being there that stopped it spiralling upwards into a family court.

I settled down on the sofa. 'No, no, I'll be fine here,

honestly.' And I slept, not even bothering to take my boots off, turning over to block out the muffled recriminations coming from somewhere upstairs.

Whose house was it where I spent the night trying to cope with the mysterious noise? I switched off the light, pulled the blanket over my head and after a few seconds the rattling sound started, somewhere in the room, not loud, but insistent. Finally I could stand it no longer, got up and switched the light back on and it stopped, instantly. I waited, switched the light off and stumbled back to the sofa in the dark. It started again. This happened three times before I found the hamster cage behind the curtains. It was three in the morning. He sat with his paws raised and an inquiring look in his black dewdrop eyes in the bottom of his wheel, waiting, politely, to get back to his nocturnal exercise.

I dreaded the mornings, especially if the mum insisted on making breakfast. 'Here, bacon, eggs, black pudding.'

'Thanks, Mrs Macey.' A long silence followed, while Macey and I stared at the greasy plates through throbbing eyeballs and pounding heads, fighting back nausea.

'Your father thinks someone was in our bed. What sort of people did you have here?'

'They were just normal people, weren't they, Rhys?'

'Yes.' Can I push this stuff around the plate without actually throwing up?

'But I don't understand. Would your mother allow this sort of thing to go on, Rhys?'

'Mmm . . .'

Well, of course she wouldn't. She would have to be got out of the way too. Because in the end, it wasn't the damage, or the recriminations, or the period of grace that would allow a modicum of tidying up, it was the loss of face that was at stake.

I have done it myself now, sat, like Virginia McKenna locked in the gun room, while a group of savages on day release from inner London day schools laid waste the governor's palace. It's a phase. Of course, we didn't believe it was a phase. We thought we had invented the genre.

Somewhere in the middle of this I had met Jane, who was a very naughty girl, and I had fallen deeply in love with her. I picked her up at a party. Or she picked me up. Yes, she picked me up. This was a rare event and what made her rather exciting. I should have known she was only dallying with me.

She was short and blonde and had been going out with someone who had just left the upper sixth. She talked to me to annoy him, but she was very direct, and I was seduced by her worldliness. The little girls – the fifteen-year-olds we were expected to focus on – were like us, tentative, but Jane snogged furiously and groped extremely efficiently. When I went to her house she introduced me to her startled mother and led me straight up to her bedroom for a bit of torrid fumbling. There wasn't any actual sex. None of us seemed to get sex, however much we boasted, though we discussed the possibility endlessly. The girls were generally far too canny. But we could rub and pant and get sticky, and Jane seemed to want to do that as soon as we met.

Jane was a wild child. I certainly wasn't. I sat and had tea in the kitchen afterwards, all flushed and wobbly, while Jane pointedly ignored her poor mother. I remember the journey home, sitting on the front seat on a completely deserted upper deck of the later bus, away from the usual rush-hour crowd, exulting in the agony of adolescent passion. This was it. I was completely and utterly consumed by the aptness of Jane, her blonde, slightly dirty hair, her nylon school shirt, her willingness, her secret personality, her femininity and understanding of my needs. We had groped in her room! With her mother downstairs.

A few minutes later, as I lurched through the night, I discovered that I couldn't remember what she looked like. I sat in a panic. But I was in love with her! I just couldn't quite recall her face. But the way she hitched her high-school dark-blue skirt around her waist. And the way a few tendrils of hair hung upwards on her cheek from an earlier cut that was growing out . . . and the way she talked to me about . . . what? We usually glued our faces to each other pretty quickly. Ah yes. I remembered her face. Yes, that's who I was in love with. Phew.

So, if I really, really loved Jane, because she was older than me and more knowing and experienced, why on earth did I tell Gotley about her at all? Why did I tell him that I met her in the woods at lunchtimes and near as dammit fucked. Not really fucked, but got pretty close.

Because the following lunchtime, when I met her in the woods again, we turned a corner heading for the bracken and there they all were, at least a dozen of them, sniggering and grinning. 'Fancy seeing you here, Stubs.'

'Yeah. Yeah.'

'Aren't you going to introduce us to your friend?'

'Bugger off!'

She didn't say anything. But she could see I was really just a kid. Come next Saturday and the next party, when I arrived longing for her, I discovered she had already gone off with someone else.

One of the girls from the joint historical society tried to comfort me. 'Forget her. She was just anybody's.' That was the point. She was as dirty-minded and sex-obsessed as a bloke. But she wasn't mine any more. But by the end of the evening I was back with my mates, getting drunk.

9. Mersea

'Is that the Peldon Rose?' my mother asked.

'Yes.'

The darkened pub flashed by. As children we liked it when we stopped for supper on light evenings on the way back from the boat. It was the first place on the mainland. We ate on furniture made of grey logs, unsawn, like branches from trees, and, since they looked so improvised, surprisingly heavy to lug about – pork pie, Scotch eggs, rubber sausages. My father liked hot mustard, and just the traces from his knife where he cut ours in half had seemed an impossibly adult taste.

The other way, beyond the pub, the road dips, the screens of Essex blackthorn lift and white fence markers appear. In the daylight, an expanse of salting stretches off to the west to Tollesbury. At night the blank coastal strip simmers under a Lucozade dawn. Sometimes at high tide the road is covered completely. The creeks on either side are shallow and clogged with mud. It felt American. So did the whole island. All the English virtues of civic dignity and properly organized pavements seemed slow to catch on. Is it still like that I wonder? It was too dark to see. It used to be characterized by private lanes with improvised road surfaces and half-developed plots. The people of West Mersea seemed in denial, or perhaps their council was. They refused for years to behave outwardly like a modern, settled 1970s community.

I turned off into Firs Road.

'Oh, you know the way,' my mother said and surprised me.

'Yes.' I knew the back route, even though I had never driven here as a teenager. I had never driven at all as a teenager. There was no chance of having a car, and my father wasn't going to lend us his, so there wasn't much point in learning. Perhaps we always took the main road through the ancient little village, another American place of clapboard houses. The boat was usually parked in a car park in front of the Victory pub. My mother wouldn't have been a regular at the Club. My father wouldn't have let her.

I was speaking at the West Mersea Yacht Club as a guest of the Royal Naval Sailing Association, East Coast Branch, and as we parked and as I helped my mother out of the car, I wished I wasn't. It wasn't a particularly focused wish, just the usual 'What the hell am I doing here?' gloom that accompanies every after-dinner speech and makes me curt and unsociable when I arrive. I would have to meet and talk with elderly strangers. (There were dozens in the bar.) I would have to eat an indifferent meal. (It was fair but hardly celebrant.) I would be sat next to the chairman, and we would run out of things to say to each other by the end of the hors-d'œuvres. (He was a nice man with a boat he kept in Bradwell, right on the other side of the Blackwater. We persevered until half-way through the main course.)

As we stood in the bar (the sort of place where you have to tiptoe carefully around the subject of why you don't drink) all I really wanted to do was look at the black and white photographs of sleek fifties racing yachts owned by brigadiers. These were the yachts we used to pass on the way out of the creek on a Saturday morning. The Kim Holman and the Robert Clarke designs that had glistened in the Essex sun and seemed so elegant, fit and organized compared with our ersatz boating experience.

I was glad my mother had been able to come. She had

been diagnosed with breast cancer two months before. This was a cruel eighty-first birthday present.

'They keep telling me it's only younger women. They even stop testing you after a certain age.'

They also told her not to worry. 'Something else will probably carry you off before this cancer does.' But that was what they had told my father at the age of seventy. It was the cancer that had quickly carried him off.

My mother was being defiantly selfless about it – talking in surprised tones about how she seemed to think about it all the time, as if this was the last thing she had expected. She had finished treatment the week before. It had tired her, but she wanted to come. 'I'm sore,' she told me, and I pulled a sympathetic face. In some polished gentlemanly society, sons can talk about the bruised and aching breast of their elderly mothers. As for me, I grunted and commiserated and tried to change the subject. She had a large and dutiful 'bosom', as she called it. This was the bosom I had rested my head on. This was my mummy's bosom. Now she was too sore to even hug.

She was a victim of too many assaults of old age: mugged by legs, attacked by arthritis, happy-slapped by a painful replacement knee, and now this. She talked about my father. The round of life brought everything up in turn. ('He would have liked this.' 'Oh, that was so like your father.') She told me that she wanted him here now, when she was frightened, more than any other time.

It seemed, despite all this, that she never faded. She just went on, my mother. This was me, in denial of the facts. There were still lunches and meetings and people calling. I accepted all the doctors told me, about how this thing would settle and how it was less virulent, because it was convenient to do so. I spent time persuading her that they were hopeful, but I knew that after all the mechanical failures this seemed like something irreparable. I was reminded of my father. ('I had to tell a woman that her husband would not survive an illness. He was eighty-seven. Do you know what she said? "Why him, doctor, why him?"')

I was speaking at the club because Derek had asked me to. Derek had retired from the Navy as a chief petty officer and joined the police. When he sailed with my father he was a detective chief inspector, the most clubbable, social, entertaining policeman you could hope to be arrested by. How on earth he hooked up with my dad I have no idea. We often sailed in a little flotilla round the east coast, bumping into Derek and his family, doing things together.

You make assumptions about your parents' friendships as a child. Or rather you don't. You simply accept these adults and you ask no questions. Why these two different men should have spent any time together only seems curious now.

To us kids Derek was the best. He told incredible long-winded and carefully performed jokes. He was easy-going in any society, confident, ready to laugh off accidents. I used to wonder, though, what he would have been like as a policeman. There were always, behind the huge smile and easy laughter and the brilliant stories, these sharp detective eyes, alert to other human beings; unlike my father.

It was a good laugh for the audience at the club that night. 'I go back a long way with Derek. He banged me up for three years.'

'No, we never came in here very much,' my mother explained in the bar beforehand. 'Your father used to say it was the most expensive loo he ever joined.'

I told them that in the speech too. In fact I got provided with half the funny stories for the beginning of my 'talk' simply by prodding memories, as we stood surrounded by all these men in blazers with their little floating garden sheds.

'Your dad,' Derek told me 'was immensely proud of *Windsong*. And one day we were in here . . . it might have been . . .' He looked around. (It probably wasn't. It was probably in the Victory. He would have gone there for his lunch because it was close to where the boat was kept in the winter.) 'And anyway, I spot Maurice Griffiths on the other side of the bar, and I was amazed that your dad had never met him, and he revered those boats.'

I wasn't amazed. My father would never have freely introduced himself to anybody.

'So I introduced him. And Elwyn went up to Maurice and said, "I'm so pleased to meet you because I am so proud of the boat I own that you designed." "Which boat is that?" asked Griffiths. "*Windsong*," says your father. "Oh, that old hulk. That was the worst boat I ever built." And your father was so crestfallen.' Derek laughed.

Is that what they thought, then, what all sons suspect about their father, that the rest of the world is laughing at them? But he *would* have been crestfallen. It wasn't my father's way to be party to the broad stroke of humour. He found social demands perplexing. If he was doing something else, he couldn't cope with them at all. I have that trait too. I had arrived at the club trying to work out where I would be talking from, fiddling with the computer that I'd brought but which wouldn't show my photographs through their screen projector, utterly preoccupied with what I had to say and unable to let that ride and concentrate on chat, small talk and the basic demands of humanity. God damn it. Yes. This is exactly how he would have behaved. I am behaving exactly like my father!

When did my father let me take the boat off without him? It was a bold thing for him to do. Would I even trust my son with my bicycle? But at some point in the sixth form, after A levels, perhaps, I took a couple of friends and we drifted up the coast one hot summer's week, going around and on into Brightlingsea. How could he let us? He was nervous. He was always so worried about safety. I have written calumny about him here, because that's the side of him that stuck to me, but he must have been understanding and resolute to do that.

We went to Brightlingsea. It was an afternoon's sail along the coast of Mersea Island and up into the Colne, the river that runs up to Colchester. I'd done it hundreds of times before. As my father got older (fifty-something) he was happy to leave me in control anyway. He would get the boat out of the harbour, hand over the tiller and go below and sleep. But it wasn't the crowded anchorage that should have worried him. (I could cope.) It wasn't the fact that the boat had to be squeezed in somehow between two upright wooden posts with a line attached to each. Although that did cause us problems when the tide changed direction and we let go of the wrong end so we drifted out and blocked most of the passage. (He wouldn't have liked to see it, but we coped.) No, it was the quantity of pubs in the little town that should have worried him. ('They're just low-grade alcoholics,' he said of regulars, neatly combining the *Lancet* with his non-conformist upbringing.)

We started in the mock-Tudor tavern near the top of the long wide hard that faced on to the river, then went up into the terraced streets, stopping at all the little terraced pubs. We drank bitter at just over two shillings a pint and eventually staggered back to the long jetty in the dark. When we started we had been sober enough to drag the little rowing dinghy right up to the top of the jetty, calculating that when we got back the tide would have reached it. We had been sensible enough in our judgement to get that right. There was the dinghy, sitting in the pitch dark. It was afloat. The water had a smear of street lights on it: squid-ink black and glossy. We were not so drunk that we couldn't slither down the green weed-covered pier and get to the little boat. It was as we climbed into it that our inexperience, mostly our inexperience with six or seven pints, really showed up. Three got in easily enough.

The fourth stepped a little too heavily on the coaming. It tipped, and the sea slipped in over the side. I remember watching it and thinking how slight a dip we needed, because within seconds we were sitting in the boat, which was sitting on the bottom, and the water had levelled off around our chests.

Oh Dad, poor Dad. If you had known about that you would never have slept. These days, I do what he would have done, which is imagine the consequences if we'd tipped ourselves those four inches sideways, half-way across instead of next to the jetty. But hey, we didn't, so who's to know?

The next day we went to Clacton. We motored the boat alongside the beaches on a festering hot day, spying on the shore through binoculars and the crowds ranged along the promenades. He would never have done what we did then, which was to take the boat right in close, throw out an anchor and row ashore, but then he was unlikely to have been overcome with an adolescent lust for pursuing bathing beauties. He would have thought about the dangers of an onshore breeze blowing up, the difficulty of holding on the sandy bottom, the possible problems of relaunching the dinghy into the waves crashing on the shore. But there weren't any waves crashing on the shore. It was merely sultry, hot and smelly. We rowed in through the sloppy wavelets between the paddlers, bought hot dogs and thought we'd done something really cheeky, though the two scrubbers sitting on the big, painted iron fence above the south beach weren't scrubby enough to be tempted aboard our lugger. They clearly weren't really impressed with our yacht. Somehow we got as far as Aldeburgh because I remember we loitered around a funfair there and drank in the Cross Keys.

My parents were trading up in various little ways. They bought a cottage in Goldhanger in the late seventies. This was a village off the twisting, looping, track-like road that ran along the north shore of the Blackwater Estuary from Maldon to Mersea, between Roman Heybridge Basin and Tolleshunt D'Arcy. It was to become Jeremy Bamber country. The mass murderer disposed of his entire family just up the road. It was an innocuous slab of nowhere, with a few pretty houses in amongst the chunks of bungalows and the remnants of Essex plotland development. My parents used it as their sailing base and perhaps, we assumed, planned it as their future retirement cottage.

My father's decision to move up a size in boats was of far more interest. The search for the right sort of hulk was picky and exhaustive. It was size that I fancied. The yellow-varnished Kestrel was still little more than two sofas and a stick. I liked the miniature sailing barge lying in the mud at Maldon quay. It had a hefty coal stove and room for a party, or at least the sort of parties that I went to, where people crouched in corners and nodded their Afros. But the hippy aspect didn't appeal much to my father. He found Maurice Griffiths' first design in the mud dock in Woodbridge, where Frank Knight had refitted it following a fire. I took possession of *Windsong* almost immediately, staying for a week on my own, in the early spring of gap year, feeling romantic in my cold cabin on the other side of the railway tracks, painting some of the bits that I'd promised I would and drinking in the Captain's Table or the Olde Bell and Steelyard up the hill of the pretty, close-packed Suffolk market town. I remember admiring Woodbridge the first time we ever went there. It took us a long week, pottering cautiously up the river system. Even the railway station was a stop on a branch line by the boat-builder's dockyard. I used to wonder what sustained this little town where Edward Fitzgerald once lived. How did this slab of middle England survive so discreetly, with its streets of 'improved' eighteenth-century terraces, fitted out with imposing door cases and balustrades by army officers stationed there during the Napoleonic wars? Now I know. There are huge numbers of retired people living there. My mother is one of them these days, living in a little cottage I could have seen from the boat where I camped for that cold week in March.

The regular certainties of my family life had started to slip away once I was sixteen. I became too busy to turn out for them to order, too concerned about the possibility of missing things in Upminster, too resentful of being cut off from the round of parties to go on the four-week jaunt my father awarded himself in the summer. On one last family holiday I struck a bargain half-way through the trip. There was a folk festival at a nearby country house. I had to go. It was my sort of thing. I was on holiday too. What do you mean disruptive? What are you doing? Just drifting around the same old places? Christ, you're lucky I come at all. None of my friends would do this sort of thing with their parents. So what if we sat in a marina and didn't move on the same as we always did? Why couldn't they hang on for me for a change? No, I was going. I didn't care. They could take the boat further up, I'd find them again.

My father interrupted his fretfully planned itinerary and they sat tied up to a jetty while I took the bus to Hintlesham

Hall over on the other side of Ipswich for the day. He probably thought that the concession would extend the relationship. ('You know your father can't really sail the boat on his own.') He probably hoped it would buy him time and initiate a new contract with his regular unpaid extra hand. But the reeds and the mud were not going to compete with the excitement of Maddy Prior singing 'All Around My Hat' in a tent in a field behind a ragged stately home. I skulked about with the slightly self-conscious body language of a single person at a hip event, added Roy Harper to my 'famous pop stars I've seen live' tally and rejoined the family holiday, sporting more itchiness than before I went. 'I should have been at the Isle of Wight Festival instead of cooped up in this hulk with you.'

'We are so pathetic. Look at us. No sense of adventure at all.'

Perhaps it was this same holiday that we anchored off Stone Point, round behind Walton-on-the-Naze. A steep spit of sand shelved down to a deep channel that drained all the acres of marsh, island and saltings every tide. It was inaccessible by land, four or five miles from the nearest town and an anchorage for larger boats visiting the backwaters. At weekends the channel could be crowded, but during the week, even in August, there would be no more than three or four yachts there. People fished and walked on the sand. Other people, not us, built extravagant fires and chattered in groups, drinking beers and laughing. 'Go on, go and say hello.' My poor desperate father was under constant pressure from my sister and me to open up, get social, meet some of these other people. 'Look over there. They've got children our age.' We were seventeen. Nothing means as much as the company of other people who are also seventeen when you are seventeen. But we were too shy to make the running ourselves so we loaded the responsibility on to my poor anti-social father. 'Ask them over for a drink, or something.' He even went. He wanted to hold on to his pressed crew so badly that he rowed himself over to other boats and painfully introduced himself, offered to play host to surprised fellow yachtsmen. But I think it was us who approached the owners of the pretty yawl when they were on shore collecting drift-wood. Their boat was like a proper version of the boat we had, slim and spoony instead of fat and cumbersome, with an elegant counter and a low profile and ten or so extra feet. Though we never got inside to see her gorgeous inte-rior, she had all the glamour of a proper romantic twenties yacht. We sat around their fire in the evening, and the tall, blonde girl whose family owned it tossed her shaggy locks back and pulled her knitted jacket around her shoulders like an illustration in a Ralph Lauren catalogue. I was a year younger than she was, so I knew my place, which was to sit on the broken shell beach and feel ashamed of my hopeless fat family.

'Do you know what they do on Christmas Day? They don't sit around and watch the television at all. They live on a farm or something and they come for a huge ten-mile walk across the marshes here. On Christmas Day.'

'Yes, darling. Well, you could go for a walk on Christmas Day if you wanted to, but last Christmas we had trouble getting you out of bed at all in the morning.'

'That's because we're so bourgeois. We're so flabby. We're so normal.'

The blonde with the boat became my benchmark. That's what proper exciting people who lived on farms and had lots of money and lovely boats that didn't leak did. They went for a long walk on Christmas Day, when they weren't making impromptu barbecues in out-of-the-way places, of course.

But then I was always a sucker for pretty, unattainable girls bigging up their families.

Why do these things stick? These tiny burrs that catch on the coat of experience. 'Don't sit on the radiators, they'll give you piles.' 'A gentleman has rugs on his floors, not fitted carpets.' Rugs, rugs, rugs. Who's to say the man was right? I don't belong in that place or this. I will have to learn what to do to enjoy myself properly and become an exciting person. I went to Cambridge to get out. And now I have lots of rugs.

Windsong was almost entirely flat-bottomed; though thirty feet long she drew no more than two and half feet. One evening, we crept up the Butley River. It was a creek around behind an island at the mouth of the Ore, and no more than twenty feet across for most of its surprising length. It could be described as little more than a drain, in a wide expanse of utterly flat marsh – not a reedy exotic marsh, but a sharp grassed, unforgiving matted expanse of half-land, crazed with runnels like a larger version of a baked mud puddle. We could not see this. The boat sat low between the banks. We motored slowly forward for two, perhaps three miles, twisting onwards. There wasn't room to pass another boat, but we wouldn't meet another boat. No boats came up there any more, though half-way up we passed a red-brick quay where, until the Second World War, Thames barges, mammoth sixty-foot wherries with tan sails, would have tied up to take hay to London. Here the land began. The tidal river unexpectedly widened. The bank built up on the northern side into a twenty-foot-high cliff which met a sea wall snaking in from somewhere towards Orford. We anchored, probably in the middle of an oyster bed.

In the last of the light I rowed away from the boat. When water is completely calm the oars break mirrors. The rowlocks squeak and rattle as if being recorded in a studio. The dinghy and the rower seem to be overpowered, scooting into glassy motion at the slightest tug. I pulled up on the shore and climbed up the sandy cliff and sat under some crouched trees, which seemed to mark the beginnings of liveable land. Away on the other side of the sea wall was a low cottage with a single light in a window. Ahead to the south and west, the Suffolk fields rolled up and out towards Bentley woods where I knew there was a priory, originally served by the river. I couldn't see it. It was dusk. What I could see was miles of fading, almost medieval landscape. I waited there as it got dark under the blackening trees, an oil lamp on the boat reflecting on the water like a connecting thread. I can hardly think of any other moment in my life which has encompassed such perfection: the solitude, the beauty, the sense of the journey made and the simplicity of the place. I got back in the dinghy, pulled the thread in and rowed back to the intimacy of the little cabin. It was what my father wanted from it all. He gave that to me.

Thirty-five years on, I went to take a look at *Windsong* while they were laying her up at the end of the 2004 season. It was a difficult yard to get to, upriver of the tide mill in Woodbridge, crossed by a railway line, and dirt tracks, where the Suffolk Heritage Coast dumped its chair manufacturers, plant storage and sausage makers. The place for a beating-up in a low-budget cop show. The winter facilities were little more than a couple of sheds and a crane, in a field full of boats on sticks.

I sat on the blue-covered bench seats, my father's uphol-stery wearing dramatically well, and as I looked around and praised aloud the cosy ergonomics of the neatly arranged shallow interior, I was thinking that I had libelled my own father in the cause of filial mockery. He hadn't loaded the boat with woodwork until it sank beneath his carpentry. His additions, like the little book case, and the 'tidy', were positioned with a good eye and discreetly made in dark mahogany. They looked good. It was good that the boat that he lavished such attention on was going to continue. It was good that what seemed to matter most to him, his claustrophobic, neat cabin, where he liked to 'get a fug up' and hide from the world, retained his stamp. Out on deck again under scudding clouds I paused for a second. I could see down to the bend in the river where, fifteen years ago, we had gone out in a boat and scattered his ashes.

10. The Wake Arms

Six miles below Epping, in the middle of the forest, I parked my car and walked into the 'Olde Orleans Eatery, a Taste of the Deep South'. It was eleven o'clock in the morning. A fat couple and a baby were eating plates of chips under a fake Tiffany lamp, but the rest of the pine-clad multi-levels were empty. I could enjoy my familiar neurotic dilemma choosing a place to sit.

'How long have you been here?' I asked the manager.

'Oh, ten years now. We're due for a refurbishment.'

It all looked perfectly new to me. 'What happened to the pub?'

'Way before my time.'

On the way to the cloakroom I peered at the photographs on the wall. They were of jazz combos: Coleman Hawkins, Bix Beiderbecke and a young Louis Armstrong, nursing their trumpets and staring out from sepia reproductions. To most of the customers they might as well have been the Siberian Accordion Stars. They were a 'theme', chosen almost at random by a marketing man. But the chip-eaters would have heard of David Bowie, or Pink Floyd, or Black Sabbath, and all of these monsters of guitar-twiddling had actually played this place. Or not this place, but a sweaty box with black walls, round the back of a biker pub that used to be on this site, called the Wake Arms. The 'Olde Progressive Music Eatery' must have been rejected as being uncommercial.

There had always been pop music at home. We had a Dansette like everybody else. My father carted its nice, gluey, fresh plastic smell home when we were in rompers. The first forty-five we bought was 'Multiplication' ('that's the name of the game').

The fanciful plot of my dad's famous puppet show was based around his experimental musical purchases. There was an elopement scene ('James, James, Hold The Ladder Steady' by Susan Maugham). There was a shipwreck (a bit of the 'March Of The Valkyrie', off a *Selections From Wagner* EP). And an octopus fandango ('Do The Mambo Jambo', a bossa nova by God-knows-who, on an old seventy-eight). My father actually got hold of a huge quantity of ancient platters from a hospital social club clear-out (including some rare Noël Coward and Gertie Lawrence sketches, which I'm afraid we thought were risible and made into plant pots. Our forty-fives included selections from *The Boy Friend* and extracts from Gilbert and Sullivan's *The Gondoliers*.

When I went back to Epping on my nostalgic daytrip in 2005, the little shop 'Chew and Osbourne's' was still operating. It had largely determined our 'collection' (since my father just marched in and bought a handful of what was to hand, to see how his player worked), though I was sorry to see that the booths with the white holey board, where you could solemnly listen to your choice before taking it home, had gone.

By the time we were ten we had become more discriminating. Woolworths used to do cheap cover versions: extended players with three tracks on each sides, 'indistinguishable from the real thing', except that they were on red plastic. A vinyl warning: 'This is not a real record'. Nobody much cared who recorded the originals of 'Venus In Blue Jeans' ('She's everything I hoped she'd be') or 'Ferry 'Cross The Mersey'. But 'Love Me Do' was different. Even we could tell it was a bit gormless to have the cover version of that.

The Beatles singles came into the house on the original discs, in the weeks that they were released. 'I Want To Hold Your Hand' was particularly significant. It was mine. I bought it with my birthday money. We were Beatles people, then. My mother watched the Stones on *Top of the Pops*, and fretted about the unhygienic nature of their hair. At thirteen we rather agreed with her. They were too noisy and had aggressive lips. The records we had in our wooden box with the lifting lid (which my father had knocked up for us) with its natty sixties red-and-white washable gingham-print vinyl sticky-backed cover, were all sing-alongs.

Then I used my accumulated Christmas money to buy a whole Beatles LP: *Help*.

It caused consternation. I can remember my mother trying to talk me out of it. I would only listen to it once. Next week there would be other pop records. It was an utter waste of money. Wouldn't I prefer to buy a telescope? But I prevailed. And I still have my copy. It didn't really fit on the record player, though. The huge disc overhung the edges of the tiny turntable.

It must have been some time around then that I fancied being a pop star and took up guitar lessons. I never practised. My guitar had particularly poor 'action', the strings seemed a long way from the fret board, and it took all my strength to play a single note. I am afraid that my favourite bit was walking through the town carrying the thing. I imagined everybody thinking, 'there goes Griff "Guitar" Rhys Jones, the good-rocking eleven-year-old,' but I didn't want to learn to play 'My Bonny Lies Over The Ocean' anyway.

Later, my brother came home from his boarding school under the influence of traditional jazz. (This is why I know of Coleman Hawkins.) He belonged to a club in Midhurst and wore a duffel coat, but Chris Barber was gradually being pushed out by the blues, and the blues were going electric. Alexis Corner and John Mayall were twanging along in the wings.

My sister and I used to go to a youth club in Epping up near the Catholic church. It had started as a Saturday-morning cinema, showing black-and-white cowboy serials to a noisy full house. It was presumably a Jesuitical plot, but I don't remember that the Lone Ranger ever converted anyone to Catholicism. Later in the long summer holidays we just hung around there. I remember the hall with its tall windows and stacking tables. The sun was shining and making glaring yellow hot spots on the parquet. There was a bigger record player there, with more powerful speakers, and we played records during the summer afternoons, but we began to play one record over and over again. When it finished we rushed to stick it back on. Suddenly, with the big noise, bigger than the radio or the piddly little gramophone in the corner, what had seemed messy began to sound glorious, what had seemed disordered began to take on a visceral excitement. 'I can see for miles and miles,' the Who sang.

At school, these discoveries got to be carefully passed along. The whole point of the group ethos of the gang era was these shared enthusiasms, determined by group loyalty. Upper Five was on the first floor of the main block. It was right at the end of a long corridor. It was O-level year. We were coming under increasing pressure 'to succeed'. The form master, Mr Best, told us, rather ominously, to enjoy the summer vacation. It was the last one free of work before the end of our finals, six years hence. This was utter nonsense, but it lodged, and I blame my entire lazy existence on it. With the prospect of nothing but work ahead, I determined to take every opportunity to enjoy myself while things were a little slack.

When the exams finished we weren't allowed to go home.

We had to take part in a series of improving activities organized to 'prevent our minds atrophying' (and to justify the huge fees charged for the boarders). There were lectures by distinguished parents, including, excitingly, George G. Ale, out of *Private Eye* (an *Express* journalist and father of a ginger-haired twerp in a boarding house). He turned up and growled at us from a podium. Someone who worked in the BBC made us pretend to be a news room, and a plainly crazed big-game hunter banged away with his walking stick to change slides of 'the six killer animals' (the water buffalo being the most dangerous). But the most vivid was made by a doctor enthusiastically documenting the physical effects of a variety of venereal diseases. It was an extensive, timely and wide-ranging dissertation, accompanied by highly coloured slides of venereal warts, and the regular chair-scraping thump as another boy fainted in the dark.

In between times, hanging about in Upper Five, no longer playing football, Holloway, Horth and I were perfecting our impression of Joe Cocker doing 'A Little Help From My Friends'.

'Eeeeee, eeeee, eee.' It was particularly enjoyable to froth and go all twitchy in imitation of the convulsive Nottinghamshire groaner. And to do the high-pitched guitar with the scratchy distorted ending. Gotley came in from his own classroom next door and, inter alia, gave us his own educative lecture. It wasn't pop we were interested in. It was 'underground'. He and Tompsett had a collection of Pink Floyd albums, Jefferson Airplane albums, the Fugs and Quicksilver Messenger Service. He and Gotley were already into Zappa and Beefheart. We gazed in admiration at the inner-sleeve pictures of men wearing fish masks, top hats and fur coats.

Gotley pointed out the complicated psychedelic graphics

of the titles of the Grateful Dead offerings. If you squinted at them, you could see they said 'take acid'. Tompsett turned the photograph of Bob Dylan on the cover of *New Morning* upside down. If you looked very carefully you could see a man with a trumpet up his nose.

A teacher suddenly came in. 'What are you all doing skulking in here?'

'Nothing, sir.'

'It's a lovely day. Get out and be in the fresh air.' But it was too late for that. That was all finished.

We were outside the science labs when I was first introduced to the *Melody Maker*. The back pages had thick and inky lists of gigs. The names were arranged like wrestling posters. You could go and see bands by rote: Blodwyn Pig, the Edgar Broughton Band, the Third Ear Band, Quintessence. They were appearing at somewhere called the Roundhouse in Chalk Farm, in central London, but there were also venues in Ilford (The Red Lion), or (blimey) Epping, where I lived, at somewhere called the Wake Arms. They weren't famous groups, but we liked the names: 'Black Sabbath', 'Uriah Heep', 'Family'. It wasn't pop. It was music. And Tompsett had been going to these places since he was thirteen.

Tompsett had bog-brush hair and buck teeth, one of which was slightly discoloured. Adam Hennicker Gotley was short and never fitted his clothes. They were both the sort of humans that authority figures tend to distrust on sight. (Adam is a probation officer now.) They were physically unsuited to conformity. I believe that Tompsett managed to annoy the headmaster simply by existing. His Christian name was Fabian. Mr Sale would have found such a gesture unusually suspect.

There were plenty of genuine rebels in the school. There

were boys like Morris, who adamantly refused to conform. He led his third-eleven team in dancing through a cricket match, and then at the termly event called 'trials', where we each had to be assessed in a sequence of athletic events, he skipped his way around the compulsory mile, while the playboy spiv of a senior gym master, Mr Shortland, looked on and went red. (Even skipping, rather an exhausting show of mettle, to be honest, got him well within the specified pass rate.) When the Corps was inspected by a general (who flew down in a helicopter) and he finally got to the field service unit – a special division, seemingly invented for those of us who were considered incapable of charging and marching – it was Morris who stepped forward and presented him with a Peace Pledge Association leaflet and a daffodil.

There were naughty and dangerous boys, who asked disruptive questions, smoked under the stage and were suspected of being on drugs, like Martin (everybody was called Paul or Martin). Above us there were serious offenders who were occasionally threatened with expulsion. But they were often protected by a magic halo of achievement. In the end, it was poor, hopeless, misguided Peters who got the sack. Boastful Peters, ever eager to please the gym masters; willing Peters, who became some sort of staff sergeant in the Corps, and paraded around with bits of coloured rope around his armpit; silly Peters, who stupidly boasted about trying a joint within hearing of a science master and was summarily kicked out.

This was meant, no doubt, as a warning, but only reassured us that the authorities knew nothing. They could only lash out in ignorance. Clever boys fielded threats.

But not me; I was perfectly content to bend either way. While Morris, Gotley, Jimpson and Tompsett looked a shower in their new Corps uniforms, I turned out quite smartly.

Mine fitted. I secretly enjoyed shooting at targets and marched quite briskly. When the time came, I was happy to become a praeposter and then a school praeposter and then a head of house, happy to join the debating society and the film club and the history society, edit the *Brentwoodian* and direct the cars on Speech Day. I was happy to keep my feet in all camps and my options open, and be enthusiastic for any old rot, as long as I didn't have to commit.

By the sixth form we were no longer expected to turn out in the sports fields. Brentwood was a football school. Even today when I meet beefy blokes in blazers at city dinners they speak in hushed tones. 'Yes, we used to play Brentwood. They were quite a good team, weren't they?' Who knows? I sort of recall the headmaster announcing successes against his rivals at assemblies. My house, East, provided a lot of the stars, but I never knew them. They were an arrogant presence at house meetings. But their prowess directly affected my sporting life. In the autumn term the whole school played football. Naturally, these talents came to the fore and led the house to victories. For people like me, it meant playing football in the third team, every Wednesday and Saturday afternoon, out on the furthest reaches of the school fields with the fat boys and the geeks, where the pitches had severe slopes down one end, and the junior master, wearing the house scarf around his neck, only finally appeared to shout at us at the very end of the after-noon.

Then, in the spring term, the goal posts were removed, the rugger 'Hs' stuck up instead, and the 'rugby term' began. In East House, however, the properly athletic stepped to one side and bowed out of taking part altogether. Half of the stars were still playing football. The school wanted to have it both ways and to pretend to be a public school for a term, but the pampered race horses of the school football squad had no intention of flopping about in the mud, so the house master excused his prima donna footballers and assembled a scratch rugby team out of the weedy stragglers remaining. That included me.

'Well, Rhys Jones, with a name like that, you'll be ideal for the rugby team.'

'Yes, sir. You said that about the choir, and look what happened there.'

'Never mind that. You know how to play, don't you?'

I didn't, but foolishly assumed that blood would out.

The rugby term became a miserable catalogue of defeat and injury. In retrospect, the sloping, rubbish football pitches were havens. The first-fifteen rugby pitches became plains of mud to rival the Somme.

Fielding a couple of fat boys from the fifth form, a weedy praeposter or two (not given to sporting prowess but gormlessly keeping the house spirit up), a few wets who had been winkled out of their usual bolt hole in the library and an extremely keen captain of rugby (who had failed to make the grade in football and now intended to lick his unit into shape by being cross with them and shouting a lot), we stumbled out, shivering and disorganized, to do battle with serious opposition.

I had probably been the youngest player in the entire first division, apart from Smith, one of those boys who shot to a height of six foot and a width of four foot at the first tickling of the hormones. Smith was in South. South had a team comprised of oafish giants, and a house master with a small moustache, who took rugby very seriously indeed. We seemed to be there to provide them with practice at throwing human beings head first into frozen swamps while they waited to get to grips with their real rivals, North.

When it was our turn to get to grips with North, naturally enough North decided to take their defeat at the hands, knees and fists of South out on us. Every week the footballing jerks would lounge on the windowsills and smirk at the sorry results we carried back to the house meeting.

It was almost a relief to get to the summer term, when I was sent back to the sloping pitches to play cricket for the third eleven. I hate and abhor cricket. I loathe cricket. I abominate cricket. There is only one thing more boring than the abysmal English habit of watching a game of cricket and that is an afternoon playing the wretched game. It is sport for the indolently paralysed. Only three people out of twenty-two are engaged in any proper activity. The rest simply sit and wait their turn.

The excruciating tedium of 'fielding' – standing about, like a man in a queue with nothing to read, in case a sequence of repetitive events, ponderously unfolding in front of you, should suddenly require your direct intervention (at which point every other listless 'player' suddenly, aggressively, demands your instant involvement in their pathetic ritual – 'catch it!') – is only matched by the absurdity of allowing the rest of the 'players' to lounge about doing nothing at all, until it is their turn to 'play'. Play! The skill is all opportunism. Cricket requires hours of pointless 'service' instead of direct involvement. It seems to have been inspired to advance the values of sentry duty and directly favours 'star players' above team involvement.

At my school nobody even bothered to teach you how to play the sodding game. Our first afternoon in the summer we were taken off to the nets, and a red-faced, fat and wheezy ex-county player who taught Latin badly, drank too much and was alleged to be addicted to rent boys bowled three balls at us. I had never picked up a cricket bat before, coming from a state school, and hit none of them. As a result, I had to spend five years of school summer afternoons hanging around, waiting. Waiting for a ball to come my way as 'long stop' when the wicket keeper failed to get the badly bowled ball first time, waiting to be asked to bowl, which I seldom was, because I couldn't, and nobody showed me how, and then waiting and waiting and waiting for the rest of our team to get bowled out so that we could go home.

Most of my team mates wanted to go home too. We desperately longed to be bowled out as quickly as possible, but the standard of bowling was so abysmal that even holding the bat above your head and standing to one side of the wicket seldom resulted in a clean hit on the stumps.

Horribly, some time during 'the match', the urge to win the dreadful contest would overtake the third-eleven captain. After an interminable 'game', which meant we had all already missed our bus home, we would seem to be close to winning. Just another few runs and victory was ours. So, as ninth or tenth man in (that's me), I could save the game.

'But, Captain, the trouble is that I only get to practise this farrago called batting for three minutes twice a week. So naturally I am a sitting target.'

After three wide balls and two no-balls I could usually get out for a duck.

These days, I sometimes get invited to take part in celebrity cricket matches. (It's my own fault. I have organized two myself.) Once I turned up at Fenners in Cambridge, on the strict understanding that I would sign autographs, pull the raffle, dance the dance of the seven veils, but not play. Naturally, when I swanned in, several unhealthy-looking men of limited imagination and unlimited lack of sensitivity surrounded me and bullied me into going out to the stump. ('You can't come all this way and not go out there . . .') I went through the familiar horror of strapping on pads and fitting protection. I pulled on the crippling gloves and the silly hat and walked out to the middle of the enormous lawn. 'Now, don't worry,' said the captain, a man who, astoundingly, made a living playing cricket, 'we've arranged for you to be bowled an easy lob on the first ball.' The bowler threw the ball, I missed it and it hit the middle wicket.

'Oh dear, out for a duck,' said the commentator, over the tannoy (so that everybody in Cambridgeshire could hear it). I turned and headed back to the hut. As I reached the edge of the grass, the tannoy barked again. 'I say . . . that's a bit unfair. He's come all this way. Let's give him another go.'

Unable to communicate my own reaction to this sporting gesture, I paused for a second or two, turned and walked back to the wicket. The cricketers smirked at me. Then I was bowled out for a duck, the second time.

Football is a game. Tiddly-winks is a game. A sack race involves energy and fun. Cricket is like a cucumber sandwich: indulged in for reasons of tradition, despite being totally eclipsed by every other alternative on offer.

By the sixth form, we had drifted out of these obligations. There must have come a moment when it was felt too humiliating to make us play sport at all, so we bunked off. We still went to the school changing rooms on a Saturday, though. While eleven-year-olds got into their blue flannel shorts and striped football shirts, we pulled off our blazers and flannels and pulled on our weekend hippy outfits.

I want this bit to appear in small writing. Perhaps as one of those extensive footnotes that runs discreetly over the page. Almost nothing I did in my youth – even the abrupt abandonment of trusting young women – fills me full of such cold, sweaty embarrassment as my off-duty clothes.

I can't blame Tompsett or Gotley. Now that I think about

it, they went to some lengths to look as if they had stolen their gear from a peasant farmer while on the run from a prisoner-of-war camp. Gotley had a sort of dirty whitish pullover and a stinking pair of black trousers that could have stood up and walked down the high street on their own. Tompsett could be a little more flamboyant and had a frightening yellow shirt. But I looked as if I was about to follow Roy Wood of Wizzard into a battle of the bands.

I had a pair of poisonous green needlecord flares that would have attracted insects in the jungle. They weren't just bright green or lime green, they were radioactive-sludge-that-ate-Leytonstone green. Only a painter in the secure wing in Broadmoor would have been crazy enough to combine them with a purple tie-dye grandfather's vest and a red scarf. I did. And he would have drawn the line at the Indian belt made of mirrored glass, and the grey astrakhan fur coat on top. I didn't. Did I wear this all the time? It was enough that I wore it once.

I emerged from the tube at Chalk Farm for a Quintessence concert one Sunday lunchtime and the others wouldn't stand in the queue with me. I probably modified it after that. Perhaps I restricted myself to the canary-yellow jumper and the bright-blue t-shirt with the Mickey Mouse motif.

Having back-combed our hair, squeezed into our leggings, primped some flowing neck wear and donned our baseball boots, we stuffed our blazers into duffel bags and strutted away down Brentwood High Street.

'I was walking with you once,' my mother recalled, 'and you suddenly disappeared. I couldn't work out what had happened to you. And then we met the headmaster coming the other way.'

It was decent of my mother to walk with me at all.

It was, I submit, a flamboyant era. We none of us had any

money. People would take desperate measures: inserting bright-red satin patches into the bottom of old jeans to make flares, wearing spotted handkerchiefs with gipsy rings around their necks, tie-dyeing elderly relatives' underwear.

Personally I loved flower-power from the very beginning. I thought I looked pretty good in my first flower-power shirt, which had a dotty, splodgy, very small, very bright petal pattern, as if a horse had been sick in a meadow. It came with a matching square-bottomed tie made of identical material and looked fantastic with a pair of black crushed-velvet hipster trousers with patch pockets and a four-inch-wide plastic belt. Not bad for a thirteen-year-old.

By 1970 Mary Quant had been overthrown in favour of ersatz personal invention. The Beatles, quite probably the richest self-made twenty-somethings in the world, took to wearing what looked suspiciously like second-hand clothes. Double-breasted jackets smelling vaguely of urine, which frightened mothers and outraged fathers, could be sourced in Oxfam shops. Collarless shirts with acres of material dangling somewhere around the ankles were found in jumble sales. Muslin shirts with round collars had to be bought in Mr Byrite. Rather better, I thought, though few seemed to agree with me, if hand-dyed a lurid pink.

The small ads in the *Melody Maker*, and a few pages at the back in the *Exchange and Mart*, began to set new standards. They advertised trousers with increasingly huge flared bottoms. 'Twenty-six-inch flares!' the ad boasted, and showed pictures of just the trousers, in ghostly isolation, stick-like to the knees and then ballooning to impossible fantasies of flariness. (A flare war might have broken out. 'Twenty-eight-inch flares!' 'Have we reached the forty-inch flare?' 'Is Britain ready for the wigwam bell bottom?' I would have happily stepped forward as a guinea pig.) Obscure small ads seemed to be the best way to get a cheap navy reefer jacket too, or what became vital to every alternative gentleman's casual wardrobe, the army-surplus winter-warm great coat.

RSM Mason, in his tin Nissen hut at the end of the Chase, happily provided ordinary khaki ones to any member of the Brentwood School Cadet Corps. He might have been surprised how many ended up on parade at the Isle of Wight Rock Festival. But mine was distinctive: a very long, darkish-grey-blue and double-breasted Russian number. Even Tompsett admired it. Honoured, I lent it to him, and he wore it to a rock festival somewhere.

Later that week I was parading about in it in the dining room in front of my cousin Jane and one of my mother's fearsome friends. Attempting to borrow some money, I idly put my hand in the pocket and pulled out a condom. It wasn't used, but I think the ladies were impressed. I blushed. 'I lent it . . . to Tompsett . . . the coat, I mean.'

I was probably on my way to spend half an hour leafing through album covers in a record shop. We were quite content to flip exhaustively through the stacks, hardly ever buying, just admiring the majesty of *Uncle Meat*, the Frank Zappa double gatefold, or the mysterious, semi-surrealist splendours of *Tales From Topographic Oceans*. Alas, it was a time when the objects of our worship were hardly ever content to stick out a single album any more. So fecund was their genius that double or even treble albums were clogging up the bins, and since we were rather keen on anything wilfully obscure, these were severe tests of a limited budget.

It was a major investment to get hold of *Trout Mask Replica*. My copy was, pleasingly, an American import, which meant that it came in a distinguished heavy cardboard, like a wash-ing machine package, as opposed to thin and wibbly card, like a milk carton. But it was a lot of money for a record which was distinctly difficult to listen to more than once. Gotley topped it. He suddenly appeared with a copy of Wildman Fisher, a protégé of Frank Zappa, discovered on a pavement offering songs for a dollar. It was a treble album of utterly tuneless hollering. Its only function was to supplant Deep Purple at a party and initiate a row.

More than anything we wanted long hair. As the seventies ground on, even newsreaders got bangs. Ted Heath grew side-boards. John Prescott must have had a magnificent hairdo to maintain such a silly pudding-basin funerary memorial to it today. But at the end of the sixties the size of your cock was as nothing to the size of your barnet. Even Tiny Tim's waist-length tresses were envied by us schoolboys, who felt silly at rock festivals. Beads and kaftans, with short back and sides? No, no, no. When we went to watch Arthur Brown set fire to his head in Victoria Park, we would have willingly swapped our snakeskin cowboy boots for five-foot-wide Marsha Hunt sprouting-broccoli hairdos or lank Dave Gilmour waist-long hirsute tents, just to allow us to pass unnoticed in the queue at the Jamaican pattie counter.

We battled the forces of conformity. But, sadly, searching out long hair was the second master's favourite pastime (after spotting coloured socks). He would stand at an upper window, bored with teaching, and pick on a passing lower-sixth-former below. 'You, Bell, see me, nine o'clock tomorrow with a proper hair cut.' Bell might invest in liberal platings of VO5 Extra-Hold. He could fold his tresses up using hair pins. He could arrive sporting a masterpiece of the perruquier's art with the consistency of a crash helmet, but the school prevailed.

By the time I got to university even the porters had long hair. Bah. I shaved my head.

As we lay and listened to *Atom Heart Mother* in the dark,

on our new stereos (mine was made up by adding a separate speaker box to the Dansette), or decided to wake up the house with a blistering burst of *Chicken Shack*, or despaired when Marc Bolan went 'commercial', or went all fey with Principal Edward's Magic Theatre; as we back-combed our hair and put on fur coats, to make little pilgrimages to the 'Third Ear Café' by the World's End Pub in the King's Road, and ate tasteless brown rice and horrible beans; as we sat under a plastic sheet in Hyde Park listening to Canned Heat and puffed on our first joint, we firmly believed we were part of the alternative society. We went off to a little wood at the bottom of the school, tootled on pipes and banged tablas, made a disjointed film and thought we were at least as good as the Incredible String Band. But it wasn't a new age. It was sixth-form age. Who could have imagined as we grooved to 'Set The Controls For The Heart Of The Sun' ('no, no, listen to the stereo effects') that what we were actually listening to was the beginning of Arts A-level Culture World.

The Wake Arms was where I first saw Ozzie Osbourne. We rather rated Black Sabbath. Uriah Heep not so much. I remember the lead singer leaning in after three cacophonous numbers and urging us to 'listen to the lyrics of the next one' and then crashing into another hugely pompous and deafening prog-rock anthem, within which any distinction of individual words would have been quite impossible. There were huge stacks of speakers for such a tiny place. We got as close as we could to them, and wobbled our heads to Argent or the Pink Fairies. We were particularly keen to catch the Edgar Broughton Band. They managed to combine two popular themes of the era, black magic and revolution, into one song: 'Out Demons Out' (which, as far as I can recall, consisted of that one phrase, repeated to the same riff for several hours).

But if the homework was relatively light and I had the bus fare, I would get along to almost anything, and leave two hours later, partially deafened, with my ears buzzing into the next morning. It was beyond comprehension why some of these pub rockers were to become international stars and others simply faded away. They all seemed astonishingly loud and equally basic.

One Saturday afternoon my father sat in his usual chair and read the *Daily Telegraph*. 'Look here,' he said, poking at the bottom of one of the grey pages of endless print. 'This article here is quite right.' There was a picture of various hair styles. 'It has been scientifically proven that various types of long hair have become a badge of degeneracy amongst teenagers.'

'Well, that's just nonsense,' I retorted, shaking my delicately coiffeured curls.

'No, look.' His voice was rising. 'Look, from the teddy boy through to greaser, you simply cannot deny that the link is obvious. I'm not accusing you,' he continued, though, by now, I had decided that he clearly was. 'It is merely a matter of association. It matters what people think. You are in danger of being naturally associated with the criminal class.'

'That's what you think of me. I'm a criminal, am I?'

Three minutes later I had grabbed my fur coat, flounced out of the house and was heading down Station Road towards Epping Underground. I simply wasn't going to stand for this sort of ignorant behaviour based on some rubbish in the *Daily Telegraph*. If I wasn't free to live and dress exactly as I pleased then OK, I would go my own way. I was old enough to live on my own. I was working hard, doing perfectly well at my exams. It was all just so they could show off to their friends anyway. Did they really think it made any difference to me? Well, sod that. I was quite capable of looking after myself.

As I reached the bottom of the hill he drove alongside in his car, begging me to return. Silly man, did he really think I had anywhere to go? He was an innocent. If it had been me, I'd have let me get on the tube. Where on earth did I think I was going, dressed like that? Not that it made any difference. I was far too much of a conformist anyway. Rebellion, hah! I was on my way to Cambridge.

11. Reunion

On a late afternoon in October, I drove myself out to Brentwood. The route was utterly familiar. I take it most weekends to get to Suffolk – down through Clerkenwell, where I once lived, through Hoxton, and up under Banksy's smiley-faced riot police mural up on the railway bridge. The car could almost drive itself. I was wearing a suit. I was on my own in the car. I felt slim and purposeful, because this wasn't routine or part of the loose fabric of my life. I was deliberately breaking out, going home for a while. I felt excited. I felt like I was in a film. I decided it could be a film. There was one already, with John Cusack. He went back to the school reunion and he was a serial killer and he killed some people. I felt like a serial killer. It was the dream of escape. I was momentarily sloughing off my present. 'Bring your wife or partner,' the yellow slip had invited, but I didn't want that. Nor did anyone else. There were to be very few wives or partners at the 'Forty Years On' reunion dinner.

The school was as one might expect a school to be at seven in the evening, deserted and too dark. I parked by the pavilion, where we had had the discos upstairs and where the fencing champions had trained. There we are. I'd never been in those lower changing rooms at all. They were reserved for the sporting stars, and the balcony above them for the headmaster and the visiting headmaster and the visiting headmaster's satraps.

Right across the way was the sacred piece of grass that boys were not allowed to cross, between the undistinguished

Queens Building for science and the back of the staff common room. But I crossed it now, for devilment, and walked towards the front of the building. Was it ever this deserted? There was no sign of anything happening. At the front the school entrance was solidly shut. It always was. There was a porch with stained glass windows, but they only ever opened that for public days. (We weren't a public day then.) The Memorial Hall was dark. I had thought we would be in there, fêted, at dinner in the heart of the school, in the smelly assembly hall with the portraits of headmasters looking down, but there were only piles of music stands in the gloom. To my surprise, the corridors were carpeted. The place had lost its stinking soul.

I walked blindly on. Everywhere the lights were off. Beyond the chapel the concrete floors had gone and the empty corridors became like the corridors of a hospital, with fuzzy carpet and fire doors and unfamiliar offices and nobody around at all. The old Big School, the original schoolroom, was lit but deserted. Stuck to the door was a list of names. I assumed they had already met for drinks and then gone on to the dinner.

I stared at the printed page. It included Horth, Tompsett, Smith, Bagnall, Thorogood, Woollard. There were other names, some that I didn't remember at all. I took it down. It might come in handy.

I walked on, past where Mr Ricketts lived. He saved me from ignominy in Latin, because he could teach the subject. How? Who knows? Enthusiasm, perhaps. He spoke his Latin with a strong Italian accent and expressive hands like a proper Mediterranean, and he got me to hurdle the ablative. We liked him for it, as we always admired those straightforward, determined teachers who seemed to have set themselves a target and went straight for it. And he had lived in that little cottage on the other side of a beech hedge in the middle of the school.

'Are you lost?' A bald man was advancing on me out of the glare of some floodlit practice pitches. He was smiling. He must be a teacher. Not one of mine, I decided, though it took a moment to accept that my teachers, looking much the same as this one did with his fringe of white hair and sensible clothes, were all probably dead now.

He was there to hurry me along, past the new floodlit tennis courts and into a noisy company of forty or so men holding wine glasses.

And now I was stuck. Who were these blokes? I started talking to the headmaster, for safety, I think. But for the most part I just stared around with an expression that I would rather not have worn. I couldn't recognize the majority of them. They seemed to be of all ages. We were unaware of it then, but I can see having watched my own son grow up, that boys at fourteen, fifteen, sixteen have no universal age. There are big, deep-chested ones who shave twice a day and tiny, fresh-faced, girly ones and boys with explosions of acne and others who attain ethereal beauty which as soon deserts them, none of which meant anything to us, then.

But that was then. This was now. Some of my former school friends looked like old men. Others were youthful, gangly and spiky-haired. I recognized Smith first. Having been the conservative and blushing giant of South, he had now become cool, with long yellow hair. But he was still the tallest.

'Is that Smith?' I asked crudely. I needed some sort of order. I needed some questions answered. I wanted a register read, or a formal presentation made. I could hardly ask Smith himself. 'So, Smith, you were always a very straightforward sort of bloke and here you are now with long blond hair, dressed in velvet. How so, old fellow?'

'Yes, Smith,' the person standing next to me said, 'and that's Horth. He looks just like he did when we were here, doesn't he? Remember him?'

Of course I did. I'd met him quite recently. It was the person talking to me that I couldn't place. They would slot in, wouldn't they, if I stared hard enough? But I mustn't stare. So I wandered Horthwards, to my own gang.

The bloke with the short hair was Graham Jimpson, my best friend. He was relaxed and laughing. They must have managed to throw off all this gawping puzzlement earlier. Perhaps they had had their shared moment before I arrived, like wakers from a frozen state, feeling their way back to life, sharing the experience of letting the mainframe boot up at the canapé stage.

Graham Jimpson saw my confusion. He welcomed me like the junior relative of a senile politician. 'You remember Fabian?' Of course I did. But Fabian was different in some way. He was stocky and plump, yes, but we were all stocky and plump. I knew it was him. I had guessed it was Fabian when I saw him across the room from the doorway, but something was different about him, and I stalled. I could hardly say, 'I didn't recognize you with your hair long and pulled back and in these casual clothes and oh . . .' I real-ized what it was. He had done something to his teeth.

'You remember Chislett,' said Graham, and I did, but not before that precise moment. It was like retrieving a file. I could even recall his house. I could see the stripes of his tie. He had every right to be remembered as well as anybody else. I knew that. He had been part of the gang. We had joked, played football, probably even had a fight, but I had wiped him from my memory bank. I had got along happily without ever needing any stored information about my good friend Chislett. But it was there. Over the course of the confusing evening I rebuilt a photo album. After the pudding he came over, and I suddenly saw him in the Corps uniform with his hair gathered up into his beret. The essence of Chislett returned.

'I see Paul Morris,' Graham Jimpson was saying. 'He was my best friend really over the last thirty years. Him and Paul Callick. You remember him. He used to play at the folk club.'

I didn't. I could see the folk club in a room in the high school and the girl with the wool-ball hair who used to pluck a Spanish guitar and that other bloke who wrote very complicated songs which were extremely difficult to play but seemed entirely tuneless, as if simple tunes with three chords were the most difficult things of all to construct, as indeed they may well be. Was that Callick? 'Veness?' I asked.

'He's in the City somewhere.'

'And Bean is second in command at the Bank of England.'

'Yes. And Martin Thomas I keep in touch with.'

Martin the bright, Martin who won all the prizes.

'He's trying to take up an academic post in Mexico.'

'He's an academic?' I liked the idea that people I had known at school were now distinguished.

'Yes. A professor, but he's giving all that up.' Martin was in love with a twenty-eight-year-old Mexican.

It was as if all of us had reached this point and suddenly needed to take stock. Perhaps they were all writing books.

'But Graham, what happened?' I needed to know. 'I just want to know the details. What happened to the people who went to Oxbridge to rule this country? Don't they rule the country?'

'No. Only you and Anthony Blear.'

I paused. Not something else that had slipped. I don't remember him.

'You do,' Bagnall told me. 'He's the Prime Minister.'

'Tony Blair!' I had misheard. Of course – Graham had been at Oxford.

'I threw a bowl of rhubarb fool over his head at a dinner party, I was so annoyed by what he was saying. He was just someone in this band then.'

We were happier talking about the little things we remembered, like the league ladders. 'With the perforated slots . . . Each team on a separate cardboard tag so that you could move them up and down . . . a sort of chocolate brown.'

When Graham imitated little me, he'd do me posh, using long words. 'Let us find accommodation on the upper deck of the omnibus.' But that was Essex talking. I was surprised to find how joined at the hip we were. He knew the boat, my sister, my friends in Epping.

'You were a good drawer of studied anatomical drawings of ladies.'

Hm. This was an accomplishment, then.

'Really big on the blackboard in Upper 5. It was a bit *Encyclopedia Britannica* anatomy section, but the idea was that you threw the board rubber and scored points – called "the Olymptits". A big thing, until Mr Cluer came in and found us.'

And then in the sixth form the two little boys drifted apart. 'You became a hot gospeller, didn't you?' I said.

Graham buried his head in his hands. 'At one party in the sixth form I went off with Martin Hope, and we made a sort of pact that we would become celibate.'

And Graham had taken on the selfless moral imperative for the rest of his life. While I went off on a cruise he went to Tanzania. In Oxford he opened a fair-trade shop called

Uhuru, still operating today, and he became a revolutionary socialist, heavily involved in student politics. He left to work in Oxford sink estates, as a youth worker, which is where I'd last brushed into him, twenty years ago.

Some there, like John Squire, watched us through narrowed eyes, standing to one side, as if suspicious of the event. Perhaps he carried too much baggage. I certainly did, but mine was a suitcase of self-consciousness. He had packed his closely around him – slipped it into his dark suit pockets. Nobody was really helping very much. I wanted some order. What was the headmaster there for if not to organize this? Get all of us, one by one, to give an account of ourselves why don't you? Forty years was a colossal time. They had lived a life which could be measured out against the patterns of the twentieth century. I had skipped off the tracks by accident and rumbled about in the fields like a railway accident: a public opportunist. I wanted to know what they had done.

Over the meal, small connections clicked into place. We were surprisingly benign. Why this warm feeling? We pitied those who had decided not to resurrect their past. We laughed when one of the masters said that one old boy had sent his wife to answer the phone and to tell the school never to bother their household again. Not us. We were here and we seemed happy.

It wasn't the school itself. Bagnall and Thorogood openly regretted the place. They felt that the academy had left us quite unprepared for the reality of civilian life. So what was it? For one evening we embraced what? Not the bland security that old boys seek in the old boys club, surely? Not even the rebellion that Fabian found there, nor the identity that the ritual offered. It was the vigour. We had allowed ourselves to taste being seventeen again.

After dinner we reverted. We gathered round the headmaster, a younger man than any of us, and told tales out of school. We jabbered at him about Bilge and the corporal punishment he dispensed so casually. We told him stories of outrageous teacher behaviour, how we saw through the headmaster's act, how one teacher was a pederast and another lusted after rent boys, and he looked on, fielding all this with a slight, bemused smile.

I was sorry that it came to an end. Most people were keen on doing it again. 'Let's not leave it another forty years.' But I sensed that we would. Perhaps we didn't really want to confront the reality of our school friends' actual lives.

I went back to my car, drove back towards the barrier and found that, while we had been eating, it had locked me in. The sports centre was deserted. Chislett and some of the others walked past and cackled at me through the side window. They had parked sensibly in the available car park, not swanned into the centre of the school like a would-be visiting dignitary. I scurried back to find the headmaster. He was perplexed. He didn't have any keys. It was a separate security operation. Eventually he found a cleaner, who traced a night watchman, and they buzzed me out, the last to leave.

And I left confused. Perhaps it was because we had returned to take the place at night, when it was just a black shell and lacked the constituents that made it today's working school. There were no inquiring grubby faces, or lines of girls in badly fitting skirts, or clamouring noise, which meant that we had been able to reoccupy it.

But the visit had also laid a ghost. We had been told we were part of a progression, a force for betterment, the embodiment of a particular education. I had used it as a prop myself. 'Brentwood was up there with Manchester Grammar, you know. Do you know how many of my year went to Cambridge?' I was still on the honours board. I had been able to see it over Bagnall's shoulder as we ate our lamb noisettes – three of us with Exhibitions to one college. Gosh. But it was just a school. We weren't some golden, blessed generation sitting in that canteen. We were just some blokes from Essex hankering after irresponsibility.

12. Ugandan Affairs

At one time or another I had possessed a box full of torrid letters from my late teens, hadn't I? My mother had dumped it on me some time in the eighties. Was I fantasizing? I could vaguely remember that I had been fascinated enough to open the box but not quite fascinated enough to read them. What had I done with all this flaming, passionate adolescent biro-work?

I found it in an old oak bureau (disappointing some future grandchild, no longer able to say, 'I wonder what's in this old oak bureau?'). The letters were in a shoebox.

This is what a 'musty' smell smells like – a flimsy airmail letter left for thirty-five years to absorb damp and rot slightly. Some of these letters were written by myself on my first trip away from home, but most of them were messages from the massed girl-correspondents of 1972. I have no idea how my mother came to collect them all together (although one of those girl-correspondents had been my mother herself). Did I really leave them lying about White Lodge so cavalierly? But I was trembling. Quite honestly I had completely forgotten that I had had so many massed girl-correspondents.

Jill, Wendy and Jane had written to me in the sixth form from their respective boarding schools. 'I'm just writing this in the dorm before lights out. Don't forget, please, please, please send me another funny letter.' Wow. But Jill, for whom I pined, was just teasing me. She may have been intimate in her letters from Felixstowe after prep, but she was icily remote in the flesh during the holidays in Epping. Obviously I could present myself as a loopily entertaining, wild and crazy guy to a trapped and lonely girl, as long as it was in writing. Could I follow through? It was worth persevering.

The other letters were from Beth, Dale, Karen, Bev and another, quite different, Jill. They were about walking the dog, the extreme cold, French exams and how funny I was with my crazy letters again. (Listen, they were seventeen and easily impressed, and they all came from distant Canada.) I turned over one of the flimsy airmail envelopes, and a photo of Karen dropped out. In blue and green tartan trousers and a tight sweater she was seventeen and pretty, sitting on the porch in front of her house in Nova Scotia, and smiling at me. Oh, Karen. I must have found this all heart-stopping then. I am pretty jealous of my former self now. There was a picture of Bev too: with red hair, a coy smirk and a purring invitation to Ontario. I must have been a letter-writing machine. I had forgotten the names, but I remembered the general idea. All these Canadians had been part of a mammoth, group, ship-board romance which had lasted no more than a week but was followed by months of diligent pensmanship all through my 'gap year'.

It wasn't a whole year. In 1970 I had sat the scholarship exams for Cambridge. The sixth form was dispersed. A levels were over. But a select few came back in the autumn to take 'Oxbridge Entrance'. For a term we did little except try to appear remote from the concerns of ordinary schoolboys and take desultory instruction in 'thinking' from the deputy head-master. The exams were taken in the 'Old Big School', somewhere I had rarely ventured before. Amongst the black beams, carefully preserved ancient graffiti, and on a wonky floor I was invited to write speculatively on utterly gener-alized subjects. Luckily, I had spent every Saturday night for the last two years in a kitchen in Upminster arguing the existence of God with Jimpson.

A telegram arrived at White Lodge. I had got an Exhibition at Emmanuel. I wrote to Felixstowe Pam to tell her. She wrote back her congratulations. 'I didn't even know you were artistic.' My father seemed pleased that this meant money and hardly disappointed at all that it was no more thirty pounds a year. What it really meant was that the palpable result of all that homework could be left on the sideboard to be picked up, smoothed off and re-read with decreasing incredulity. But it was Christmas. I was eighteen. Cambridge started in October. 'Oh that magic feeling, nowhere to go.' Did we call them 'gap years' then? It was nearly a whole year off as far as I was concerned.

I had to earn some money. If in a very good mood I sometimes try to get friends' children temporary work in television. Wielding her more limited influence, my mother found me work counting lamp posts. If their street lights went phut, the residents of Epping complained. They were told to make a proper report and furnish the council with the number of the malfunctioning lamp. It was stencilled in black on the side of the pole. Unfortunately, the council had no record of which number corresponded to which lamp post. So to prevent council bulb-replacement operatives, who only worked in daylight, aimlessly meandering down mock-Tudor avenues, they hired me to make a definitive survey.

Luckily every man-hole, every fence, every fire hydrant and every unenumerated lamp post in Epping was marked in voyeuristic detail on huge maps in an office near the library. I needed my own version of this Big Brother document to take on the road, before I biked out into the streets in that cold Essex January, so I grappled with a bath of viscous liquid and rollers which clanked and whirred and produced sinister-looking blueprints in a suspicious purple colour. Nobody would have thought of trying to copy their arse on the roller and acid machine in the Epping surveyor's office.

Gap years provide an education. I learned that the wearying fiddliness of pre-photocopier seventies office infrastucture was ripe for Japanese intervention (and indeed that was to come). I also learned that there were some mind-numbingly boring work-environments that I never wanted to share again. I was quite keen, though, and still innocent enough to be surprised that nobody wants you to be keen in dull work places. But I was just visiting. That month I walked every street and cul-de-sac, every close, avenue, crescent, lane and terrace of my home town. Then I left for the Mediterranean to take up another temporary job.

This looked a more cushy number. In the autumn of the previous year I had been interviewed by a charming codger in a grey suit in my first open-plan office. In early March, after working in a petrol station, trying to Christmas-wrap lamp stands in a design shop in the high street, taking baby-sitting jobs (where I thumbed through my mother's younger friends' sex manuals secreted on the upper shelves of their cherry-wood G-Plan units) and sorting the Epping illumination, of course, I flew out to Malta to join a school educational cruise ship as a school office assistant.

It was a significant departure for me. As a family, we didn't 'do' abroad. I had been with the school to Denmark, where we learned to row and had an accident with the hanging light. I had been on a trip to Wuppertal to stay with Doris, the former au pair, to 'improve' my German. But the Rhys Joneses had never gone to the beaches of the south. We had certainly never taken package holidays, but neither had we ever jumped in the car and taken the ferry to wander off through France and eat pâté. Never. It seems an extraordinary admission now. I am thinking, 'Well, we must have gone.' There must have been some foreign adventure. We were a perfectly ordinary middle-class family. Didn't we ever get as far as Calais? No. Not by ferry anyway. Until my father decided to captain his own boat across the Channel we ignored Europe completely. But then I don't suppose this was particularly rare. Miller, who had ginger hair and a languid manner, was considered slightly exotic at school because he went to France every summer. We were aware that he did because we thought it gave him an unfair advantage in French lessons. Rhys Jones never went anywhere because his father had that boat. It was the holiday of choice. We never had any choice. We just went on holiday on the boat.

I wrote home, excitedly detailing the circumstance of the flight, the food served on the aeroplane and the fact that I had met some of my colleagues on the way. I was delivered to sandstone Valletta, the capital of Malta, and thence to a white boat, towering above a wharf in the docks. ('This is not a boat. It is a ship!') It was the SS *Uganda*.

We were four 'school office assistants', two of whom I liked immensely and one of whom was called Adrian. We were effectively junior pursers, charged with mundane jobs like making meal announcements and handing out torches, setting up lecture equipment and printing the daily news, but we didn't wear a uniform and were considered to be under the authority of the headmaster as opposed to the captain. We were also paid four pounds a week, which we spent on bonded whisky at eight pence a shot. The ship was a floating embodiment of 1950s values.

It was divided into two classes. At one end (the smaller and the back) there were dormitories, classrooms and dining halls, painted a battleship grey, floored with lino, smelling of hot diesel and patrolled by sergeants at arms. Here they shoved about six hundred schoolchildren. Up the other end (the larger and the bow) there were individual cabins, lounges, a library, a decent restaurant and a ballroom, where an Indian band played jazz standards every evening. Here a small number of fee-paying passengers stretched themselves out. They were joined in this paradise of inlaid wood and starched napery by the teachers.

It was an ingenious scam. The teachers worked hard all year. It was their task to persuade reluctant parents that their children deserved to enjoy the privileges that other children would be enjoying as soon as they had persuaded their equally reluctant parents to take part. As a reward for press-ganging the kids, the company gave them a luxury cruise. The teachers had to take the occasional lesson. They would be responsible (sometimes) for showing their charges a pyramid or two. For the most part, however, the pupils attended lectures given by the intelligent, plump ship's headmaster, ate fattening food and went to the disco under our tutelage.

My first letter home, out of an envelope with a red Britannia crest on the back, was to my mother. I was confined to an empty ship, picked on at work and not really homesick at all. The ship's officers had glowered at us when we tried to visit their bar. The Maltese security guard had ordered us back to quarters. And she would be relieved to know I had not managed to spend any money yet. I assume my letters to my future girlfriend correspondents were a little racier. (But only they can tell me. Perhaps they have them somewhere in their own shoebox.)

Our work station and the hub of shipboard existence was the school office, a metal turret at the meeting point of various corridors on the lower decks. In the morning, we opened for business by rattling up shutters on three sides and facing out to meet inquiries. It was run by Michael – tall, languid and practised in queenly disdain, particularly, so it seemed, for us.

'You can sit over there and keep out of the way,' he started. We had a few things to get straight. This wasn't 'school' at all. Not our school, not the pupils' school and not the head-master's school. It was 'shipboard' and on shipboard sailors like him (he was a junior purser) were in charge. He was equally dismissive of orders from above ('Oh Lord, what are they trying to do now?'), keen to put us in our places and determinedly lazy.

Before we left, waiting in the empty ship for our comple-ment of pupils, Michael was expected to provide some sort of an inventory of equipment. Lounging back in the only chair in the office, he summoned two of us over. 'What have we got in that cupboard over there?' he asked.

It was filled with boxes of Monopoly and Scrabble.

'There are supposed to be fifteen, aren't there? Give them here.' He started idly picking through the contents as if intending to count the houses, silver top hats and hotels but quickly grew bored. He scooped all the games up into a cardboard box and handed it to us. 'Go and throw that over the side,' he said. Then he picked up his clipboard and pen. 'Fifteen replacements needed, I think.'

Michael's deputy Nigel was short and ginger. Both of them had the comic assurance of the minimally experienced. They busied themselves with organizing visas and stamps for pass-ports and trying to pass their duties on to us, while I prepared my own inventory of their shortcomings in my letters home. 'He hit the roof last week because I played a record at reveille that he didn't like.' (Hm. King Crimson not so popular then?)

'He has produced a rota whereby one person is on duty all the time and then complains because we are not all present when he wants us,' I huffed peevishly.

Four weeks later, things improved. 'The School Office Purser has finally bought us a drink.' (And at eight pence a shot too.) I must have played 'Bye, Bye Miss American Pie' at reveille.

On the morning of our first day the four of us hovered in the margins, newly oppressed by petty rituals. The pursers ignored us. They were leafing through the passenger manifest. 'They're all from Canada,' Michael snorted and threw it to one side.

Given a break, we clumped up to the open-air decks. The crew were at their perpetual task of chipping rust and painting. We leaned over a rail and watched the passenger coaches arrive. Way below us they drove in a great curve around the dock, as if in long shot, and stopped next to the companionway. We stopped singing Beach Boys hits and leaned forward as six hundred Canadian schoolgirls aged fifteen to eighteen were ordered off the buses and marshalled aboard. Well, that's a slight exaggeration. There were only five hundred teenage girls and about a hundred boys, but I don't think we noticed the boys particularly.

It was strictly forbidden to 'fraternize' with the pupils, although over the next two weeks we spent a huge amount of time with the pupils. It was our job to spend time with the pupils. The pupils thronged around us. We gave the pupils visas and advice and smiles. In the evenings, we were expected to organize a disco for the pupils. But there was nobody for these pupils to disco with, except some of the junior officers (unfashionably short-haired and just a little straight), those hundred or so Canadian boys (well, never mind them) and us. We quite badly wanted to fraternize with the pupils. There were, it seemed, rather a remarkable number of pupils who wanted to fraternize with us. They weren't our ruddy pupils. Some of these pupils were older than we were. And we weren't teachers either. We were like prefects, weren't we?

Alas, there was absolutely nowhere on the ship where it was possible to 'fraternize' in private. We looked. It was reputed that a previous school office assistant had decided to use the ironing room to get to know a pupil better. It had two open doorways and an ironing board. Unsurprisingly, he had been caught in the act. Apparently there had been a bit of a fuss.

I dutifully informed my mother that the passengers were 'either very fat or very beautiful', that I was making 'an awful lot of friends' and that my bar bill was £1.45 for the week.

But day by day the sensation increased that we were taking part in a not very convincing late-sixties sex comedy. It was a new experience, having come from a boy's school, to walk down corridors and be greeted with winks and endearments by either the fat or the beautiful. The dashing Leslie Phillips had been pursued around the decks by his female passengers, but it couldn't happen in real life, could it? When it did, it became acutely difficult to remain responsive to six or seven admirers at a time.

The ship sailed off to Greece, passing down through the Aeolian Islands and into the Corinth canal. And it was spring too.

The *Uganda* carried a full complement of old-fashioned Empire certainties. The crew, for example, were Goan. Dinner and lunch were 'three-course blow-outs', enlivened by kofta curries and tarka dahls. We ate well away from the steerage pupils, at tables of gleaming silverware, with teachers and officers and passengers. 'Do the crew all eat at this dinner?' I asked one of the third lieutenants.

He scowled at me. (It was central to officer-training to be

able to scowl authoritatively.) 'The *crew*,' he said pointedly, 'make their chicken stews in their own quarters.'

One of the 'matrons' recruited exclusively from ex-captains of hockey teams leaned across. 'The crew is black, darling. Never call the officers crew.'

'You should try to eat one of their chicken curries if you can,' said the deputy headmistress between mouthfuls. 'It's a real treat.'

The 'crew' were paid four pounds a week, same as us. But unlike us, they had been recruited as entire villages in Goa and would serve four-year stints. Their 'quarters' were squeezed into the stern of the boat.

'Most modern ships have black crew,' I was told.

One of the other junior officers giggled. 'If white crew don't like your orders, you can disappear over the side in the middle of the night.'

But this knowledge didn't seem to make the officers much warmer to the black Goans. 'The problem is that these natives have to be doubled up. We have twice as many of the blighters on board as we ought to need.'

My letters home, when not about my search for the perfect Afghan coat, are full of righteous indignation. 'My steward shouted at me,' I wrote, 'because everybody shouts at him and that's how he thinks English is spoken.'

Our duties were not taxing, but two of us had to get up at five in the morning and deliver the daily news. It was my second encounter with a seventies office techno-nightmare in six months. Two or three typed pages of 'the news in sentences' arrived from somewhere up in the radio room, each with several backing strips and a flimsy. They were attached, by means of punched holes in the top of the paper, to matching holes on the Roneo machine and then had to be smoothed on to a drum. Once in place, the backing pages were ripped off. The machine was turned once with a massive handle to ensure that the ink was oozing through the punched type face, and then we pressed a button. It was supposed to clank out fifty copies.

It was a deadly business. Too little ink and fifty pages of blankness would emerge. Too much, and the black, adhesive gunge would spit out over my Mr Byrite trousers. The pages of used paper had to be delicately transferred to a bin without getting them stuck to a shirt. None of this was made any easier by the early hour, the cramped space or the hangover. We would run around the ship, trailing paw marks up the companionways to the chef's office in his smelly kitchens, delivering the news-sheet to the thunderous engine rooms (where an engineer would mutely hang it on his clipboard), up to the bridge, into the lobbies of senior officers and under the doors of the cabins of the passengers. The ship, of course, chugged on all night.

Reaching Kos, the headmaster of the ship and the captain went ashore at dawn. Callow as I was, I never really spotted that the headmaster looked out for us. He took two of his school office assistants, although we had no function at all except to look on. We clambered down into a lifeboat and chugged over a limpid bay in that early, violet, tremulous Mediterranean light, before the rest of the ship had even woken, slinking to the town quay, on an insiders' visit, always the most exciting way to go. It was the best way to arrive anywhere – by boat. Waiting at the top of the steps was a little knot of men in suits – the mayor and dignitaries of the town – probably seeking assurance that the ship's juvenile complement weren't going to pillage their island.

By nine everybody else was ashore. The islanders somehow found a bicycle for every passenger aboard. The girls pedalled off across the island. A thousand sturdy Canadian legs pumped through mountains smothered in wild flowers, up to the temple of Hippocrates and along empty coastal roads. We set off in pursuit. I was with Jon. A handsome bearded Canadian himself, he had wildly overstretched his fraternization. He had planned at least six or seven separate liaisons. We pedalled furiously around the island to pre-assigned meeting points. But wherever we settled with one of his girlfriends, another would come cycling along the street calling his name and waving plaintively.

It was a relief when the ship docked back in Malta, even though my vicarious fraternizations with Bev, Beth, Dale, Karen and Jill had all, somehow, to be concluded simultaneously. On the last night, the band played 'Auld Lang Syne', all the girls burst into tears, and I collected a lot of Canadian postcodes. I had to explain, where I could, that poor Jon had been held up by his duties, while he hid in his cabin.

The school office assistants decided that we would plan more carefully for the next voyage and try to stop behaving like starving monkeys in a banana shop. Unsuccessfully we attempted to make sense of the passenger manifest and repaired to our eyrie above the dock as the buses took away our girls. The returning coaches disgorged six hundred screaming Scottish schoolchildren between the ages of eleven and fourteen, and they roared aboard. With the hiss of a pneumatic coach door, *Adolescent Lust at Sea* became *The Pure Hell of St Trinian's*.

During five cruises in twelve weeks I visited almost every port in the Mediterranean for six hours. We trudged in a mob down the streets of ancient Ephesus. I spent an overnight anchorage in Istanbul haggling for a rhomboid leather jacket in the grand bazaar. (It was made of 'lamp leather'.) In Santorini we ate a kebab lunch while the ship disgorged its screaming horde, mounted them on to hundreds of donkeys for a ride to the top of the volcano rim and promptly took them straight back down again. In Izmir I found the Afghan coat which had become more smelly than fashionable by the time I got it delivered home. ('You will have to have it treated for flies,' I wrote to my mother. 'Don't worry, only ten per cent of them are infected.') In Tunisia we peered at three or four disconsolate lumps of stone, pondered how efficiently the Romans had razed Carthage and then hurried back to our 1950s world for supper. Later in the year, we sailed to the Baltic. I went to Finland, Stockholm and Denmark, with more Scottish kids aboard.

One morning we woke up in a fjord in Norway: the ship like a model in a slab-sided stone bath, and, at the far end, a tiny village, a needle spire and a whiff of smoke waiting in the clear back-lit air. The boats were lowered. Six hundred hollering children jumped in. A Viking invasion in reverse, we were ferried to the hamlet, and they sacked the town.

Five hours later, the masters at arms stood at the companionway, reaching eleven-year-olds out of the boats, turning them upside down and shaking them vigorously. Key rings, model churches, souvenir pencils and bottles of illicit beer tumbled on the ridged steel deck to be gathered up into a hamper and returned. The ship delayed sailing that evening, so that the frightened shopkeepers could come aboard and reclaim some of their looted stock.

It was around then that the staff captain, a small man with the demeanour of the Duke of Edinburgh kept waiting by a pop star, took to glaring at me. I think it was my hair. Lounging in the saloon, running up bar bills on a chitty or chatting up the younger teachers, I would glance up to see him on the other side of the wood-block dance floor, incinerating me with a glare. Once, I was asked to set up a microphone for a lecture. He stood at the back of the empty hall for five minutes, sporting an expression of malevolence that would have felled a dog.

Perhaps it was this that made me feel that I was in an early George Orwell novel. Before we reached Alexandria, it was patiently explained to me, once and for all, that 'these Goan people are simply not as intelligent as white people'.

I protested. 'What on earth makes you think that?'

The officers at the table gaped in bemusement. One of them laughed. 'Look around this room, for Christ's sake. Who are sitting at the table? White men. Who are serving them? Black men. Do you think that would be the case if black men were as intelligent as us?'

Everybody seemed to have run away to sea. The banquets, so lavish, became repetitive. The horizons so broad, were, in fact, bounded by the bow and stern of the ship. The lovely girls, who swooned over the handsome third, were there to romance but never to touch. The visits were to the same docks, year after year, cruise after cruise, and only the intelligently curious headmaster and his lecturers seemed bothered to go ashore. The rest preferred their world hermetically sealed, but were in reality suffering from island fever. And I was only a visitor. Nonetheless, after I stepped off the boat in Naples, my letter home was filled with regret at leaving.

I disembarked from the *Uganda* with a tightening around the chest. For the first time in my life, my days were completely unregulated. As I write this, I am trying to check whether it can possibly be true. I was eighteen. I must, surely, have separated myself from social connections before. I must have been responsible for setting my own bedtime, or finding my own meal. For Christ's sake, I had been to Glastonbury and eaten boiled kale, hadn't I? But I had never faced an entire country like this.

A flush of panic washed over me. I bought a pair of bargain

sunglasses to assuage it. Aviator-style, satisfyingly cheap, they were black enough, I hoped, to hide my wide-eyed innocence, but probably silly enough to mark me out to what, in my credulity, I imagined was a wholly rapacious population. I was a straggle-haired eighteen-year-old would-be cool dude, humping a suitcase through hot streets, brusquely fending off propositions from taxi drivers: 'Where you wan' go?'

Yes, indeed, where did I wan' go? That magic feeling. 'Nowhere to go.' For the first time in my life I had nobody to talk to in the evening, nobody to share a meal with, nobody to make a joke with about the rank smell emanating from the drains, nobody to expect me to get in, nobody to tell me whether the place I was going to sleep was safe. Oh, Mummy!

I went to Rome. The train had seemed the safest emergency option. I could stick my luggage on the rack and sit down for a bit, while the auburn country wound past. I don't think I admired the railway system. I put any differences from suburban London down to Latin primitivism. But I was happy to get away from the confusing south and anxious to distance myself from the cruise ship. Moving on felt safe. It delayed decisions. Besides, I had to see Rome.

In the autumn of 2004 I went back there for a fortnight. Was it the first time since? It seemed so comfortable and familiar and so unchanged. At about half past six I hurried my wife Jo out into the street. It was Sunday night, and Rome was alive like a dignified cocktail party. Most of the shops were open, and the passeggiari full of people just walking, many arm in arm like us, a few with dogs, husbands and wives, men together, girls laughing. They were peering and assessing, presumably spotting tiny variations in detail in the goods on offer. Women's fashions do, after all, change, but Roman men wear muted colours, cashmere pullovers, tweed jackets and soft shirts in subtle stripes and delicate fabrics, and a hundred small stores seem to offer them infinite tiny varieties of their discreet, unvarying, preppy taste.

Even as we joined in and thought about some serious shopping ourselves, we noticed that the shops were closing, that the streets were thinning. The carabinieri let the cars through along the Corso. The cafés were still busy. The flower stalls would stay open until late – someone might want to offer apologies or take an offering. It's not the brisk, alienating outdoor life of Paris, London or New York, where early evening is all a frenetic rush to get on to mid-evening entertainment. There aren't many cinemas round the old city. Theatres are thin on the ground. The promenade was the main event, and by eight it was seriously over, and the stragglers were thinking about getting off home.

Nothing seemed to have changed since 1970 except me. Then, I was burning with A-level artistic pretension, part of which involved a mini grand tour of 'great art' and 'important architecture', but I had standards. I was a good, cold, northern chapel sort of a chap and on my guard against curlicues. The Baroque dismayed me. Gold things worried me. I could just about cope with the grotesque, but was suspicious of Bernini. On first walking into St Peter's I recoiled from what seemed an Aunty Betty, gold-plated, glittery notion of the sublime.

But I was prepared to mug up, and public collections are good companions. In Rome I busied myself with the sights. Pompously, I seem hardly to have bothered with the seventeenth century and addressed myself exclusively to the historical certainties of Ancient Rome, trudging to the Forum, tramping on to the Colosseum, wandering out to the baths of Caracallus, even managing to walk to the Appian Way, and then indeed some small distance along it; a restless vade mecum, following other people's noses, ticking off the guide-books' five-star attractions on a forced route march. As long as I was planning my budget, carefully calculating where to eat, comparing prices in small restaurants, estimating which place would serve me the cheapest spaghetti, or which pantelleria could provide me with three huge slices of white-spotted mortadella, I was fully engaged with my quest. Overnight I had changed from spendthrift financial hooligan to a pennypinching ascetic. I filled my letters with accounts of my cheap meals and careful budgeting. It probably gave me comfort too. By following my parents' instructions, by living up to their standards. I was still in Epping in my purse.

When I had exhausted my restlessness, I went back to the little room I had rented near the station. It was a 'walk-up' and smelled of cooking. The owner wore a vest. I sat and wrote up my accounts in a tiny room behind a sliding door while television jabber echoed down the marble staircase. In the morning, I pushed through a beaded curtain and ate dry rolls and apricot jam with black coffee at a Formica-topped table and then hurried out to pound on, talking to no one all day, until finally leaving the cats to the dusk around the Trajan's Forum. One night I went to a concert presented by the British Council in an ornate room full of stacking chairs. It was sparsely attended by earnest pairs of girls in glasses and thin men, leaning demented faces on one hand. In the second half, the musicians got to their feet and plucked randomly at the piano strings through the lifted lid of the Bechstein. I felt deliciously separate from everybody, so much so that when my school friend Andrew arrived, I actually resented his presence.

So, now in 2005 I have in my hands a plastic-backed exercise book. I would have bought it in a 'tabacchi' in Italy. It records everything I did from 1 April until 19 April 1972. Here, at last, is a proper record – a gate, a window into the real obsessions of the eighteen-year-old me.

I have written 'Griff Rhys Jones' on the first page ('Now get out your exercise book and write your name clearly in the front of it'). There were some other vaguely figurative decorations, including bald-headed space-rulers, a female resembling Sandy Denny at a woodland folk meet, and a booted space soldier firing a ray blaster.

Despite the missing first half of the journal, I know that Andrew joined me in Rome. I know I despaired of losing my pensione, until a woman realized my dilemma and took me downstairs to find another, bigger, double room. I know that when Andrew arrived I dutifully tramped round all the ancient sites again and showed them to him as if I owned them. I know that this began to irritate him. I know that we left for Siena for three days before we headed to Florence to start our art course.

Blimey, I was reading Nietzsche, 'taking it in easy stages because I'm not sure whether it's deceptively easy or deceptively difficult'. We were always in the library or the pensione reading for a couple of hours before heading off to visit museums and churches. We are behaving like a louche version of *Room with a View*. We seek out the restaurant recommended by my school friend Douglas Adams. (I was dogging his footsteps.) A meal is described in detail and followed by a short sentence: 'Was a bit ill in the night.' I recount the prices of food and the lecture on Raphael ('very interesting') and the story of the chair: 'I sat down rather heavily on a chair.' (I jumped on it actually. The leg broke off, and the 'old dame' made us take it to get it mended amongst the fakers of the old quarter.) 'We went to see *A Funny Thing Happened on the Way to the Forum*; well, we watched very hard, but we didn't see that funny thing happen.' Great. Not only that. By 28 March I am solemnly recording that I had received six letters in one day.

13. Jill

I can't take the Canadian letters. But I must. I must sit and piece this together.

The smell, the stamps, the addresses on the back, the photographs, the washed-out snaps of tiny girls in tartan trousers with long hair, the shame. I led them on. I led them on. Oh, Dale, Jill, Karen and Bev! On the back of Jill's envelope in bold writing it says, '6, Cod Road, Nova Scotia, Canada'. Cod Road? A cold, exotic, fishy place it sounds. Near Halifax. Halifax? I shall have to get an atlas. I have never even checked whether this was west or east Canada. I must have guessed it was near the water. 'Read this page last.' The growing confidence still stings. 'I miss you.' She didn't want to send a photo, but I pressed her, and she obliged me.

'Read this last,' so I did. 'Well, you asked for it! Here it is – my passport photo which was taken two years ago – 1970.'

But it isn't there. I go through the box, but I haven't hidden it in any other envelope. The other photos all survived with their letters. There's Bev and Dale and Karen. I must have taken Jill's and put it somewhere safe. But Bev was writing in April: 'Remember that I'm thinking of you every day.' So I had hardly settled my attentions on Jill. Or perhaps I had, but I hadn't told Bev, or Karen, or Dale.

It takes me time to sort the letters out, because the handwriting looks so similar. What did I write to them? To get them going. To encourage them. To lure them in. 'You sound a slob,' Dale writes chidingly. Did I duplicate? Did I reinvent? What doodles did I send? Why did I write about the 'gippos' quite so much? (All of them write back asking to know what I mean.)

Karen was still writing in May. She was still walking the dog and doing badly at her exams. I have got the atlas out, by the way. Toronto is hundreds of miles from Halifax. I had lumped them all together, but they had come to the boat from different parts of Canada, as remote from each other as I would be from Germany. Whew. They weren't likely to have met at a party and compared letters, anyway.

And who was Margot from Bowman? My goodness, turning the pile over, I discover another girl altogether. Dale was jolly – full of news and practicality. Karen was wistful. Bev and Jill chatty and direct. Margot got straight to business: acid and speed and a story of the OPD (the Ontario Police Department) raiding her house at six in the morning. Her face 'was redder than my hair'. She was planning to travel across North America on her ten-speed bike. 'But most of all I want to see you.' Oh, Margot. What would have happened if you had bicycled over the Atlantic? There isn't any photograph of Margot.

Did I churn it up? Did I urge them on? Jill's first letter is a largely formal one. 'Which one was she?' I must have thought, ungallantly.

'The page is running out unlike my thoughts,' she writes but she goes on to mention that she is planning to come to England in August – in that very first letter. I must have planned it all. By March she was writing again, having apparently got my postcard – from Florence (spelled like her middle name). 'After reading your postcard I wished that I was in Rome and about to go to Florence . . . and most of all to see you.' Heavens, I don't suppose we even danced together. Oh, Jill, did you know that I was writing to all the girls?

She had a photograph of that last night on the boat – the last night of a mere thirteen days. In the photograph she has her hand in my pocket, so she tells me. She had gone to work in the movie theatre and in a small boutique for $1.50 an hour. By June she had saved $135 and was 'almost there'.

This is horrible, reading all these letters – the innocence, the trust. The hard work she went to, based on thirteen days and that hand in my pocket and all those long replies I must have sent. By now she's telling me to eat properly and wear galoshes in the rain.

Could my mother write to her mother (49) and formally invite Jill to our house?

As I read these letters the sound I can hear is me making groaning noises. What do they mean? Her reaction to a photo that I sent . . . I can't repeat it. It's too intimate and trusting. And the letters have got ten pages long. She writes so cautiously, dropping her little hints and indications, venturing into possibilities of intimacy. Her emotional state seems such a fragile thing.

Suddenly I wonder what would happen if I tried to get in touch today. If I wrote to Cod Road, would someone pass it on, would she answer? Unlike all my school friends, these girls couldn't know anything about me. It could be an anonymous trip. I would just be this guy from the past. I could visit them all. I could see if any parents still live at those addresses, in their eighties now, I suppose. Is it possible? 'Dale and Brian live near Calgary now and have three children.'

The letters are so potent. All those junior excitements. All that promise of, well, let's face it, sex.

I finish sorting them out. They lie in front of me in bundles. Margot stopped writing first. Why? She only sent me three in total, but then she was the acid queen, so that's understandable. Dale's practical, chatty ones finish in mid-correspondence – mid-endearment, almost – but some time in the summer they all stopped, even, eventually, Jill's.

There isn't a letter in the pile, though, that asks, 'What happened? Why did you stop writing?' By June I must have settled on poor Jill. Did I simply just stop sending letters to the others? I suppose I did.

I have identified the last letter, I think, from Jill herself. I can hardly bear to read it. It is sent from Hampshire, in England, on her way to stay. The one before it is full of excitement. 'See you Friday,' she ends.

Now I am in a forties thriller, feeling through the envelopes, double-checking, turning them over, searching in the box. Surely there is more. Where's the next letter? Where is the one that forgives me? Where is the one that pours hate on me for treating her so badly? Where is the conclusion to this? My only personal memory is the slight icing of recollected shame. I have completely lost the cause, erased it. I cannot remember any real details, how she packed, how we must have taken her back to the airport. Did my mother commiserate with her? Was I even courageous enough to discuss this with her? I doubt it. All that remains is the electrical charge of a residual negative emotion.

(Of course it would have been tidier if I had gone there. I like the notion of those frozen places. 'We have the best climate in the world,' Dale wrote with all that enviable Canadian pride. I could have gone and visited them all one by one. Instead, I waited for Jill to come to me.)

I came home from that first adventure in Italy by car with the Haydens, our local doctors from Epping. It wasn't late in the season. It can't have been, because I had finished the month in Florence and headed north to Val-d'Isère by a sequence of trains that left me confused and cold at a small station high in the Alps. I got down from a powerful express which I'd boarded with an illegal ticket and transferred to a branch line. I came out of the station and walked through the town to the practice slopes, where I finally spotted my doctor, his family and my sister learning to ski on the crowded hill. It felt like a miracle of personal organization to make these connections. I had never been skiing. I had no clothes and no money to buy them, so I spent the weekend in flared denim jeans and a reefer jacket, falling over until the wet froze them like cardboard, and my legs became ready for amputation.

So it was after a second tour of duty on the boat that Jill came. I must have taken the Baltic trip and then headed south. Yes, I remember we passed through the Channel on an upper deck in bright early-evening light. One of the assistants danced for joy in his platform-heeled boots, and we all gave an impromptu exhibition of cod Fred Astaire. A junior cadet was sent up from the bridge directly below to scream at us. We had disturbed the captain at a crucial moment as he tried to steer the *Uganda* through the Straits of Dover. On to La Rochelle and La Coruña, then Lisbon, where we went to the brothel by mistake, then down to North Africa and Carthage, and then home for the rest of the summer, which was when Jill came to stay.

Of all my regular correspondents, Jill was the cleverest and most passionate. I had studied her lost photograph closely. Remembering that photograph now and comparing it with my own from 1970, I see she also had the dubious accolade of looking almost exactly like me. Her hair was parted in the middle, black and wiry. She wore flared jeans and sweaters. She was of average height. It was a unisex thing. We could tell the difference, even if the *Daily Telegraph* couldn't. We were very excited by the difference. She seemingly as much as me. She was a sweet, intelligent girl and I treated her abominably.

For a start, when she announced that she was coming to England, I decided that this was quite probably the opportunity to lose my virginity. She was coming a long distance and would be staying with us, in my home, which would furnish the opportunity (though quite where and how might need to be carefully addressed). She was Canadian. That seemed to augur well. American girls were notoriously loose. Essentially, Canadian girls were American girls in pullovers, weren't they? 'Love, love, love,' warbled the Beatles. Jill seemed bright enough to understand the ethos of the era and the unworthiness of my intentions.

I hoped I would recognize her. I did. She was, as girls so often are, polite and considerate. I gabbled ceaselessly. My mother's eyes were shining, as mothers' eyes do when their male offspring bring girls home. I know from my own experience that dads want to grunt and get on with the previously undisturbed tax returns, but mothers look to the companionship, they like to poke their noses in and they like the hint of nookie. Or at least my mother seemed to.

There is no doubt that I was in love, by my own standards. I knew the beating heart and the state of excitement that led to lingering gazes. I was pleased that she was a better, more considerate person than me, and that everybody else immediately recognized it. This all helps enormously at the beginning of any relationship. It can become something of a problem near the end, though. Other people will grow attached to nice, friendly girls.

Of course, there was no sex in White Lodge. This may have been the tail of the swinging sixties, but my parents were born in the twenties. Jill enjoyed the cooking and was happy to be quizzed exhaustively by my mother and help with the washing-up, but there was a granny lurking about. My mother and father never seemed to go out. I had never noticed before that my family came and went with such noisy regularity; in and out of every room in our house. Then at night Jill went to one end of the upstairs corridor, and I went to the other.

I lost my virginity on the boat. You might imagine that a twenty-nine-foot yacht was a less promising boudoir than a large detached house, but somehow, at the time, it seemed a better opportunity.

I went sailing without my parents. How did that happen? My father must have been 'on duty' at the hospital. My brother was certainly aboard, though, and my sister too, I seem to remember.

Jill was given 'the cabin', and after lights out I rustled up there to join her. It was my first experience of wearing a condom. We can't have managed that with the lights out. Perhaps we used a torch. The 'cabin' was separated from the rest of the boat by a small, bright-blue curtain. It was a cupboard. If you slept in it, the centreboard casing formed one side, the hull the other, and your legs went into a sort of cubby hole. There was barely enough room for one person to scramble up there. It must have been a challenge to accommodate two. A novice couple engaged in screwing must have been highly audible in the utter blackness of this tiny boat. It was probably made worse by extreme caution. A long zip of a zip-fastening on a sleeping bag being unzipped, followed by a circumspect pause during which only breathing could be heard, followed, after enough time had elapsed to allow the false assumption that the other occupants of the boat were now asleep, by a rustling noise and a squeak.

On the wedding night of a Bejar nomad, the groom leaves the men's tent in the middle of the night, creeps across the desert and clambers under the tent flap to find his betrothed. Then, in the women's tent, surrounded by her mother, aunties and sisters, he ravishes his bride. This was similar, though at least I knew where to find her and didn't have to stumble around in the dark and inquire where she was. I obviously thought that siblings didn't count. I would have done the same for them. They had to pretend, for form's sake, that they were asleep. If they woke up and tried to eavesdrop, that was their look-out. But I wasn't really concerned about them. The extended courtship by letter and now an attempt to take each stage as slowly and quietly as possible must have stoked up the ardour. The condom smelt rubbery, but it was real sex, and Jill was a bona fide visitor from the more straight-forward Americas. I had joined the sixties sexual revolution at last, and only two years late.

After that we worked hard at it. I did a lot of babysitting. We would stand at the door, see the parents off and get at it amongst the toy cars. Thank God for dinner parties. I meet grown-up people today who could have choked to death in their cots for all I knew. We loved the sex, but, alas, I gradually realized I didn't love Jill.

'I thought she was staying for good at one point,' my mother told me. I should have realized that no trip around Europe was really planned. Jill didn't suddenly reach for her backpack and wave a cheery farewell. I took her to see the Tower of London, but the sites of major European cities weren't the reason for her visit. I was. I had made the poor girl cross the Atlantic, and as the summer faded so did my passion. In September I would go to university anyway.

Jill was far too grown up not to guess that there wasn't any real future, even if I was too immature to be able to broach it. I took her with me to Cambridge a few weeks before I was due to go up. I hadn't had the guts to talk to her, but by now I was walking separately from her. I can feel the dipping, draining slide of the stomach and the heat on the back of the neck. It's called 'shame'. I simply grew cold towards her. We had talked a lot, now I didn't talk at all. We had walked hand in hand, now I took my hand away. We had been friends, now I acted like a stranger. And she was thousands of miles from home.

She finally got the message and flew off, and I was relieved. Everybody was sorry that she was going except me. They were just more polite than me. They could say sensible words and talk to her. I just let things drift and behaved obtusely until she told me that she thought she had better go home. I hope her parents hugged her. I hope she got married. I hope she's happy.

I hope she doesn't read this.

14. The Whiff of Nepotism

In the autumn of 2003 I went back to Cambridge. I was taking George, my son, there to start his university career. I should have been many things at that moment. I should have been proud and a little in awe of his youth and attainments and I should have been happy for him. I should have been supportive and easy-going and helpful. I should have been at the very least a little decent. But I suppose I have never really been very good at being the things that I ought to be.

The year before, he had quietly come to me to ask me my advice about colleges. 'My advice?' Once I had accommodated the mild shock, I had given my advice freely enough. I was an expert, after all. It was one of my favourite subjects. 'I can only recommend two things.' I was exploring a tone that I gradually recognized as being magisterially paternal. 'Go for a college by the river. You will be spending time in university activities, not college ones . . .' (how speedily one becomes an utter arse under these trying and exceptional circumstances) '. . . and the river colleges are much prettier. But, hey, it doesn't really matter, just whatever you do, don't apply for my old college, Emmanuel. They hate any whiff of nepotism. And anyway,' I added, 'it's become some sort of academic top-runner, apparently, first on some ladder list or other, and there's no point in making things difficult for yourself, is there?'

George ignored my advice, applied to Emmanuel and got a place easily enough. The director of studies was apparently utterly unaware that his father had been at the college at all.

And when the time came, I offered to deliver his bass amplifier. It was the least I could do. Had my own father come with me at that point? Probably not, but I wanted to be at least a little parasitic. We drove out through east London, actually passing within sight of Epping on the way.

'This is actually what I'd like to do,' I said by way of conversation half-way up the M11.

'What?'

'Oh, I don't know. Spend a few years studying architecture at undergraduate level.' University was wasted on young people. 'They only want to shag each other and explore the shops. Ha ha. We should go to university at sixty. Then we'd be fascinated by the lectures. God, I'd attend all the lectures these days.'

My wife Jo shifted in her seat and laughed gently. 'Are you trying to compete with him?'

I laughed myself, loudly. I was trying to make conversation with an eighteen-year-old, wasn't I? OK. I was dumping my neuroses on him as I did so, but then he was old enough to understand that, wasn't he? By the way, had he actually read any of the set books on that list they sent him? Had he?

By the time we arrived, I had the grace to feel moderately ashamed of myself, and he was a nervous wreck.

'Oh, for God's sake, it's always *you*!'

But it *was* me. This was the unacknowledged elephant sitting in the back seat of the family Zafira.

We arrived at the back of the college, my college. They had built a cream-painted wall where there had once been internal windows looking down into the Junior Common Room, but otherwise the building was utterly unchanged. To an undergraduate returning from the 1940s, Cambridge in the 1970s would have been a different planet, but as we heaved the trunk through the same heavy sprung door up the same spiral staircase and stood in the same corridor I felt I had entered some sort of cruel time warp. George wasn't actually in my room. He was in Andrew's, next door.

This was the real reason they discourage nepotism. The experience is too traumatic for the older relative. George's room had the same bed, pushed back under a sloping double cupboard, with the same adjustable shelving above. There was the same desk with the same wide, shaded anglepoise light. The same plate-glass window ran along the width of the north side looking out on to the same roof garden, where the same shrubs now seemed surreally overgrown, reinforcing the impression that it was a looking-glass dream, because when I say 'the same' I don't mean it in a comparative sense, I mean it in its absolute sense. Why hadn't they, at the least, changed the colour scheme or replaced the lino?

When I was at Emmanuel, according to 'the alternative guide' for college undergraduates, I flooded the North Court passages after an accident with a washing machine. (Heh, heh.) But this was completely untrue. Surely I had felt nothing for my college? Emmanuel had merely become a place to sleep, hadn't it? I sneeringly rejected the beery Junior Common Room and its habitués, dressed like a Marks and Spencer knitwear catalogue. I pompously spurned everything that reminded me of school (the sports teams, the head of the river, the rowing bumpery-frumpery, the college societies, and the Master's wife, with her well-thumbed copy of *Who's Who* resting on her nest of tables). My college scarf had lain for years at the bottom of the architect-designed chest of drawers, wrapping up some china. So why was it affecting me so oddly now?

'We should go.' My wife was standing by the door, having said her goodbye to George.

'Yes. Do you want to meet later? Anything you need? Hadn't we better get you a kettle?' I was grasping at utensils. 'Shall we meet you for tea?'

'Perhaps.'

We went out via Front Court and I started to slow my steps. There were the same posters for what looked like the same productions of *The Bald Prima Donna*. I furtively glanced at the stairs up to the pigeon-holes. I had to fight a residual urge to go up and look – as if there might still be something in mine. No, no. This was ridiculous, but what my wife could not understand, and what I could not admit, was that I had never finished whatever it was that had started here. I was standing in the cloisters looking across the square of grass at the yellow stone hall and trying to leap across thirty years, but the leap that I was trying to make was forward, to accept the present. Thirty years? My father once told me that he had never felt a day older since he had been at university.

'What on earth is the matter with you?'

'Nothing.' My son had usurped my life. He had thirty years on me, stretching ahead of him. This was where my own life had suddenly become what it had never been before: exciting. It had remained exciting, but never as much fun. I was fiendishly envious of my own flesh and blood. 'We can get a kettle in Robert Sayle, if it's still there,' I said.

In 1972, my mother was impressed by my place at Cambridge. My father, apparently, had been bright enough and qualified for Oxford, but the War intervened, or his father died (the exact circumstances varied), and he had had to stay at home and become a doctor in Cardiff. Mummy had to admit that she wasn't quite sure what it was all ultimately 'for'. She hoped, I think, that I would eventually become as successful as David Frost, the Cambridge graduate who most seemed to epitomize varsity success amongst the middle classes in the late sixties.

At school, only the senior chaplain, 'Sexy' Gardiner, ever stopped the roar of the qualification machinery for long enough to allow the Oxbridge factory to examine itself. 'Why are you all going to university?' he asked, in the middle of a general studies lesson. We stared sullenly back at him. Eventually Horth stuck up a hand. 'Because you told us to,' he said.

There was no 'beyond' Oxbridge. It was the edge of the flat world. This was the era of *The Graduate*, with that party scene when the man comes up to Dustin Hoffman and says, 'I have one word to say to you – "plastics".'

Nobody even said 'plastics' to us. Nobody said 'law', or 'civil service' or 'City of London' either. Nobody said anything beyond 'get a degree.'

At Cambridge I was to bump into a few seemingly deluded would-be rulers of the country wearing waistcoats who liked to bray loudly and publicly at either basset hounds or rowers or the Union. (They ended up editing major newspapers and running political parties and were not deluded at all.) But they were not us. We had no sense of destiny, only mild shame. How could we do anything other than blush and groan slightly when our mothers introduced us to some pompous friend with the dreadful words 'He's going up to Cambridge next year'? We learned to mutter to our contemporaries, 'I'm at college.'

We were, after all, products of the *Melody Maker* and *NME*, of earnest endeavours to persuade teachers that the lyrics of Procul Harem were the equal of Shelley, that the bass rhythms of Deep Purple were as musically complex as Scarlatti, and that Bob Dylan was as clever as Auden (and decidedly more important because he was populist, egalitarian and youthful). A whole generation had been corralled and seduced by the marketing ambitions of a self-important youth culture. Nick Hornby was somewhere over the park in Jesus, preparing for an early career writing for music magazines.

'My father tells me you were at Emmanuel,' a different famous novelist I interviewed for *Bookworm* once said.

'Yes.'

'When?'

'Seventy-two.'

'Oh.' He looked bemused. 'Same year as me. What did you read?'

'English.'

'Gosh, same subject.'

I was in a different set. 'Funny we never met.'

'Yes, well, I spent most of my time at Cambridge lying in my room smoking dope,' he said.

In *Brideshead*, they drink themselves insensible in panelled halls. In *The Adventures of Verdant Greene*, Verdant spends most of his waking hours chatting up shop girls. Betjeman never did any work. Byron ran up debts furnishing his rooms. Peter Cook spent most of his time in London, writing revues for Kenneth Williams. But they were all self-consciously, unashamedly, *at* Cambridge or Oxford. Not us. We were the egalitarian generation. The 'Oxbridge seventies lot' rather scrupulously avoided any national presence until Stephen, Emma and Hugh came along and were clever in public again. For years, the most outwardly famous product of Cambridge of my era was 'the Cambridge Rapist'.

There is an undistinguished triangle of open space, just off the river, at the corner of Grantchester Road. In 1972, my mother drove me off the main A11 and through the suburbs to start my own first term and it was this bit, ringed with low Victorian villas, rows of almshouses and the tall trees of the meadows by the river (not collegiate Cambridge at all) that spuriously hit me with the promise of cloistered academia.

There were enough bicyclists wrapped in scarves, purposefully crossing the green on old-fashioned machines, enough breezes picking up the first autumn leaves, enough rays of sun, weak in that high east-of-England white sky (shining on distant cupolas and spires) to fool me into believing that I had immediately captured the essence of the university. I would become a tweed-clad, mole-like scholar myself, studying in my private world of difficult books, hurrying like all these others to lectures, supping the odd half pint of beer but otherwise burying myself in the routine contentment of serious study.

Over the next five years I spent in Cambridge I was intermittently seduced by this fleeting madness again. The town encourages it. The Victorian leafy, bricky fustian could sometimes wrap me up like an old don's cardigan, for, oh, at least a minute at a time.

I got a gown. I had a bicycle. I was shown my room in South Court. Then I went up those stairs for the first time and visited my pigeon-hole. It was already stuffed with instructions on supervisions and lectures, which all seemed to start in a week, but it was also crammed with dozens of advertisements for extra-curricular activity of a vaguely Christian nature, and one hand-written note.

'Need someone to play a part in the *Rivals*. Interested? Get in touch, Douglas Adams.'

Douglas had been in the year above me in school. Like me, an enthusiastic schoolboy actor, he had, like me, never been given much to do. But I had got to know Douglas sitting in the changing rooms waiting to go on as the Bloody

Captain or Julius Caesar. In the sixth form, along with a
bloke called Paul Johnstone, who subsequently threatened
to sue Douglas for calling him the worst poet in the world,
he had started a thing called 'Artsphere' ('Fartsphere' Mr
Baron winningly called it). It put on concerts. My last school
memory of Douglas had been of him plucking at a Donovan
song on a shadily lit platform in the Memorial Hall. He
had so many self-conscious twiddles in his guitar finger-
picking technique that it went on for about twenty minutes
and the lighting crew ran out of colourful gobos to match
his invention.

I went straight to Heffers and bought a copy of *The Rivals*.
Douglas was playing Sir Lucius O'Trigger. It was a character and what's more it had more than six or seven lines. Fag,
the servant, had more lines than I was accustomed to as well,
but they were, thankfully, in separate gobbets. Perhaps I could
learn them without getting them wrong. I hurried off to a
rehearsal room in St Catherine's College and read some of
these lines to a marvellously clever, older woman director
called Sue Limb. (She was probably twenty-one.) She and
her partner, Roy Porter, appeared to be fully grown adults
and yet somehow they were my equals – a novel concept
to me then. Roy, who was reassuringly scruffy, had such
pertinent ideas that the process of getting them out made
him twitch spasmodically.

Whoever had been playing my part had run into a little
spot of bother with his tutors, but they skated over that,
and seemed perfectly willing to tolerate me as a baby.
Everybody in the production looked as sophisticated as
shit. Some were even postgraduates. Some were third-year
students with important-sounding titles in university
theatrical bodies I had not yet heard of. This was more
entertaining than sitting in the bar with the new fresher

intake watching a geek demonstrate how he could write his signature backwards.

Towards the end of the week, I managed to fit in a preliminary meeting with my tutor, Gerard Evans. After some chat about settling in, he asked me if I had any extra-curricular ambitions.

'Well, I'm interested in the theatre side,' I said.

He flinched. 'Yes. My best advice would be to possibly get involved in a little college production and then next year, or perhaps in the summer term, you might audition for something at the ADC.'

'Oh, I'm already in something that's on at the ADC,' I chirruped blithely.

He didn't groan. He was too dignified to make noises. But if the eyebrow he raised had been capable of a sound, it would have come out as a sort of extended, low creak. He looked into the middle distance.

'Well . . . In my experience the amateur theatre can become rather demanding on an undergraduate's time,' he said. 'Some people do rather overdo things. I would caution against letting it rule your life.'

Yes, but what did he know?

Eventually, towards the end of my first week, in between feverishly rehearsing *The Rivals*, I was able to squeeze in a meeting with my teachers – though we quickly learned to differentiate between teaching as we had understood it at school and teaching as it was practised at Cambridge. Our first supervision was a meeting with two crazed enthusiasts for the historical process. They seemed to have descended from some heady and complicated research undertaking to spend an hour trying to focus on the requirements of a group of defective novitiates.

Both of them were relatively new to the process of taking

supervisions. This accounted for their enthusiasm. (The rather more usual distracted weariness was left to others later.) They divided us into two sets, alighted seemingly at random on a topic for our first essay and then vied with each other to suggest reading lists. A spew of titles and articles gushed forth, running to thousands of pages. It was followed by a colossal fountain of supplementary reading. 'Oh, while you're there, have a look at . . .', 'Actually I suppose you ought to read . . .', 'Don't bother with the opening three chapters, but do look at his other book . . . If you can manage the original French . . .', 'I tell you what is rather fun . . .' Transported by the possibilities, they threw in dozens of works and, eventually, entire oeuvres. ('You should try to get up on Althusser generally over the next few weeks. Walter Benjamin is essential. I suppose you've all read *Das Kapital*. Engels is good on revolution in general. Read him tonight.')

Lectures? Lectures were more knotty. 'The obvious ones, of course,' though we were cautioned against paying serious attention to some of the leading academics of the university. On the other hand, it was thought a good idea to attend lectures quite unrelated to our subject, in disciplines far removed from our papers, just as part of our general education.

I reeled into South Court feeling slightly queasy. I was tasked to read three library shelves more than I had ever read before, over the next five days. History had become rather more than a dilettante exercise in hypothetical surmise. History was a science. It was an adjunct of dialectic. I had better try and find out what the hell that meant.

But other differences between school and university quickly became apparent. Having been hosed down by a water-cannon of sources, we were then left entirely to our own devices. We had no obligation to re-encounter these terrifying founts of bibliography for another whole week. Nonetheless, I bicycled straight to the James Stirling faculty library and I arrived for my evening rehearsal carrying a sack of books. This, in itself, raised a few eyebrows.

By the end of my first term, I had realized that morning lectures could be skipped and nobody was going to find out. (Or, at least not until I showed my miserable ignorance in an examination paper.) I diligently applied myself to the reading-lists until I was expert at filleting them, skilled at avoiding the longer paragraphs and hugely practised at skipping any detailed bilge presented as research. This released time not merely for rehearsals but for other important undergraduate skills: lying in bed until lunchtime and habitually staying up all night, which was when essays finally came to be written with the aid of Pro-Plus, the caffeine tablet.

But what the hell! The exams were a gratifying two years away. My college was staffed by revolutionary historians under the tutelage of Roderick Floud. They decided that examinations were retrogressive. We were not expected to take prelims at the end of the first year, like everybody else. They were a distraction from 'the real work'. This was accurate as far as I was concerned. My 'real work' was already in Cambridge amateur theatre.

15. In the Sweet Shop

By November 2004 I was back in Cambridge again and in another febrile state. In the spring, my former director of studies, John Harvey, the man who had engineered my jump from History to English at the end of my second year, had telephoned my house. Would I come and open the 'new English building'? How could I not? My son had now been at the college for a year.

'Tell me . . .' I asked, trying to remember to which of the pamphlets from Emmanuel this could possibly relate, 'I don't think that I have actually made, er . . . a contribution, financially, as it were, as yet. Is it finished and everything?' Well, obviously it was finished, since they were opening it. 'Sorry, that was a foolish question.'

After thirty years I was still anxious to try not to sound foolish to my director of studies. I had to find out later from my son that the building wasn't a college building as I had imagined, but the faculty building. I had already made a contribution to that. Perhaps that was why they were asking me to open it. But what had originally seemed to me a casual trip to my old college began to get laden with baggage. Three months later, at a party somewhere in the Cotswolds, standing by a bar made out of ice blocks, wondering whether it was time to join the other seven hundred guests for a tented sit-down dinner and a free funfair, I was joined by a noted QC and defender of radical causes.

'I've just been reading about you in the paper,' he said.

I prepared for a chat about old buildings.

'You're going to Cambridge or something.'

'Cambridge? Am I? Oh yes. In the autumn, I think.'

'Well, you seem to have caused a bit of a scandal.' He chuckled with the conspiratorial warmth that lawyers reserve for the discomfort of others.

'A scandal?'

'Some dons have complained about you being chosen to open their building. You know what they're like. Something about low comedians blah, blah . . . when they have so many distinguished graduates and so forth.'

This was the moment the *Tatler* chose to take a candid snap of the two of us, 'enjoying the party of the Cotswold season'.

'I wouldn't worry about it,' he continued after studying my expression. 'The paper seems to think the dons are being rather snooty.'

I didn't care about the newspaper. I was thinking about my speech. I had assumed that I could get away with a couple of blandishments and a platitude. It was all very well for him. He was used to facing a hostile crowd and cowing it with rhetoric. I advertised cars for a living.

They wouldn't let me out of it.

'No, no. Pay no attention to gossip. It is you we want,' the faculty secretary told me firmly.

Three months later I arrived early. They usually want you to get there early and then they don't know what to do with you. So they opened up a room and stuck me in it. Then they found a professor and stuck him in it too to make small talk with me, except that the professor was, as professors are, self-conscious about small talk and felt obliged to put up a running critical commentary on our conversation. ('I see there are two punchlines to that story . . .' though he laughed at neither.)

In return, I started talking nonsensical persiflage about architectural language. We warily circled each other on the new roof terrace

The rest of the faculty itself at last arrived and stood by, clutching glasses of warm wine and gawping at their new apricot terracotta building. A jazz band played in an improvised tent. These were ordinary men and women, who had other jobs to do, who undoubtedly felt obliged to turn up, just like me. They were curious, not judgemental; indifferent, not pompous; a little distracted, but a forgiving audience. One after another, we speakers stood on a coffee table and talked across a waste of beards and pale suits.

'I suppose you fell on your bottom as a baby and have been making jokes ever since,' said the professor wryly, as we went out for photographs.

As soon as I decently could, I trotted away from the new faculty building, past the Sidgwick site and across a de Chirico dreamscape. The building block lumpiness of Stirling's library, where I had fumbled after history journals, still looked like an unused plastics factory. There were no Japanese students standing outside the famous sun trap waiting for bits to fall off it today, but I could see exactly the same rows of bent-wood blond armchairs, facing out now on to a new Law faculty, designed by Norman Foster. On the other side was a recent, round, multi-coloured blob, the faculty of Divinity and beyond them, the old Brutalist blocks, where a big sign baldly announced 'Criminology' like an unusually literate advertising hoarding. Despite these new additions, little monuments to architectural caprice, plonked-down pavilions of some forgotten twentieth-century international exhibition, it all felt far more familiar than I expected. I had clearly been here enough times to get by.

Next to the east entrance to the Sidgwick site is a

curious keep-like building, the Lady Mitchell Hall. It is a lecture theatre. In the middle of my second term we 'occupied' it. The notorious 'Garden House Riots' had taken place in Cambridge three years before we arrived. Students were arrested for besieging a hotel which had organized a 'Greek' night. Greece was then controlled by the Colonels. 'You couldn't eat kebabs and dance to Zorba the Greek when that sort of thing was going on, man.'

Was it too late for us, we wondered? Could we still get a taste of that sort of freaky student protest ourselves?

Up until then, I had been a little disappointed by the groovy side of Cambridge. Undergraduates in my college did not seem hugely 'alternative', certainly by the standards of the Third Ear Café up the end of the King's Road in buzzing alternative London. Luckily, I had fallen in with a college group who thought themselves amongst the more forward-thinking in their year because of their shared interest in coloured trousers. 'The occupation', however, looked more like the 'Societies Fair' than the Sorbonne. There were just a few fewer Christian Union and Tiddly-wink clubs and more Anarchists and Workers' Revolutionary stalls.

We all had enough A levels to recognize a futile cause. There were murmurings about college restrictions. This was the seventies. We were expected to be back inside our rooms by ten-thirty. The college gates were locked and visitors had to leave. But even by this second term we knew how to climb in over the walls, so we weren't intending to lie down in front of any police cars for that.

Otherwise, 'World Revolution', an end to poverty, the recognition of trade unions in South America and free food for everybody were the vague themes of the protest; delivered in that hectoring way that helped to create pragmatic

Conservatives or bossy Labour cabinet ministers, depending on which side of the microphone you sat.

By the evening of the first day, Friday, when I got there (it was a perfectly civilized occupation and coincided with the weekend), the sit-in had given way to country music and short films borrowed from college film clubs: now being shown back to back, or front to front if you included the flickering 'Keystone Cops' pornography.

'Sexist!' someone shouted from the darkened hall.

The film changed to some cartoons of early flight.

'Balloonist!' another voice added.

I arrived late, because I was now in my second play. Written by Heathcote Williams, *AC/DC* was set in an amusement arcade and required almost continuous off-hand cynical abuse from the character I played. I had been auditioned by a bloke with shoulder-length hair and granny glasses who habitually wore a fur coat, which even by 1973 was slightly retrograde. Nobody dressed as mushrooms or harangued the audience. But my character pissed on a television set at one point, trepanned a friend using a Black and Decker drill and aggressively demolished the fluffy opinions of the other characters, who were all hippies. It was an early punk drama, I suppose, and when we mounted the play in a tiny theatre in the back of Christ's College, a forbidding concrete oblong with the dimensions of a giant's shoe box, and the only theatre designed by Denys Lasdun apart from the National, we attracted an audience of ten.

I was happy enough. I wasn't doing any of this for anyone's gratification but my own. But the night of the occupation the audience dwindled to two. It was difficult to persuade some of the other performers to turn up. They were itching to get off and play at being revolutionaries in the Lady Mitchell Hall instead. Scratching his ginger beard, and blinking behind his granny specs, the director wrestled with his dilemma.

'Let's take the play there!' he announced.

Was a two-hour, self-indulgent gnomic diatribe on the counter-culture quite what the revolutionary student body wanted to interrupt their festival that evening? Of course it was.

Back once more, I wandered across the Sidgwick site again last year, during an alumni weekend I had been asked to address. 'Come with me,' I said to Jo. We had arrived with half an hour to spare. 'Come and see the building I opened,' and we walked back under the raised History faculty building and along past the Stirling library. It was out of term, and a Saturday. The buildings were all shut. I took her up to the plate-glass door, and we peered inside. 'Look, there's something on the wall.' The wall was at right angles to the door and across the entrance vestibule but we could just about make out the inscription. It said, 'This building was opened by her Majesty the Queen.'

'Oh yes.' I remembered. The vice-chancellor, Alison Richard, had written, sweetly, and only a tiny bit circumspectly, that since Her Majesty was to be in Cambridge it had been decided that she might as well visit the new English faculty while passing through. Alas, there was no diminutive plaque saying, 'after a trial opening by Griff Rhys Jones'.

They let us in to the alumni weekend event at the Lady Mitchell Hall through an emergency exit round the back. Simon Singh and David Starkey were already waiting in an ante-chamber thronged with families and speakers; a dressing room for lecturers, I supposed. David Frost was tidying his shirt front and peering at his clipboard. He went on stage ahead of us and we heard him being introduced on a distant platform by Alison. We moved up to a space below the stage,

Singh, Starkey and myself, half listening to Sir David's practised jokes on the tannoy.

I had no recollection of the cream-painted concrete
seventies interior. It was an interim space, neither a room
nor a passage, half a platform, half a set of steps, a non-
functional waiting room with no view of the outside world
at all. It was the sort of place I had found myself in all my
adult life, behind studio spaces or just off church halls, round
the back of theatres or down beside huge speakers in the
Queen Elizabeth Hall, cheerless limbos, where I waited to
be ushered up, like a politician to the hustings, but with no
constituency, or party, or platform to represent. The excitement of being out in front of lots of people was momentarily
held in check. The slight tension expressed itself in listless-
ness. Like dogs waiting for a walk, we were all ready for
hyperactivity but holding it back. 'You never feel as tired and
ready for nothing as just before that big speech or performance,' someone once told me.

I must have felt that here, in 1973, in this place, when I
went on stage at the demo. I can only recall that it was very
dark, so perhaps that was why the layout of the rooms beneath
the lecture hall sparked no memories of any kind. But perhaps
I was self-absorbed. I can remember the swagger out into
the hot light and the ease with which I enjoyed it then. I
liked the dark spaces of an offstage corner from the very
beginning, but in Cambridge, doing boffo comedy, the tran-
sition to the stage became a defining excitement.

AC/DC made a thrillingly successful transfer. I couldn't
pee on the television for the excitement. I stalked the stage,
waggled my curly locks and played up to the self-satisfied
mood that overcomes students en masse, particularly ones
occupied with the organization of anarchy. After a shaky
start, we elicited indulgent laughs from our audience of six

hundred undergraduates by shouting louder and swearing more. Here I was, the toast of alternative Cambridge, cheered to the concrete rafters, slapped on the back and offered drugs in a match-box by a passing stranger. In my naivety, I rattled it and threw it away. The director dived after it into the crowd, never to be seen again (by me, anyway).

The occupation of the Sidgwick site in 1972 changed nothing in Cambridge except me. 'The happening' had been witnessed by the vice-president of the Cambridge Footlights, Robert Benton.

Short, dapper and with a habitual slightly surprised manner, Robert, like Douglas, was part of the 'old school tights' network. My former prefect asked me to audition for the May Week revue. Footlights had been mounting revues since the late nineteenth century and during the 1960s had gone through a short period of brilliance, largely thanks to Peter Cook. It was considered utterly defunct by the cognoscenti, but it was always considered defunct by the cognoscenti. It is still considered defunct by the cognoscenti. It was certainly more fashionable to consider it defunct than to be in it. But everybody had heard of it. Even me.

'I'm in the May Week revue,' I explained to Gerard Evans, at the end of the summer term. He raised another eyebrow.

I think I wanted him to be impressed. It was rare for a first-year undergraduate to make it into the end-of-year revue, which played for two weeks at the proper professional Arts Theatre after the exams had finished. I had auditioned and been accepted, rather to the chagrin of some, like young Clive Anderson, who had worked their way through the termly 'smokers' but been put to one side for later.

'It can vary a bit from year to year,' he said, trying to

appear interested, and rather presciently encapsulating the opinion of reviewers wherever we went.

'Well, it does seem a bit more Dick Emery than Monty Python,' I offered.

'Oh dear,' he murmured sympathetically.

It had shades of Jack Hulbert too. Stephen Wyatt, the director, was keen to put on a bit of a show, so we danced. I didn't know what to make of this. It was meant to be ironic. We would dance, but not seriously. The audience would work out the spoof element for themselves. I saw no evidence that they ever did, although they may have worked out that we couldn't dance, but it was the most traditional and in consequence the most successful of any undergraduate revue I appeared in. (They became my regular summer employment for the next four years.) We began dressed as cigarette packets, twirling around the stage, and sang a reggae song – 'Every Packet Carries a Government Health Warning' – and then continued with sketch, blackout, sketch, blackout, a few more songs and a bit more dancing for two more hours. I have been in some sort of sketch show pretty much every year since.

The funniest person in it was a tall and intensely serious man called John Lloyd. (John went on to produce *Not the Nine O'Clock News*, *Spitting Image*, *Blackadder* and latterly *Q.I.*) 'I remember I was invited to an upstairs room in Trinity Lane for an early meeting with the rest of the cast and sat on a bed while they discussed what they might do. 'Lloydie' started improvising about badgers. A new boy to this sort of thing, I laughed, choked violently and snorted coffee through my nose over a purple Indian bed-throw. The others studied the carpet.

The Arts Theatre was sold out for two weeks. Everybody admired the 'Oedipus rewritten by Oscar Wilde sketch' – 'to lose one mother may be considered a misfortune . . .' I rather preferred the slow-motion slapstick where two elderly toffs at either end of an extremely long table took turns to order their doddery old butler, played by Lloyd, to plaster each other with food. A lanky north Londoner, Jon Canter, sang a song comprised of French clichés. Today he's a successful comedy writer. Robert Benton performed a typical private-eye sketch. 'The name's Parker: Parker Fifty-one. It's not my real name, it's a nom de plume.' Mary Allen sang a mawk-ish torch song. And the two musicians, Nick Rowley and Nigel Hess, demonstrated a staggering professional skill with a pastiche of Bach played at tremendous speed on joint pianos. We finished with a sort of pantomime set in the jungle with Jeremy Browne and Pam Scobie playing a pigmy king and queen. Now where are Jeremy and Pam? I don't know, but have kept a sort of unbroken continuity with the rest.

The revues toured throughout the summer vacation. We went to Oxford, Southampton and the Robin Hood Theatre near Averham in Nottinghamshire before arriving at the Roundhouse in London for a savage mauling from *Time Out*. The rest of the vacation was spent preparing for and appear-ing at the Edinburgh Festival. I hardly went back to Epping at all. I don't think I made any serious effort to go home again during the next four years. And I began to realign my connections.

Of the seven from my school who went up to Emmanuel that year, Andrew had been the closest. We spent a lot of time together. I can visualize him. He had a lick of greasy mouse-coloured hair, a grown-out style – a residue of a former parting, hanging down over one side of his forehead and his long face. He seemed to have no background. His parents were off in Ilford somewhere. We had no cause to visit them. Instead Andrew was there, clever and beady-eyed, perpetually thin and hunched. He adopted a Peter Cook voice, a distancing effect, a comic persona to hide his own detachment, a snort of derision, a sniff of disdain at the world. ('He's probably something in the City. That's what her daddy is. Something. Nothing particular, just some *thing* in the City.') And he slipped further into his adopted persona, wearing suits where the rest of us wore jeans, with a tight, double-breasted waistcoat, and self-conscious desire to be a journalistic bar-fly. He did Medieval History too, and English and possibly French at A level, and I grew close to him in the sixth form because, like me, he rejected the wave of muscular Christianity that suddenly seemed to engulf our friends. We sat together in our narrow classroom, the medieval set, lobbing cynical arguments at the earnest junior chaplain, not even agnostic but arrogantly certain. 'Your superstitions seem to lead you to suppose . . .' we might begin. 'Why does your God, as you call him, require me to worship him? That's very arrogant of him, isn't it?' As if we were some Chinese mandarins quizzing a Jesuit. Pretending we had never heard of God, the Church or Christian values. 'And if I don't then I am doomed for all eternity, for *questioning* this woolly authority figure.'

At one point the junior chaplain's mask of synthetic indulgence fell away. 'You are not going to worship God because you're too busy worshipping yourself,' he spat and we smiled. We had angered him, and now he was lashing out ad hominem. Yes, yes, we notched that up, or drew a little tick in the ceaseless map of doodles that we scribbled as we talked or listened.

I dropped Andrew, didn't I? To begin with, in the alien environment of university, I needed to hold his hand. We went to the lunchtime greeting parties together and sat around in each other's rooms nursing the colossal waking hangover that five glasses of sherry delivers by three in the afternoon. We went down to attend a debate at the Union and watched the boys in waistcoats preen. He was reading English. I liked the people that he met and he settled in with them. I kept my distance from my own History set, but I found the English group congenial. I hung around with Andrew, hoping to hang around with them. It was easy to do. The rooms opened out on to a roof garden. On the other side was Charles Lambert's room. If the light was on late at night I walked across and usually I found them talking about Bryan Ferry or Robert Palmer or David Bowie.

Thirty-three years later, the current Master of Emmanuel told me he had just been up on that roof garden for the first time. I was taking tea before addressing the Emmanuel Society in 2005. Back yet again.

I always returned to my past through unexpected entrances, as if someone was protecting me from too much exposure, sliding into ponds of nostalgia slowly, a limb at a time. Did I recognize a single bit of the Master's Lodge?

I had only been there once before. We had been ushered in to meet our Master in little groups in the first week, to drink tea. I went with Andrew. We noticed the collection of Tang dynasty pottery horses in a glass case, implying some level of sophistication and money too, we supposed. But Sir Gordon Brims Black McIvor Sutherland had the dour distraction of a senior man. What did any of the senior politics of Cambridge have to do with our lives then? I had been brought up to be intimidated into excessive politeness by elderly figures of authority. In Cambridge I was permitted, perhaps even expected, to ignore them, so I did.

Now Lord Wilson presented me with cake and Earl Grey tea. We talked about my son. He wasn't going to be at my lecture. George was working in the architecture studio. 'He looks quite an academic around the college,' said the Master. That seemed a good if slightly surprising thing for George to be. But my wife and I nodded wordlessly.

Lord Wilson mentioned my vice-presidency of Footlights. He was thinking of the reason I had come. He was going to mention it again in his introduction. He'd looked me up on the internet, not something I would ever be able to do myself.

'Yes,' I said, 'but I was president of the Mummers and the ADC too and directed for the Marlowe. The Footlights was really a rather small part of my Cambridge life.'

What was I doing? Setting the record straight, then? There's no point in being a golden boy, a great white hope, if when you come back they don't realize that. 'Nick Hytner and I divided up the world really . . .' I was warbling on now. 'He directed half the productions, and I directed the other half . . .' The Master was smiling encouragingly. He told me about his own appearances with Richard Eyre. How ridiculous was I trying to be here? I was anxious to establish my Cambridge undergraduate amateur theatrical credentials with the man who had once been Secretary to the Cabinet.

Some time early in my first term I walked into Andrew's room and killed our friendship. The exact circumstances of the quarrel have completely gone. I can sit here now and revive the tightness. But what on earth was it about? We hardly did anything more elaborate than walk to other colleges to look at their bars, or take a rowing boat on the river, or go to a late film at the Cambridge Arts Club. I can remember that I was convinced he had excluded me from his set. Perhaps he had. I was the one behaving like a girl in a *Jackie* comic though.

For a year Andrew and I continued to live next door to

each other, exactly where we had been put. We shared a communal kitchen and a fridge. At some point in the summer term, I sat again in Andrew's room, talking about some plan, probably a play that I was doing, and I reached across and moved some books on the heavy coffee table that was part of the furniture in every room in that block. It would have been the same coffee table that my son would have in that same room in his time there. As I got up, feeling myself now somehow remote from him, someone who had been such a close friend, I noticed that he reached out carefully and reordered the books. He lined them up exactly as they were supposed to be, one on top of the other, spines facing towards him, edges carefully touching, and waited until I left. Did I see Andrew much in the following two years? I don't think I did. I moved on, didn't I? I moved on from the friends across the roof garden too.

'Yes, I've just been up on the roof garden,' said the Master.

'Where is that?' His wife, Caro, asked.

'Up on top of South Court.'

'I had no idea.'

'No, the head gardener has barely touched it in the thirty years since the place was built. There are all these shrubs in beds. They are completely overgrown. He's going to cut them back for me.'

But I had been elevated to the Footlights. I had been chosen by open audition for the May Week revue. I had been on tour and visited the Edinburgh Festival. Now, at the beginning of my second year, I was expected to appear in a smoking concert in a lecture room in Trinity. I didn't need Andrew.

There were no backstage facilities. On one side there was a set of steps and a couple of drapes behind which the performers ineffectually tried to hide themselves. And shortly after the beginning of my second year, I hid behind them myself, waiting to go on for the first time. You took responsibility for your own material, and it seemed that the more old-fashioned that was, the better you were likely to survive. I was a second-year now, still a relative junior and a smoker-virgin compared to Clive Anderson.

Clive had come from a clone of my own school, further around the London compass – Stanmore in fact – along with someone called Michael Portillo. At least, I don't remember Portillo ever getting up in the Trinity lecture hall wearing a skirt and horned helmet, waggling his hands around and stepping back and forth distractedly making puns about Vikings, but that's how I first encountered Clive.

For my first appearance, I wrote a pirate monologue. The entertainments at a smoker were entirely derived from an already extinct tradition of concert parties. Comic songs were popular. I wrote some myself: 'The Fork Lift Truck Driving Song' and 'Cow Poke' ('I'm an old cow poke, and I surely do miss the range now. There were no ladies there but we didn't care. We were too busy poking the cow'). Sketches were performed wearing rudimentary costumes. There *were* women about, but it was quicker to wear a dress and guarantee a laugh even if the script didn't. Nobody performed 'stand-up'. Stand-up comedians had gone into a temporary cultural abeyance, in working men's clubs up north. We wanted to be Monty Python. So we put on a silly hat and pretended to be an improbable Frenchman or a Viking or a pirate.

I hobbled into the lights with one leg tied up behind the knee and a broom as a crutch stuffed up under my armpit. I had a stuffed parrot too. The parrot sat on a heap of white plaster. There were lines – 'He adjusted the albatross around his neck with his good hook' – but I wasn't delayed by them for very long. Half-way through I pretended to become increasingly distracted by the pain from my broom handle and carefully transferred to my other armpit. I then fell heavily sideways. That got a laugh too.

But Footlights was only one of my distractions. That autumn term I was also the newly appointed president of the Cambridge University experimental theatre group – 'The Mummers'.

By the beginning of 1973 I was already sitting at meetings with a furrowed brow, trying to decide what 'experimental' theatre was. I bought books on Antonin Artaud and the Theatre of Cruelty. I mugged up on Mayakovsky. I prepared myself to confront the inevitable challenge: 'was I Brechtian enough?'

It was the 1970s. We were all eager to be alienated by our theatrical experiences. Equally clearly, nobody understood what that meant.

The great actor Ekkehard Schall was asked to define 'alienation'. I was grateful that he was prepared to do so. He was reassuringly brisk. 'Alienation,' he explained, 'is a character on stage performing a double take.' This was more like it. I understood double takes. I could even do them myself: look, think, look again. Mug for a laugh.

So, it seemed that the experimental theatre was not so very far removed from the completely un-experimental theatre as advocated by the more conservative members of Footlights. I decided that cinema was the natural home of the natural and that theatre should be the home of the unnatural. Music, lights, dance were what we needed, properly alienated of course. 'Let's put on a bit of a show, then.'

Having wrapped the two opposite poles of Cambridge theatre into one convincing whole, and since I was now in charge, I would decide what was 'experimental' anyway. I went in search of 'epic' plays to direct which would allow for plenty of mime, posturing, effect and alienation, and lots of double takes, of course.

Naturally, I had no real idea of what a director did. I had been subject to Mr Baron's emotional tyranny in school plays. I had watched at least two others try to tell me what do at university but I had no idea what constituted 'stage craft'. I had hardly been stage-struck as a boy, though in the last few years I had discovered matinee tickets in 'the gods' and I had been, on my own, to see everything accessible in the West End – staring down from a great height on remote explosions of glittering brilliance like Adrian Mitchell's musical version of William Blake or Peter Nichols' biographical play *Forget-Me-Not-Lane* or Alistair Sim in *The Magistrate*. I lived my early theatrical excitements from up high. Perhaps this was another reason why I needed a lot of arm-waggling and plenty of bangs in every student production that I directed.

There was a photograph on the wall of the Amateur Dramatic Club theatre. It had been long enough behind the glass to have the slightly wavy corners of a dried-out print. The sleek and comforting visage of Peter Hall beamed out, and underneath he had written: 'To the ADC. Thank you for allowing me to learn from my mistakes.' It was timely.

Yes, as well as the Footlights, it was from this little theatre that the titans of British theatre had emerged. They had, in the last twenty years, revolutionized not only productions, but more particularly, from our point of view, the very status of the university-educated director. The notion of actors being bossed around by uppity, bearded teenage know-it-alls (instead of semi-retired actors) was relatively recent and still enjoying its peak. What had filtered through was not so much the methodology as the hierarchical implications. Were there any more glittering exemplars of creative and artistic power than Jonathan Miller, Trevor Nunn or Peter Hall? They bestrode the arts pages – colossi in cable-knit sweaters – without even having had to write anything, or anything difficult like that; just by 'interpreting', organizing people and reading 'the text' carefully. We could do that! There were Cambridge actors, of course: McKellen, Jacobi, Redgrave (Corin, not Vanessa or Michael). They had all burst out of this great period of fecundity too, nurtured by the frightening Dadie Rylands and the brainy John Barton. But you didn't need a degree to have acting talent. It was spawned all over the place. It was a bit of a liability to do too much thinking as an actor, and acting was a rather crowded field. There were plenty of acting heroes with no A levels. It was directors who cracked the whip.

Years later, David Tomlinson explained over lunch in Boodles that senior actors of the post-war period subscribed to Robert Morley's dictum. The director was someone who got your coat if you happened to have left it in your car. By the late sixties the director was the one who arrived in the car. God knows, it wasn't that we wanted to direct professionally. I had no coherent forward thinking at that stage. I had been propelled entirely by circumstances to a Disneyland in the fens. I had no sense of beginning, planning or auditioning for a career. But just as little boys had once wanted to be engine drivers, so little undergraduates like me rather fancied being stage-directors, and there was Peter Hall on the wall to tell us this was all right. Off I went to make as many mistakes as I could, so that I too might learn.

The ADC was a strange warren. Its white gable end was decorated with a black lion. Inside, a blank staircase led up to a corridor and beyond that to an unprepossessing entrance and a very dark and bare auditorium. It had none of the trappings of a theatre – no curly plaster detailing, no cherubs, no red walls or half-shaded boudoir lights around the balconies, because there weren't any balconies. The seating raked straight backwards. The walls were painted a grim battle-ship grey, and the stage had a stripped proscenium arch with two black entrances cut in the fabric like pillboxes on the Atlantic Wall. It wasn't that modern-looking, either. The ambience owed something to the 1930s and Edward Craig. It was an almost charmless place, tacked on to the back yard of the Union and sharing space with fire escapes and a bicycle shed, but from now on I was to spend a lot of my time there (certainly more than in college), hunched around one of the low tables in the bar which, even if no one was attending the play, filled up towards the end of the evening, as the pubs shut, with the camp, the loud-mouthed and the ambitious.

Eventually I was to end up president of the ADC, and vice-president of Footlights too. I became obsessed with running committees, organizing meetings and directing plays, allowing time for a little acting on the side. I returned to my college late at night, too late to see if Charles Lambert was still up, or any of my college friends were hanging about in the JCR. I was hurrying on.

For the time being, at the beginning of my second year I decided to put on *The Dream Play*, Ingmar Bergman's version of Strindberg's rambling answer to *Peer Gynt*. It was my duty to direct it. At the beginning of term, I held auditions in a room in Emmanuel above the old hall, and for the first time, in 1975, encountered the divine Charlotte Chesney.

It was a long room with a slightly twisted floor. Two girls came in together. I wonder if the distance contributed, because I can remember I had the leisure to assess their calf-length tweedy skirts, their striped red and blue tights and their startling manner. I would have been with Lawrence Temple, of course, who was going to teach me about lights and staging and all the other skills that I felt it unnecessary to learn before pushing myself forward to be in charge. He was a London day school boy. He must have known Charlotte and her friend Cassandra already. They were London day-school girls, in their first term, and despite being convulsed with laughter (bold enough in itself) they seemed to me to have at least two coats of sophistication that my suburban friends in college rather lacked.

Charlotte in particular had a strong, giggling voice which I found exciting for its unabashed poshness. Medium height, dark hair and a snorting upper-class manner – it was very sexy. They both wanted me to give them a part, which would mean that I would be required to boss them around a bit. Yes. Well, I was up for that.

There weren't all that many women around in Cambridge in 1973. All colleges were single-sex. Girton, New Hall and Newnham were admittedly a single female sex but they were deliberately situated a little out of town. Meeting women involved a series of chivalric challenges – social braggadocio, followed by acts of physical bravura. There were college bars (Caius springs to mind) dominated by men from single-sex schools huddling in knots, clutching comfort pints and swaying slightly as they cast agitated glances at the three per cent of females lured into the place, but it was a bold move to cross the borderline under these circumstances. Nonetheless I managed the romantic challenge of chatting up a trainee nurse. That was the braggadocio. She invited me back to the nursing home for the physical bravura. She took me round the back of the building and showed me the twelve-foot wall and then disappeared to use the front entrance. I scrabbled up, sprained an ankle, limped across a darkened lawn and waited in the shadows of a fire door, before finally getting to share her narrow bed.

It was the sleeplessness of these arrangements that bothered me. There had been a couple of perfectly nice, wispy girls, studying at the technical college, who had made the mistake of acting on an invitation from a friend to visit him in his rooms. Six or seven wild-eyed youths mobbed them in a tiny bed-sit, laughing rather too loudly, smoking Number Sixes and passing a guitar around to pluck the opening chords of songs they didn't know how to finish. Gradually, by a process of elimination, they dropped out to go to their own beds. The engineers would have gone first with their early start, the English undergraduates last, and after a raid at about four in the morning to steal biscuits from a food cupboard on the other side of the college, a relationship formed on the basis of utter exhaustion.

With Jani, the exhaustion never stopped. She was such a tall girl. If I clambered into her bed on the floor of the room she shared on the other side of Castle Hill, then we had a sleepless night trying not to wake her room mate. If she came back to Emmanuel it was usually a late decision, because, with some justification, she remained uncertain of the extent of my commitment until we had both drunk rather too much to cope. She had to climb over the gate into the back of the college in a long printed cotton skirt and fell on top of me. In the morning she went to classes. I had to stay in bed until noon.

I wrote to my mother in the summer of my first year. I told her that I no longer had a girlfriend. 'She said she had always been out with nice people before,' I explained, sheepishly.

I was surprised to find that letter. It was one of about six from my first two years, folded away along with school reports from Conifers, hand-made birthday cards and my three swim-ming certificates from Epping Junior, and collected together in a Basildon Bond writing-paper box. I must have been replying to one from her. Every single one of my letters begins, 'I'm sorry I haven't written for so long.' I was frightened to look at them. What self-perpetuated myths was I going to destroy?

There was nothing to fear, except perhaps their innocence. As I scanned their bald, one-page accounts, only one directly addressed to my father, I recognized the tone, because it was the same dose of filial reassurance that my son dishes out to me today by mobile phone. I was working at my studies. I was proud to tell them that my supervisor had called my essay 'a monumental and sane piece of work'. (On what, I wonder? I can barely recall the individual papers on the History syllabus.) I was even arranging to get a travel grant to work in a library in the vacation. What touched me, because my memory has suppressed them, are the little nuances of, if not homesickness, then at least home-aware-ness: my concern for my sister's exams and my interest in the pets: 'Have you got a wig for the cat?' I inquired. Epping was not as far away as I imagined.

16. Mr Big

At the beginning of my son's second year I had to hump the bass amplifier back to Cambridge, knowing perfectly well that he never played the damn thing, suspecting that our ferrying was wholly unnecessary and trying to persuade him to plan ahead a bit more.

'There isn't room for him to leave it,' Jo explained. 'His room has to be used by a summer-school student.'

Did it? Is that what happened when I was there? All that sort of stuff, the arrivals, departures, even any memories of contact with home had withered. 'No, no. He must be able to store it. There's a room somewhere where you put it, surely.'

'It's not like it was when you were there.'

'There are Chinese students now. You don't think they take all their stuff back and forth to Shanghai every term.'

'Yeah, yeah. The storage room's full. It's too late now.'

It was the principle. 'You have made this up. As if I don't know what I'm talking about. Your mother and I have now had to have an argument. I know what goes on.'

But I was grudgingly there to help. I was prepared for atonement, except that I needed to retain my own ground. He became itchy when we got there and stood to one side with his hands in the front pockets of his jeans, the thumbs on his belt, looking tense.

'Lunch?'

'I've got people to see.'

'I'm not coming all this way . . .'

We ate in the Loch Fyne franchise. He telephoned Rupert, and Rupert said he'd come and meet us there. We talked about his term in the stop-start way of fathers and sons. He was serving in the college bar.

'That's the limit of your extra-curricular activity?'

'There's too much work for anything else. I'm on the college catering committee, but last term I had a meeting on the Sunday night, and my supervisor told me that I had to make a choice between architecture and college politics.'

'After one meeting?'

'That's what I thought.'

I poked my halibut. His life was at the college and in the Architecture department. They worked until nine at night. When they weren't in their studio they were hoarding time to prepare for their studio. It was better to change the subject. I recognized that I was veering into a middle-aged paternal foolhardiness. I could feel it welling. It needed self-control.

The books about this are always written by the sons: little Edmund Gosse, junior Samuel Butler, delinquent John Betjeman, adolescent Nick Hornby. The poor, stupid, emotional, domineering, wet, weak-minded patriarch is dissected from the pitying child's angle. Did any one of those arrogant young bastards have any conception of the base and violent feelings that fathers have?

We walked away back to the college after lunch. Rupert and George became animated. We turned right at Fitzbillies' cake shop and along past the Museum of Anthropology, which I had always proposed to visit some day. They drifted on ahead, talking and giggling animatedly. They were making plans. George, in fact, was perfectly happy, perfectly integrated, perfectly independent, perfectly satisfied. I dragged along, ten steps behind. Then I left them at the college gate and went around the back to collect the car.

Sometimes I wonder if they feel that I betrayed them, my own old, original college friends. The people I seldom meet again with whom I wandered around Woolworth's and Burgess's, had coffee in the Copper Kettle and went to the Arts Cinema late at night to watch Fellini's *Satyricon* – all those vital, critical pleasures of quality, nothing time. But if we got back together now, how would we revive that? 'Let's go for a walk down to Woolworth's like the old days.' 'Let's play three chords on a guitar for hours.' 'Let's actually do absolutely fuck all for an afternoon except walk down by the river and make remarks about the tourists.' Today, if I want to catch up at all, I have to make an appointment. It would be so much simpler if we all still lived in one square mile.

Charlotte was playing 'the daughter' in *The Dream Play*. We rehearsed it all that term. Jane Rogers, now a novelist, was quietly impressive as the mother figure. My directorial contributions were to arrange people prettily, design a surreal album-cover poster, order colour gradations in the costumes and leer coyly at Charlotte. We had our dress rehearsals in the concrete theatre in Christ's. It seemed to go together briskly. I suddenly thought of something I had overlooked. 'How long is it then?' I asked Lawrence Temple, my helper. 'Where should we put the interval?'

We looked at our watches. It had lasted about forty minutes in total. The whole play was shorter than an average first half. We went straight ahead without an interval. It should have been a key part of my expensive, state-subsidized education. Nobody has ever complained about a play being too short.

Charlotte, who remains a friend, came to stay over this last New Year and told me what happened next. (I would say 'reminded me', but it was all new.) 'Finally, in the pub

the night before the last night of the production, a group of
people were discussing what to give you as a present.'

'As a present?'

'Well, you had been the director. And Rose Bechler said,
"Well, I know what he'd like as a present, but that's sort of
up to Charlotte."' (This sounded unexpectedly erotic.)

'But what did you say?'

'Well, I was . . .' Charlotte pulled her lips down and
shrugged her shoulders. 'I didn't think anybody else would
have spotted it.'

So, engineered by Rose, Jane Rogers, Johnny Brock and
Andy Finkel (who is now Turkish correspondent for the
Times), Charlotte and I were set up to 'get off together'. And
later that night she took me back to Newnham.

I remember that the procedure resembled a slightly ritu-
alized James Bond feint. The porters just weren't there at the
desk very often. Charlotte went on ahead, checked the way
was clear, and I sneaked in, in plain sight. We turned right
and scuttled down the corridor in an exaggerated hush.

I liked Charlotte's room. It had a high, institutional ceiling and a settled, rather ordered atmosphere, with a velvet
cover over the bed, a kettle in the hearth and teapot on a
trivet. There was some sort of undergrowth in a pot too –
a plant, in fact. There was plenty of junk in my room, but
nothing that needed tending. Just being in her quarters
constituted a little invasion, staying seemed like a conquest
of alien territory. It was feminine. It was a carefully arranged
and detailed room with patterned fabrics. She kept things in
little hand-chosen antique boxes brought from home. I say
that it was feminine – it clearly was – but only feminine in
a Virginia Woolf, masculine sort of a way. There weren't any
teddy bears or rag dolls in Charlotte's room. Charlotte had
strong ideas about taste and ornament, which were new to

me – not the Laura Ashley, that was common enough, but the aesthetic touches; the patterned stuff, the wooden stuff, the textile stuff. I was only gradually to discover that these were not chosen at random. Her taste was important to her. Rather vitally important to her, I was to find out.

'But then you went to America on tour with *Romeo and Juliet*. And you instantly started messing around.'

'We *had* only had one night together.'

'Yes, but you wrote me a letter.'

'Did I? I'm impressed.' (All these letters are making me feel like some sort of Victorian lady novelist.)

'So was I. You confessed. Juliet had a thing about you.'

I was happy to let Charlotte believe that. What sort of cowardice was this, thirty years after the event? I could have said, 'No, no, I strung her along. I toyed with her affections. I encouraged her, went to bed with her all through the tour and then refused to talk to her on the bus.' But I didn't. I was still ashamed. Mortification can flare up long after the details are ashes. I wanted a settled, long-term, intimate relationship and I wanted to shag anything I fancied too.

And I wanted to go to America. So, Footlights, the Mummers, a new girlfriend – that should have been enough, but I joined the Oxford and Cambridge Shakespeare Company too. 'Educational elite, fine speaking, travel abroad, hands across the sea, special relationship.' Like Richard Hillary, popping over to Heidelberg to row against the Germans just before the Second World War, the combined amateur theatrical talents of Oxford and Cambridge would vault the Atlantic every year to recite the bard in Boston.

Rehearsals for *Romeo and Juliet* took place upstairs in a big pub off the Euston Road, just like for proper actors. This was during the summer of my first long vacation. (The same summer I toured with the Footlights, went to Edinburgh and played the Roundhouse. We took a break to do some minor academic work in Cambridge and appear in a few other plays before heading for the States in the Christmas vacation – 'No, no, I won't be with you for Christmas either, Mummy, I'm afraid.')

I had been cast as Prince Escalus and 'old Capulet'. Not 'Capulet' himself. He was the one with a lot of furious speeches about his daughter marrying a Montague. '*Old* Capulet' crosses the stage during the party scene (the one Romeo crashes) and has a single line. But I was also the Prince, a significant influence on Veronese affairs in the tragedy of *Romeo and Juliet*.

We were under the languidly watchful eye of a real professional director, Eric Thompson, famous as the father of Emma Thompson, except that Emma Thompson was yet to come to Cambridge and become a film star, so, as far as we were concerned, famous as the father of *The Magic Roundabout*.

On the first day, after buying up a couple of large Victorian hat-stands he had spotted in the corner of the pub, Eric stood in front of the entire cast and stroked his luxurious Mexican moustache. 'I have decided,' he said, emphatically, 'that our main purpose in this production must be to tell the story.'

We sat with half smiles and the fixed attention of sheepdogs. Privately and separately, we thought, 'Doesn't everybody know the story of Romeo and Juliet?' Eric wanted to focus all his attention on the lovers and their passion, and a lot less on fair Verona where we laid our scene, and of whereof I was the noble Prince.

Essentially my very important part was to run on stage and command the unruly young persons to stop fighting. Two days after rehearsing my first scene I sat with my half-smile and my tongue lolling out, ready for my next rehearsal while Eric fingered his Zapata again. 'I think we'll cut this scene,' he announced after a pause. I gagged, half raised a hand and then went home.

At the end of the first week's rehearsal we had reached the end of the play and were to rehearse the tumultuous final scene and my last great speech summing up the whole sorry mess with appropriate authoritative pomp. Again Eric twirled his moustache. Again he looked off into the half-distance. 'I think we'll cut the final scene and end the play here,' he said. At the point where you might expect the Prince to come rushing on stage and do a big speech on the 'woe and Rom-ee-o', there would instead be a sudden and conclusive blackout.

So at the very beginning of the Oxford and Cambridge Shakespeare Company's production I descended a set of elegant steps, 'like an animated mustard pot', in a comically large yellow hat. Having delivered my speech, I rushed back off stage, tore off my Velcroed codpiece and my bright yellow tights, held up by improvised elastic braces, feverishly covered my face with purple lines, smothered my head with a manky wig, and rushed back to the wings from where, panting heavily, I re-entered, gurning and gibbering as an unexpectedly sweaty old man. As I reached the other side it was all over. I spent the rest of the play and the majority of my trip around America slumped in a dressing room waiting to take part in the 'noises off' and the curtain call. 'Crescendo and . . . blackout.' Cue furious applause.

Well, cue muted applause. They quite liked the production in places like Clarion, Pennsylvania, where the set, big enough to fill the Oxford Playhouse, became a doll's house on the prairie of a university hall stage, but Philadelphia was a tougher call. They were used to giving pre-Broadway shows a shake-down. ('I'd rather be in Philadelphia' is written on

W. C. Fields' gravestone.) The critics there, in Cambridge and in Oxford or virtually anywhere they had seen Shakespeare staged before, didn't much care for our simplistic, story-telling approach. Heck, I was only on in the first five minutes anyway. Besides, we were off on a complete tour of the eastern seaboard of the United States of America in an old bus, driven by a wise-cracking black driver, through snowstorms, along 'turnpikes' and 'freeways', past fire hydrants, Howard Johnsons, mall strips, truck stops and all the romantic paraphernalia of a fantasy United States spun from a childhood spent watching old black-and-white films on a Sunday-afternoon sofa.

We went to New York. Later that week, we also managed by some absurdity of scheduling to call in at Raleigh, North Carolina, where it still appeared to be late summer. Christmas was spent homeless in Washington. But usually we stayed in university dormitories, or 'student rooms' in expensive New York hotels, or were put up as 'house-guests' by well-meaning friends of the theatre, miles out in the suburbs. Lazing in bed in the morning, we could hear the muffled shouts of husbands and wives arguing somewhere in their breakfast rooms, perfectly aware that they were probably arguing about us. I barely remembered to call home and wish Epping a happy Christmas.

Our 'allowance' was three dollars a day – one dollar per meal. But there was no dollar if food was 'provided'. After our flabby first night in Philadelphia, a reception was organized by the Friends of the Shubert Theater. We were herded into our bus and driven across the city to an elegant eighteenth-century mansion in an elegant eighteenth-century street. Beyond the veil of snowflakes, we could see an open door and a sumptuous interior. At the top of the steps several distinguished orthopaedic surgeons and tax lawyers were waiting in dinner jackets. Wiffin, our manager, stood up at the front of the bus.

'There is food provided here,' he announced, 'so this will be counted as your evening meal.'

'No dollar?' someone wailed.

'No dollar.'

Twenty-seven student ambassadors charged through the slush, ignored the outstretched hands of philanthropic dignitaries, scampered across the parquet and fell ravenously upon three or four plates of dinky canapés, consuming everything, including the parsley.

We were Oxford and Cambridge together, but rather more Oxford than Cambridge, as I recall. Nurses, friars and apothecaries seemed to come from Cambridge; Lords, noble Romeos and fair Capulets from Oxford. Originally, the part of Mercutio was going to be played by a bloke from Oxford called Mel Smith.

I had been introduced to the male Zuleika Dobson of OUDS at the Edinburgh Festival the previous August – not, that is, to the man himself, but to his reputation.

In 1973 there was some sort of joint charity event involving both universities. The two groups put up a couple of their sketches. 'The thing about you Footlights people,' Richard Sparks told Jon Canter, 'is that you ignore any pretension and just concentrate on the jokes.'

'Yes,' Jon replied. 'Unlike you Oxford people. You're all pretension and no jokes.'

But I was probably listening to Steven Pimlott, now a distinguished stage director, reciting M. R. James stories in a darkened room off Leith Parade. Only certain senior undergraduates had been invited from Leith Transport Hall, otherwise I might have encountered Mr Smith then. As it was, the day afterwards I was sitting in a gloomy pub on the south side of the hill that runs down from the Royal Mile to the Grassmarket, when Jon Canter nudged me.

'That's him, that's that Mel Smith bloke from last night.' Jon pointed at a pasty sort of bloke with a protruding jaw, hunched over an unnecessarily large selection of drinks. I was unimpressed. I had not gone to university to be impressed by anything, least of all by someone from Oxford. And when all was said and done, he looked rather like me.

When Mr Smith's tutors heard that he had been offered the opportunity to eat hamburgers in fake wood breakfast bars on the other side of the Atlantic, they counselled him not to go. I believe they told him that if he did go, he need not bother to return. They were anxious, after his under-graduate career igniting explosives on the Playhouse stage, that he should make an attempt to master a little of his chosen subject, Psychology. He stayed and was chucked out anyway. I was not to concern myself unduly with old potato face for another five years.

Smith's part was taken by the dashing Geoffrey McGivern. Nobody would have considered Geoffrey especially dashing except possibly Geoffrey. But at this stage of his life he did, and it was an advantage. Geoffrey played all the big roles at Cambridge. He was, and still is, an excellent, flamboyant actor, constantly in demand as 'the other bloke' in sketch shows.

Like Charlotte, he had come to stay with me for Christmas 2004. It was the same time of year as the trip, and we were driving around the outskirts of Colchester, the same sort of place. With its Essex straightforwardness, its hoardings and semi-industrial hinterland, it reminded me of the States.

'There was the very cool dude who drove the bus through the snow, and one of the girls wanted to be sick and asked him to stop, and he said, "Can't do that, honey, you go right

ahead and do it on the step there," so she did. And did you
go to that small woman with the big breasts' house?'

'I might have done,' I said.

'She had the embroidered gold piano.'

I asked him whether he remembered the trip to the hunting lodge in northern Pennsylvania.

'Oh my God! Yes.'

What a thing, to open these memory banks. Geoffrey was
smiling and rocking forward with delight. 'Weren't there girls
there?'

Oh, I see. He was hoping for *nostalgie d'érotomanie*. 'No.'

'But we must have gone all the way there, miles to get
there, and then got back by first light to catch the bus . . .'

I temporarily lost Geoffrey to the miserable business which
afflicted whoever I reminisced with, of trying to put the
events into a logical order.

During the tour, Geoffrey's involvement, like mine, finished
early on in the drama, though I think it is fair to say that
his performance had more impact. We shared a dressing room
with an ex-Territorial Army historian with bad teeth and a
manic laugh called Richard McKenna, who had been cast
as 'the apothecary'. Richard had over an hour to perfect his
make-up before going on stage and liked to find ways of
'improving' his part. As he waited, his false nose grew ever
huger. He spent his daytimes searching out stuffed birds and
voodoo dolls to hang on his costume. He started tottering
on stage on miniature stilts. Geoffrey and the others helped
him. One night, when Romeo hammered on a flat and
shouted, 'Apothecary, apothecary!', six separate ghostly wise
old men, clad in flowing robes, appeared from every dark
corner of the stage, clutching lanterns, and chorused together,
'Who calls so loud?'

It was Christmas 1973. The Philadelphia Sound was just

becoming fashionable, and we were in Philadelphia. Geoffrey and I were head-hunted in a disco by two charming women in their mid-twenties. They had greatly admired Geoffrey's swagger and declamatory voice in the play, and I just happened to be with him. 'Ooooh, ooh, oooh! Oooooh! Take me in your arms and rock me, baby.' Eventually we went back to their place. My friend escorted me to her bed on the third floor of the dinky little terraced house, leaving Geoffrey and Dee to take the room below.

We were woken at six in the morning. A man's voice was shouting in the street outside. 'I know you are in there with someone! You whore! You're in there with some guy. How could you do this to me, you bitch? I'm going to kill you both.'

If you had swung the front of the terrace open (like my sister's doll's house) you could have watched two men, one above the other, leaping out of bed.

'Oh my God. It's Frank!' said my girl.

Frank. Her Frank? Or Dee's Frank? It was a significant distinction. I was wrestling with my fashionably skimpy hipster flares, which had pulled themselves inside out in excitement a few hours before. There was a furious hammering on the door. ('Who calls so loud?') One American fantasy was merging into another.

'I'll kill you, I swear it!' The voice had become slightly hysterical.

'It's Dee's old boyfriend. He gets mad. She'll send him away.'

Whew. That Frank. So Geoffrey could climb up on the roof and run across the chimney pots then.

Dee was now calmly telling Frank to go away, or she would have to call the police again, and he would remember what happened last time. My friend turned softly to me.

'Come back to bed,' she whispered. But I was fully dressed and somehow I was thinking about the school bus and my British friends.

I became close to Geoffrey but ended the tour resentful of him. We had a few days left before we went back to England. It seemed a good time to go off and explore the States together. But Geoffrey went to New York to catch up with Dee instead. This was no good. He was my new soul mate, but Geoffrey dropped me for some intimate, grown-up, mature thing like a proper relationship with a girl. I felt betrayed. I was having too much fun to have to spend hours talking sensibly with one woman.

Besides, I had all the responsibilities of my own proper relationship waiting for me back in England. Was I quite ready for this? It had been prearranged. The spring term beckoned, and Charlotte and I began a fierce skirmish that was to last seven years, with intermittent periods of cease-fire.

From the very beginning, I loved her. I loved so much about her. I loved her straightforwardness, her handsome good looks. I loved her briskness and drive and enthusiasm. I loved her bonkers impetuosity. I loved being with her. I liked her settled existence in Newnham. She was a pusher of Earl Grey tea and a fierce advocate for the importance of civilized trappings – new to me, but I loved it. Her friends were not only called Cassandra, they were called Penelope, Hero and Oenone, as if their distempered corridor was some Greek grove, and I liked that. I loved the fact that, like me, she fussed very little about the notion of coupledom. I loved her determined domestication. I loved her courage. Where I would nervously approach the water hole of social inse-curity, Charlotte had the conviction of a cobra, the fastidious discrimination of a lynx and the loyalties of a water buffalo.

She was to be my education and my indivisible self for nearly a decade. And I disagreed with her about absolutely everything — degree, value, commitment and intent. Everything.

One night, after I had shared the neatly embroidered, bevelveted and cushioned tidiness of her existence for some time, we left a production at the ADC on our bicycles (Charlotte naturally had a splendid antique sit-up-and-beg version with a wicker basket in the front). We turned left up Bene't Street. It was one o'clock in the morning. A young policeman hailed us. He was quite calm. 'Were you aware you were cycling the wrong way down a one-way street in utter darkness without any lights at all?' he asked.

Cravenly, I was ready to apologize. But Charlotte felt a pressing need to say something.

'You're enjoying this, aren't you?' she started in an admirably forthright tone. 'Haven't you got anything better to do than *harass* us!' She grew a little more strident. 'We're not harming anyone, there's no danger, but no! You have to stop us!'

It was fantastic. A *mélange* of Margaret Rutherford and Vanessa Redgrave, it somehow gave the status of 'the pigs' a social nuance as well. He didn't take it well and grimly took our details. We were eventually handed a fine we could scarcely afford, though I seem to recall that Charlotte continued to rant on about abuse of police power as he scribbled. When we got back to her room, it was my turn. I became incandescent with rage and, as became increasingly common, we enjoyed a mouth-watering, life-enhancing five-hour row.

Charles Maude called Charlotte 'la Belle Dame Sans Merci'. It was elegant. Others knew her as 'Shut-Up Charlotte', because that was how I habitually addressed her. Whenever we were together (and we feared minor traffic fines because we increasingly spent time spending non-existent money on dog-meat moussaka in restaurants), friends would quietly remove the cruet and breakable plates.

'I remember the time Rory and you pushed me into a ditch after a May Ball and just left me there,' Charlotte recalled, thirty years later.

'I suspect it was more likely that you fell in the ditch in a drunken stupor and they just walked on,' said Jonathan, her husband.

But we had a fierce attachment too.

'Apart from having a thing about Michael I was faithful to you for seven years.'

'Yes . . . What thing about Michael?'

'You must remember.'

I didn't. I know who Michael is now. He is that tall, bald bloke with the strange taste in ties who runs a major institution. But I thought I had met him for the first time at a fund-raising dinner. He was always rather cool towards me, but I put this down to the natural disdain that the director of a world-famous institution who wore frock coats would entertain for a low comedian. I had no idea that it might be because my girlfriend had a thing about him when we were students.

'You were rather incredible about it. One evening Michael and I were in front of the fire in my room in Newnham, and it got dark. We were sitting there together in the gloom and you suddenly came in. And you switched on the light and said, "Hello you two," and just sat down at my desk and immediately started writing an essay.'

'Did I?' It only sounded incredible to me that I was writing an essay. I certainly didn't remember any suspicion of hanky panky. Jealousy is a strangely permanent stain. (This was thirty years ago. We're both married to other people now, with grown-up kids. So is Michael.) But I take consolation from the fact that I nearly said hello to the sort of undergraduate who would go on to run important national institutions after university, even though I didn't know it then and appeared to ignore him altogether.

Charlotte was in the meantime perfecting a balancing act between the demands of her strongly held principles and a hectic social scene. She knew quite a lot of posh people. We were all invited to a party in the Lake District by someone who owned a lot of it. I was there as the entertainment, not to present *The Chinese Airman Reports Back to His Comrades*, but a Footlights cabaret.

I lodged with a mad vegetarian and ate nettle soup for supper. Charlotte was a guest in 'a stately'. She was driven back there afterwards by Hoorays who crashed their cars for fun. (Cambridge in those days was quite a broad social mix.) She walked up some hill with Michael, and he got terribly interested in things, or so I discovered thirty years later. This was all going on behind my bloody back, while I was performing, without my trousers on, for the benefit of some of Charlotte's poncey friends who never liked me anyway.

I met plenty of proper public schoolboys at Cambridge. I assumed that their louche assurance was a direct result of their education. How great to know how to behave. How comforting to have the assumptions of your caste so ingrained that you even know which are proper shoes and which are not, which are the right shirts to wear and which are not, how to talk to people at dinner parties and how to belittle them with confident disdain. Naturally, I despised them for it. I hated them for never having been beaten up in a play-ground in Harlow because of the way they talked, for treating 'going on a bus' as quite an adventure, for having no taste in music beyond the sickly sentimental pop they played each other in their studies. But I envied the easy assurance. I was a trimmer. I adjusted my sails to the prevailing wind.

'A born-again Marxist, he spouts dialectic while sitting at the helm of his father's yacht.' My biography in the Footlights programme was written by the son of a naval captain from a public school. But of course they were all only pretending too. They were just better at it. What I liked was the ability to enter all these worlds, the politics and the theatre, the Pitt Club full of Hoorays and the poetry society, and find there were always people playing at it. Everybody was pretending. It wasn't an elite, it was a cloister. The inanities of Oxbridge were a background against which anyone could shine as long as they had the brass neck.

I was celebrating at the end of a second year. I had been happy to kick on: a fake, intense Brechtian, a grotesque for the Footlights, a director of spectacles at the ADC and a party-going sophisticate with a girlfriend too. Nothing seemed to be falling off as yet.

The only thing I was losing confidence with was History itself. After two years of galloping, I was about to face a Beecher's Brook: Part One exams. Apart from the papers on Political Thought the whole subject had become a little too mature and objective for me. Besides, if I was going to read under pressure, I might at least read well-written literature, instead of mock-scientific turgid journals (although whether literature would be as susceptible to speed-scanning as articles on the three-field system in thirteenth-century Leicestershire was questionable). I had an interview with the director of studies in English, wrote a trial essay on E. M. Forster and now prepared to jump horses, but only if I did well enough in the forthcoming exams.

Ah, yes, those exams. I somehow had to fit 'Part Ones' into what was already a rather busy term. Geoffrey McGivern and I were both in *Chox*, the May Week revue at the end of the year. It was Geoffrey's first. 'All that silly decadent stuff,' as he described it.

It was 'silly', because of *Cabaret* and Bryan Ferry. Being camp in public had become fashionable. But we weren't camp. We were just spotty undergraduates. The opening 'ironic' dance routine was even less ironic than usual. 'What do we all have in common? What do we all do together? If it's just a bar on your birthday, or a ten-pound box bound in leather . . . we eat Chox! Ba – tuppity, tup tup – baaa . . .'

We rehearsed during the Easter vacation, got everything ready, and then took a break to sit some exacting papers.

My second summer vacation was fully occupied with the Footlights. In Averham, where the tour stalled for a week, we decided to re-enact the alcoholic excitements of *Days of Wine and Roses*. We stayed in dormitories above the theatre, in a sort of farmyard by a church, under huge electric pylons, just a few fields away from a massive ditch at the bottom of which the River Trent slopped along. We had no transport and no pub.

Donald Wolfit had begun his career at Averham. His bust leered out from a corner of the stage. But it was understandable that he left. The theatre was merely a hut with a tin roof. When it rained, it rattled so loudly the audience couldn't hear anything the actors said. This might have been a good idea. They had been shipped in by tractor. The authorities shut up the drinking facilities ten minutes after curtain down, and it was a long night in the middle of nowhere. 'Binge drinking' is an inadequate description.

Struggling to place orders for six or seven pints, we had to jostle with our audience at the foyer bar.

'You were a very quiet audience.'

'We didn't like to laugh in case we missed the next joke.'

The first night we said farewell to the charming old ladies

who ran the place, sat staring at the walls for a few minutes and then forced the padlock on the bar. We drank ourselves insensible. They were a little upset the following morning. 'I know you're prepared to pay but you must promise you won't do that again.' So we promised and the second night we didn't even wait until their car had hit the main road before we took a crowbar to the hatches.

The audience were being polite. They weren't laughing because the show was getting worse. The 'actors' in the revue (less inclined to drink) were beginning to gang up against the 'writer-performers' – Clive Anderson, Jon Canter, Martin Smith and myself (more inclined to drink). We wanted to sort them out. We wanted them to do the scripts properly: the funny way, as we saw it and as we had written it. To our annoyance, Geoffrey, who sometimes pretended to be a lad with us and sometimes to be a camp nonce with them, sided with them.

Thirty years later he was outraged at the suggestion. 'I did not. I was the voice of calm reason!'

'You joined the side of the actors.'

'I wasn't *with* anybody!'

'Traitor! You just pretended to be all grown-up and adult and sided with those bastards.'

'I remember you sitting underneath the sink with a saucepan in each hand banging them together because you couldn't get your way,' he said.

I also remembered crawling through puddles in the pouring rain at three in the morning howling with rage, but I can't remember what on earth for. I think we were on the point of calling the whole thing off, packing our bags or having a stand-up fight when a telegram arrived: 'congratulations stop michael white will present you in the west end stop telephone me stop'.

Geoffrey snorted. 'I remember saying I thought we'd be mad to go. We'd be slaughtered.'

'We were.'

'I got some very good reviews.'

'What are you talking about, Geoffrey? The whole show was slated. Michael Billington's notice started "If this dismal little revue . . ."'

I had read all the critics on the top of a bus coming into the West End. Outside the theatre I stood watching a man from an advertising agency balancing on a stepladder. He was desperately trying to find some words of good cheer to stick up on his hoardings. Literally scratching his head, he saw me and scowled. 'I don't know what you've got to laugh about,' he said.

It was a strange way of spending a summer. We dug in for four weeks and were filmed by the BBC. After a few days, Michael White came to see us and took away the meagre subsistence we were paid, in order to save on overall costs. ('Well, you're students, so it won't matter to you.')

I stayed in London at Charlotte's home and took to exploring the life of her parents, who lived amongst piebald cats and potted plants in a cluttered flat in West Hampstead. They were exemplary student accessories. Anne, Charlotte's mother, related to the Thackerays, was kind and judicious, and one of the founders of Britain's social services. Kellow had written a whole book I had heard of called *The Victorian Underworld* and had been a Communist in the thirties, when such things had been the height of fashion. Now he was working on a history of sporting life, a project sadly never to be finished, but he would throw up his hooked nose with a fruity chuckle and disconcert visitors to his green-baize-covered dinner table by assuming that their knowledge of eighteenth-century London, or nineteenth-century boxing or Byzantine bishops was as detailed as his own. When he asked, 'Oh what was the name of that fat chap in Tom and Jerry?' he meant the nineteenth-century popular novel not the cartoon. I learnt to mumble distractedly, as if the name had just eluded me too, until Kellow grew impatient and pressed on. I would leave this little capsule of literary bohemia to sing the 'Fork Lift Truck Driving Song' at the Comedy Theatre. 'He's the best forking forker in the whole forking world.'

Geoffrey remained resolutely sober until the final night at the Edinburgh Festival. It was like bookends. The extravagances of 1973 had bankrupted Cambridge drama at the Festival so Footlights went alone, sharing a hall with Oxford. We put on extra shows and took the money for ourselves, and, despite London's critical outrage, it was a well-honed popular show by then. We did three performances on the final night, with a midnight matinee and then an extra, extra-late, performance at one-thirty in the morning.

As the festival finished, it was almost time to go back to Cambridge. And I had been given an extra year to finish the race to my degree. 'Two more years before exams! Wow.' Now I could really enjoy myself.

We blundered on into our next year, feeling light and feeling free. Or some of us did. Simon came from a conventional enough middle-class background. His father was a pathologist. Simon specialized in gruesome comic monologues about syphilis and disfiguring ailments, but just like everybody else he took part in any play that was available. When Simon's results came through his father ascended from a trap to drag him back down to hell. He failed the first exams of his two-year Part Two in Law. There was to be no more play-acting. He had to leave and take his bar exams separately. (He is a successful barrister today.)

We were in Southampton footling about in *Paradise Mislaid* when the phone call came, as if from another world. Never mind his public, Simon had to go back to Cambridge to face his tutor and then, worse, his dad.

At the time, we discussed it in hushed awe. This was like the past coming back to haunt us. We had managed to artificially mature beyond our real responsibilities. We had used the last two years to mark out our own territory. We weren't doing this for our parents any more, were we? Or were we?

Simon's father was a powerful presence. I met him ten years later during the height of *Not The Nine O'Clock News*. He quizzed me about whether I was earning a living, nodded a little curtly when I told him I was, and then leaned in closer. 'How's your father taking it?' he asked sympathetically.

I like to think that I never went home, but I probably skulked back to Epping in September. Around this time my father had started to venture across the Channel in his boat and he needed help. I had certainly gone with him on his first trip, sitting callowly to one side as he fretted about his navigation and became convinced that we had drifted a hundred miles north in the space of an hour because he spotted an oil rig. (It was being towed down the Channel.)

I definitely joined the boat on some canal in Belgium for a week at the end of my second year, when my father's prickly self-justification and anxiety at unfamiliar foreign lock etiquette, his fear for his topsides, his daughter's embarrassments and his son's headstrong independence all shaken up inside a twenty-nine-foot cask kept threatening to detonate into a blistering family row. On the day I arrived, I met my sister storming along a jetty, off home, with my father chasing her down the dock apologizing. I don't suppose I made it any easier, berating him for his dithering as he vacillated about squeezing his precious cargo into a slab-sided lock shared with four two-hundred-ton motorized Rhine barges.

'But who will go with him if you don't?' pleaded my mother. Who indeed? Len and Derek had their own boats and had stayed the other side of the Channel. Twelve months later I managed another trip, but only by taking my Footlights friend from Middlesbrough, Chris Keightley, as a fender. Chris was a scientist. He was uncomplicated and interested in things like diesel engines. He could talk with my father, or at least talk at my father, who couldn't sail a boat, worry about future hazards and make anything approximating to conversation all at the same time.

For my part, his northern frankness was what I admired – no trimming there, but I wasn't sure how to respond one evening when we went strolling along Ostend promenade. We had bought ourselves a paper cup of 'warme wullocke' – whelks boiled with onions and cabbage. We chewed a whelk for half a mile, but the mollusc remained obstinately intact and increasingly flavourless. It was either swallow the whelk or spit it out. As I discreetly gobbed it into the gutter and noticed six or seven other well-chewed whelks discarded in exactly the same place, Chris suddenly turned to me and said thoughtfully, 'I tell you what. I don't half fancy your mum.'

17. The Burdens of Office

'Um . . . I know we have a supervision planned for tomorrow, but I haven't actually managed to get the entire work done . . . would it be at all possible to postpone it a bit . . .'

There was a pause at the other end while the supervisor riffled through his diary. 'I'm afraid I would be unable to accommodate you until next week . . .'

'Oh dear. What a pity. Perhaps we could make it then.' Put the phone down, breathe steadily, walk out into the sunlight and into the nearest pub.

Supervisors got used to my phone calls – so did I. It took guts the first time. Can I ring? What will he think? Shall I pretend I am ill? But like most self-deceptions, with practice they became surprisingly routine: 'I'm not going to be able to make the supervision this week, bye!'

I had been given a year 'to catch up' for what was a fairly simple Part Two in English. It took monumental extra-curricular commitment to comprehensively waste it. I directed a lavish pantomime version of *Babes in the Wood*, starring Clive Anderson as Buttons. I chaired committees, shaved my head to take part in the Marlowe, sang comedy songs at smokers and wrote a convoluted play called simply *Dracula* on the expectation that the name itself would shift tickets at eleven o'clock in the evening. (It did and the preposterous, wordy nonsense went on to sell out at the Edinburgh Festival too: 'A mild thrill at midnight' – the *Scotsman*.) John Lloyd directed the best of the Footlights revues, *Paradise Mislaid*, and I rushed about a huge set designed by Tanya McCallum.

'You had that big place in your second year, out towards the Newmarket Road,' Charlotte reminded me. While I was astonished by my amateur theatrical career, she had quite a good grasp on the accommodation.

'By the Zebra pub. Yes, I remember.'

'But you swapped it in your second term.'

'Did I?'

'Yes.'

I had forgotten. I remembered the ugly modern accommodation block. I remembered the large, separate bathroom with the huge bath. I remembered that after Charlie and Charles, my non-acting college friends, had helped me drink an entire bottle of Southern Comfort I had brought back from America, we foolishly decided to smoke the souvenir comedy cigar that came with it. The cigar was ten inches long. It was real tobacco, but green, the Southern Comfort was sweet, and the three of us filled the bath with vomit. We were so drunk it seemed like a bizarre medical experiment.

Later I swapped rooms with Charlie. Charlie moved out into my rooms in the Newmarket Road, and I got Charlie's suite, back in the centre of town, in exchange. I think it had something to do with access to supplies of Scotch eggs.

It was a pretty little set of rooms, at the top of a staircase in North Court, with an 'oak' (which could be sported), a minute kitchen and separate bedroom and sitting room, and (particularly lovely this) a gas fire with glowing asbestos bars, in front of which I could fall asleep whenever I picked up a book. I kept the rooms for my third year too. They should have eased the stresses of finals, except that I didn't have any finals. Mine were postponed a year. Still, there were plenty of other distractions.

I had arrived at the university looking like the bass guitarist in the Sweet. I left dressed as a science master in a costume drama. The seventies presented bewildering options for the impecunious popinjay. In the early part of the decade, I thought I looked pretty dashing in a pair of navy-surplus canvas button-front trousers. I had a baby-blue tank top and a round-collared muslin shirt too. Perhaps I should have been wary about wearing the lot together, but I was nothing if not sartorially willing.

I was just an amateur, of course. There was no money for any of it. There was bound to be an element of improvisation. Perhaps everyone would have started wearing duck canvas bell-bottoms eventually. There was barely time to find out. It would have been simpler to stick to moss-coloured jummies from Marks and Spencer.

Then Bryan Ferry went and looked excessively cool in his white tuxedo on the front of *These Foolish Things*. It was time to dump the glittery-coloured things and take to Casablanca. Charles Lambert and I went to see Louis Malle's *Lacombe Lucien* and decided that members of the French Resistance had exquisite taste in tailoring even when being tortured. *The Sting* was a bit tight-arsed, but the French riposte – a film starring Belmondo and Delon called *Borsalino* – unequivocally demonstrated to us that people just simply didn't know 'how to dress properly at all any more'. *Bonnie and Clyde*, *Ma Baker*, *Casablanca*. Look at those beautiful suits. If you wanted proper bags, there they were.

I'm not sure that Charles, who was rather more scholarly than I was, did more than pass comment. He was all mouth and no change of trousers. I was less inhibited. On a quick tour of Cambridge's charity shops I turned up dozens of elegant if slightly smelly outfits. 'Demob suits', my mother might have called them, but it seemed more probable that they were hand-tailored, slightly conservative, professorial degree-ceremony wear. King Street was lined with old-fashioned tailors – yellow gel in the windows to protect their old-fashioned stock – but they were not quite old-fashioned enough for us. Generally, the jackets looked mimsy, mid-sixties and dull, but thirty years before, the Emeritus Professor of Greek had splashed out on a dark navy wool barathea suit from the same source, and it was lovely.

My uncle in Cardiff proved an unexpected ally in all this. Ieaun must have seen in me some slight respite from the trend to dowdiness in the rest of the family. He recognized the faltering gene of dandyism. He could see that at least one nephew was going to try to pass himself off as a piss-elegant fraud. Things started arriving, jolly nice things too. He gave me a 'cast-off' watch. Well, he called it cast-off, and I believed him. I realize now that he was excusing his gift, the unexpectedness of it, playing down the generosity. Insensitive as usual, I took it at face value and failed to spot the nuances.

I still have it. It is a Movado gold fob, biscuit-slim, on a white gold and platinum chain, for wearing in your breast pocket – exquisite. It was attached through the button hole, but only useful, of course, if you happen to have a breast pocket and a proper 'cut' button hole to hang it in. There were six jet and platinum studs too. And you could only wear those if your dinner shirt was starch fronted and pompous enough to need studs. Not with a tie-dye t-shirt. The signet ring had once been the property of the first Lord Mayor of Cardiff. It was made of gold mined in the Welsh hills and bore the great boyo's seal. He had been related to my uncle's wife, Aunty Joan, so it cannot have been without sentimental value, but the circumstances of his giving these things to me have gone, except that he subtly informed of their 'prettiness, what?'

I don't have the ring any more. I once gave it to a dresser on a set for safe keeping while I tottered off to do a sketch. He lost it. If I had reported it he would have got the sack, so I had to let it go, unremarked.

I had little to give my uncle in return except my attention, and I wasn't very generous with that. When Aunty Joan died and left him alone, my mother in her own widowhood gave way to mild implied triumphalism. 'I am so lucky to have my children all about me. Poor Ieaun,' although poor Ieaun, older than my father by ten years, survived into his late eighties.

Still a student, I went to call on his glamorous split-level residence in Cardiff. What had seemed unbearably stuffy to a six-year-old became exotically seductive, if utterly bonkers, as I grew older. Every square inch of wall was covered with dazzling pink and yellow flower power wallpaper and hung with sickly-coloured paintings. Joan and Ieaun had imported the Nice Corniche to a suburb of Cardiff and sat amongst their glittering bibelots looking down on Radyr Golf Club. He would show me round his treasures before, inevitably, launching into his lengthy war saga.

I was an attentive listener. He had left Cardiff when called up, gone by ship to South Africa. The garden railroad had taken him to Durban for training and Aden, where he had been a Wing Commander in charge of a hospital. (I had his tin trunk inscribed with his rank in my set alongside his old Imperial portable typewriter in my room in college.) With all its details, of cocktails and verandas, of encounters with girls in flowered frocks, with his post-war difficulties building a practice and accounts of pre-war anaesthetical inadequacies, the story usually lasted most of an afternoon.

It was like sitting opposite a distorted mirror vision of my father. Ieaun was tall, elegant and spare, with delicate gestures and a nervous, half-stuttering manner – donnish, you might have thought, if he had read anything other than that week's *Country Life* – but rather remote from the picture of a short-tempered tyrant that my mother always painted. Elwyn was short and tubby, but with the same translucent skin and the same round features and the thin but not receding hair, and inescapably the brighter. It was as if there had been a division, though. Daddy had taken the ordinary share. He wanted to be an unpretentious person, with a family and children. Ieaun had taken the rest. It was impossible to imagine Ieaun allowing his wife to choose his clothes: his alpaca mono-grammed dressing gowns, his Turnbull and Asser shirts and his hand-made plus fours. My father looked at style and fashion and parties and dancing and declined them all, mooching around in his Morris Oxford and his Gannex mac. Or perhaps my uncle had already taken the lot, and there was no possible point in competing. All the same, it explained something about my father. It explained his origins in pomposity. It explained the trappings and his almost disguised dignity.

Later in life, I rather proudly brought my uncle out to show him around a bit, to demonstrate that I had trappings too, so that others might appreciate that I had stylish antecedents beyond my dumpy old dad – not that they had ever met my dumpy old dad, but Ieaun was an agreeable substitute though he habitually embarrassed me far more than my father would ever have done.

When *Bookworm* went to Cardiff I sold Ieaun to Daisy, my producer. 'Oh, he's terribly stylish,' I promised and brought the wizened old stick to join us in our hotel, dressed in a purple shirt and a yellow suit far too big for him, with a tartan tie and correspondent shoes. He looked bemused by the new Holiday Inn, peering about as if the lobby and its flaming torchères had descended on Cardiff from outer space, but he rattled out most of his war stories before getting up to dance a little too intimately with the girls one by one. (He was then seventy-nine.)

A few years later I invited him up to London to a Royal Variety Show, where he did the same at the party afterwards, taking straight to the dance floor and smooching with a startled agent. I didn't know her. She just happened to be sitting at the table where the rest of us were gradually falling asleep. He was dragged away at two in the morning begging for one last dance. He was a ladies' man, then. He must have taken all of that side of the sibling share too.

When Ieaun died he left all his wealth to his accountant. It was his accountant who had decided that Ieaun was too ill to look after his own house and arranged for him to be moved into a nursing home near Newport. I visited and discovered him alone in a little room looking out over a bleak garden. He may have detested us as children but he had lost none of the good manners he had shown us as adults. He was wearing a rather fine cashmere lemon-yellow cardigan with the buttons done up wrong. The nurse brought us both tea and presented him with a chocolate bar. 'Oh, you like the Twix, don't you, Ieaun?' And he nodded and reached for it. He munched with the concentrated attention of a toddler. He started talking earnestly about my Fellowship. 'That's quite a thing you know, your Fellowship . . .'

I demurred.

'No, no, to be a fellow of the Royal College of Physicians, it's recognition.'

He wasn't talking about any honorarium of mine, but my father's. It had been the subject of a row with my mother on the night of my father's funeral, and now with tears in his eyes Ieaun was somehow trying to acknowledge his younger brother's qualifications.

I didn't stop him. It was a fragile and telling genetic connection. I was content to play the part of my father, to acknowledge that he was a better man than me and deserved the praise. I took it on his behalf. Confusingly, in this befuddled sibling, there were all my father's mannerisms again, the little feminine reassurances, the same grey look in the eyes, the slight earnest urgency. What was this? My father mistaking me for my father? But Ieaun knew as he talked that he wasn't right in some way and faded. A look of panic overwhelmed him, and I tried to encourage him to talk on.

'Yes, because you went to South Africa in the war, didn't you?' I finally said helplessly.

For a moment he calmed. He nodded and smiled. 'I went on the Castle Line . . . all the way down because . . ?' And he stopped. He faltered and sat quietly, and I felt bad for what I had done. Tears rolled down his face. I had only succeeded in prompting an awareness of his current condition. He was happier with his chocolate bars. He was suddenly conscious of the complete absence of memory. He was reduced to the present, to a drab room, a candlewick bedspread and a regular, rationed Twix.

His will pre-dated his Alzheimer's, but I got his clothes. They arrived in five or six large cardboard boxes: dainty Lobb shoes with trees, monogrammed shirts, a Sulka dressing gown, dress collars and studs in little leather boxes. I keep them for sentimental reasons.

There weren't many intimations of mortality in Cambridge. After wallowing in relative luxury, designing posters and directing plays and dressing up in borrowed clothes, I now faced my final year and had to go in search of somewhere to live.

Three days before term began in October 1974, I went back a whole day early to study the small ads in the *Cambridge*

Evening News. A room was advertised in Eden Street in the Kite, with a viewing at six o'clock.

I left that late too. When I arrived at five past, a considerable party of students from the tech, several men in cheap suits hugging carrier bags of clothes and a clutch of desperate-looking pregnant girls were already waiting in the queue. An estate agent came and unlocked the front door. He turned to the crowd. 'I have only two rooms in here,' he announced. I could have left then, I suppose, but speculated that the thirty desperate people in front of me might just possibly be very, very fussy, so I waited at the utter end of the line. Both rooms were taken immediately. The estate agent marched briskly out and along the queue. 'There's another round the back,' he said. We turned on our heel as one. Nobody protested, though they should have done, because the last to arrive (me) was now miraculously at the front. He unlocked a lean-to outhouse. I glimpsed a folding table and a bed. 'I'll take it,' I said. Twenty-eight people behind me groaned softly.

It cost me five pounds a week. To open the door I had to fold the table away. There was a shiny oval electric bar heater high on the wall. If I switched the fire on, the room instantly became sweltering. This seemed promising. The space was little more than the length of the bed. As the winter progressed, though, the cold out-performed the bar. The wall was only one brick thick and the heater struggled to warm up north Cambridge. So I spread my Russian flag over the bed and went to sleep at Newnham (easily done as long as I got in before ten), padding down 'the longest corridor in England', squeezing into Charlotte's single bed. I was just one of a large number of illegal male friends sneaking about the nunnery.

Life wasn't exactly formless. I spent almost five years at Cambridge. That's only a little less than the time I spent at secondary school. At school I had grown. At school I had progressed. My balls dropped, my voice broke, hairs sprouted on my chin. But university is a blur of repeated impressions, as if nothing really changed, while everything was changing. But though I feel no different now – somehow damned to remain forever eighteen, with an increasingly bad back – I started a journey at Cambridge which I suppose was to become the rest of my life and I never stepped off. I never pushed the boat out. I never started the engine. I don't recall exercising choice.

But one day I looked up from my crud-covered trousers and realized the end was approaching. I stayed in Cambridge for another vacation to try to catch up.

'I remember being furious because you got a dispensation for an extra day on your long essay,' Charlotte told me in 2005.

'Did I?' This was marvellous. I had no recollection of that at all. It was enjoyable to reconstruct my forgotten life, to live it again, vicariously. 'Why were you furious?'

'Because I had finished mine on time and, instead of being able to relax and celebrate, I had to go around and proof-read yours.'

'Incoherent.'

'Yes, but clever; on Ibsen and Nietzsche.'

How sweet: Charlotte was flattering me after all these years. I remembered it as being a colossal error. I had to read the whole of Ibsen, the whole of Shaw and quite a lot of Nietzsche in one vacation, only in order to point out that they had nothing in common at all.

Six Hamilton Place was a house of postgraduates: Rose and Charles and Ian (who was in fact still an undergraduate, but a bearded one) would emerge from their studies, blinking and tottering, and make tea in the back kitchen. I moved there after a German count playing a small part in a play I was directing borrowed the room in Eden Street to change for the squash courts and lost the only set of keys. Finals were coming. The women's college was getting tense. I knew I had to give myself over to monkish cramming in order to get by myself, and, lo, it was good. I can remember the warm spring nights, getting back up the hill under horse chestnut trees hanging over a wall, heavy with waxen candles.

Was it then that I was trying to earn extra money by working in the ADC bar? Was it then, unable to get through the month, that I sold all my books in a shop opposite Magdalene? (I watched as the owner picked through the box and came to a leather-bound seventeenth-century tract I had inherited from the wreck of frizzy Aunty Betty's house, assuming that it would be worth a fortune, only to have him sniff at it and add an extra pound to the total.)

'I remember the carp you bought and cooked,' Charlotte said.

I remembered that too. 'In red wine and sultanas.'

'It was disgusting.'

I had taken up experimental cookery too. How did we fit it all in? Why did we fit it all in?

I was directing a musical version of Cyrano de Bergerac composed by Peter Fincham, but I finished a busy rehearsal one afternoon in 1975 and I decided that I ought to try to reread my essays. There weren't that many of them, but I had Finals the following day. I especially needed the one I had written on James Joyce. I spent the evening I had allocated for revision trying to track down my supervisor. He still had it somewhere on his desk. I had never finished his sequence of supervisions before my exams intervened.

So I finished my education and drew breath to look around

me. There was no sense of panic. I had been crawling along the baby-boomer pipeline since 1953, doing pretty much everything that was expected of me and enjoying myself; possibly a bit too much recently, but as far as I was concerned, I was top of my class in shouting at other undergraduates in university plays. Something would come of that, surely. If it didn't, I wasn't sure that I minded unduly. Frankly, I was exhausted by the last four years. I needed a bit of a rest.

I would become 'a director', of some sort. I had never invited anybody up from London to look at 'my work'. I did write a letter to a man at the Royal Court, who promised that he would try and kindly pointed out that he had retired ten years before. (The library copy of the *The Theatre Yearbook* was a little out of date.) I vaguely assumed that I should work as some sort of assistant to begin with, but for whom? I decided I had better start writing letters in earnest.

A decade and a half before, a clutch of directors had left Oxbridge and persuaded the world that it owed them a job. Some of them seemed to have had theatres built for them by northern boroughs. But they had no intention of giving up ten years later. But I wrote. I worked my way through the entire list of theatres in the *The Theatre Yearbook*. I got shown around the premises at the National by the staff director and I was invited for an interview by Michael Bogdanov. I wore a suit. That could have been avoided. But I came from an elitist university background. That couldn't.

While I waited to see Bogdanov at some little theatre in Leicester, I went to visit the big theatre in Leicester. Two friends with whom I had appeared in revues, Geoffrey McGivern and Crispin Thomas, had joined the real world a year before and were 'getting their Equity cards' by appearing in play-as-cast parts. I sat in the corner watching them put on their make-up, feeling as useless as any interloper in a dressing room does, especially before a show, but feeling particularly useless in this real world of theatre too. Was this what I wanted? Did I share any of their excitement? Where was the intellectual stimulation in being a bit-part actor?

Mr Bogdanov had no jobs and certainly no job for me. He told me he had a policy of interviewing everybody who wrote. I crumpled and went back to London. (Perhaps I should have persevered. About a year later he hired Mel Smith as an assistant director at the Young Vic.)

Immediately after finishing at Cambridge I was still much too busy to look down. There was a hiccup for the exams, and technically I left, but some employment came in the form of the Cambridge Gilbert and Sullivan Society. It was considered an honour to be asked and probably one to be resisted, but they had money to pay for a director and, thanks to my father's early selections from Chew and Osborne, I could sing whole verses of 'Take a Pair of Sparkling Eyes' and quite a bit of 'Tit Willow' from *The Mikado*, the operetta already chosen by the committee. I got the general idea anyway: lots of enthusiasm, plenty of lusty singing. They were sort of pantomimes, weren't they? It wasn't a job, but it was a postponement.

We were a little restricted by the fact that the production was to take place in the open air. The Minack Theatre had been cut out of a natural amphitheatre in a granite cliff and has, as a permanent backdrop, the boiling Atlantic Ocean. Depressions marched in regular succession through the summer to break on the Cornish coast. The audience were prepared for this. They simply clambered into their oilies. The technicians were prepared for it. They wrapped their electrical equipment in plastic bags. I am not sure that my production was prepared for it. I had planned that the granite surroundings would be transformed into Ko-Ko's garden, with the addition of dainty strings of Japanese lanterns to light up and enchant us as night fell towards the end of the first act.

I stood up in the church hall at rehearsals and made my usual rabble-rousing speech, outlining my general plan of attack. With a week in hand to get them up and trotting around, I was rather taken aback by their unwillingness to jump to it. Matters came to a head when we rehearsed Ko-Ko's first entrance.

'Now,' I said expansively, 'Jeremy, come on from stage left and the chorus will part hurriedly, with little steps please . . . is that OK, Jeremy?'

Jeremy muttered. The chorus twittered. We tried it. But Jeremy didn't appear.

'Jeremy?'

Jeremy appeared. He stalked to the centre of the church hall, and I could see that he was exercised. 'You don't seem to understand,' he said. 'I have to come in from the centre of the stage.'

'What do you mean you have to come in?'

'That is where Ko-Ko comes in from!'

I looked blankly at my script. There were no instructions of any kind. 'In what?'

'In the D'Oyly Carte production!' the entire chorus thundered as one.

I stared blankly back.

'You're leaving out all the fan business!' a member of the chorus wailed. Then they all started shouting at me. This was not the same as the production which each of them had seen at least a hundred times and memorized in every particular detail.

I restored order and approached Jeremy gingerly. Luckily I had my own snicker-snee to disable them. 'Jeremy, chorus, my friends . . .' I boomed. 'I would love to do an authentic D'Oyly Carte production, really, but I think we have to be aware that the Minack does impose restrictions on us. The only way that Ko-Ko could make his entrance from the back of the stage were if he were to arrive by boat, scale a hundred-foot cliff and surmount a ten-foot concrete wall. There *is* only a fucking side entrance!'

I think that did it. From that little crack in the fabric I managed to effect a demolition of the Gilbert and Sullivan Society's preconceptions and ended up with something that was, I fear, more *42nd Street* than Titipu. I was perfectly happy to interpose business of our own. I seem to remember that Ko-Ko made one entrance carrying a large wet fish in a chamber pot.

On the opening night, my *Mikado* was carried on stage in a magnificent lacquered palanquin across a sweet little Japanese bridge. He was accompanied by beautifully costumed aides. It was supposed to be a willow-pattern plate come to life. Alas, a howling gale, accompanied by a sea mist, had blown up during the first half. The Minack never became a Japanese garden. It reverted to being the blasted heath it always had been.

It was a beautiful summer. I was going to Edinburgh to redirect the Footlights, but it would have seemed apposite to get into at least some sort of minor panic. I had no money. My prospects were virtually non-existent. A quick look at my friends who had left the year before could not have been encouraging. A few were working as actors. Douglas Adams was holed up with John Lloyd, who was now going out with my sister and living in a flat in north London. He had been taken up by Graham Chapman as an 'assistant', but nobody seemed to have an occupation you could easily describe as a job.

So I had time on my hands. I embarked upon a rabid affair with the leading singer in *The Mikado*. We used to meet up in London, get over-excited during lunch and jump into a taxi to Putney when her rower boyfriend was away sculling.

One afternoon I arranged to meet my diva in a little room above Maison Bertaux at the bottom of Greek Street, for a cake. I wouldn't recommend taking your mistress for tea in a small room with only one exit if you only know the place because you've been introduced to it by your regular girlfriend. It is quite possible that your regular girlfriend's father will have introduced her to it. It's very possible your regular girlfriend's father will be sitting taking tea there. You can brazen it out, but he's likely to be a canny man of experience.

He never said anything at the time, but a year later, when it all went rather messy, he told Charlotte that he had sensed something was wrong because I went to such great lengths to introduce my companion and actually remembered her name.

I might have been expected to start taking some responsibility. Apart from anything else I needed to earn some money.

18. A Short Visit to the Real World

In 1975, at the end of a summer directing the Footlights and Gilbert and Sullivan and sailing my father's boat, and with no immediate prospects of employment, I stood waiting for a man whose brow had been furrowed, whose fleshy and unshaven jaw was set with Desperate Dan determination and who was thinking, 'This is fucking mad.'

The man sitting next to him was thinking. 'But fuck it! It sort of makes sense.'

Both of these men had had the well-greased probity of ex-police officers, because they were ex-police officers. They still wore their coats, despite clearly having been in the room for some hours. There was a tray of coffee and some half-eaten food in front of them. They hadn't asked me to sit down.

'Would you be able to start tomorrow?'

'Yes.'

As job interviews go, it was short. I signed nothing. They told me to get to a room in the Hilton by eight the following morning. The man sighed, and I left the room.

When I arrived the next morning, the corridor I had been sent to was empty except for a squat-looking figure sitting up the other end in front of double doors. He seemed to be distorting the normal perspective, like the illustration under a greaseproof sheet in my mother's big blue cut-paper edition of *Grimm's Fairy Tales* – the dog with eyes like saucers. As I tentatively approached, I thought the corridor had shrunk to accommodate him.

His massive frame was encased in a navy blazer. He wore

tight, light-grey slacks. His hair was greased back in a
flamboyant pompadour. He was perched on a small upright
chair, hunched slightly forward, as if about to launch himself
up the corridor and devour me.

'Yes?'

'Oh, I've come from West Security.'

He paused. 'Are you doing this shift?'

'Yes.'

A look of pain crossed his face. He snorted derisively.
There was another chair on the other side of the doorway.
'I'm Big Mike. That's your chair.' I sat. He turned away and
continued staring up the corridor.

It was the comedy science-fiction-novelist-to-be Douglas
Adams, formerly of Brentwood School, now happily un-
employable, who had once again taken an interest in my
welfare. Thanks to his telephone call I was sitting outside the
hotel door of the Sheika of Qatar, masquerading as a bodyguard.

'Your sister tells me you're looking for a way of earning
a bit of money?' he had begun intriguingly. 'I found an advert
in the London *Evening Standard* offering four pounds an hour
for bodyguard duties, and I thought it might be *quite* a silly
idea to go along.'

Douglas' interview apparently took longer than mine. The
ex-coppers who ran West Security feared that a namby-
pamby, wet-behind-the-ears, over-educated slop like Douglas
might not pass as a creditable bodyguard. But they were up
against it.

'What it was,' Big Mike explained to me, 'was that West
Junior took over the company and he thought his dad was
a bit *slow*, behind the times, as it were, so he went all around
the embassies of our Arab friends, like, and he laid out a lot
of the old baksheesh.' He rubbed his thumb and fingers

together. 'Only it all went much better than he expected, 'cos they all come over for the summer, see. It's too hot over there, so they're all over here in London. He's got jobs coming up all over the shop, but he's not got the operatives, not the trained ones like me.'

The company needed bodyguards. They put an advertisement in the paper, but every old lag and con man turned up, intent on fleecing the clients. And then Douglas sauntered in. After appointing him, they wanted to know if he had any friends. The thing about students, it was agreed, was that they were too naive to be bent.

We were also rather weedy. Douglas, to be fair, was an impressive six foot and a lot. His hooked nose rivalled Big Mike's, his hair was just as lustrous, but somehow he didn't give one confidence that he was a killer. Gillies O'Brien Tear (another Douglas find) frankly looked like Little Lord Fauntleroy. Barnaby Dickens looked like someone called Barnaby Dickens. Candidly we decided the job was largely a question of 'presence'.

Though I was to work for West on and off for another six months, it was nothing like regular employment. The phone rang intermittently and a man called Roy handed out an assignment. One night, quite late in our relationship (indeed pretty late that night) he asked whether I could come down to the Dorchester 'sharpish', because somebody had failed to show. I dragged on my only suit and found myself padding up a narrow staircase, disconcertingly like the back stairs of a country house. A bullet-headed, villainous-looking six-footer emerged from the shadows. 'What do you want?'

'I've come to take over.'

'Fucking hell. Are you a student?'

'No. No. Not a student, no.'

I could only see the whites of his eyes, but I gathered they were glaring. He looked at his watch. 'Well, listen. The bloke downstairs is Para. The two blokes on day-duty are ex-MPs.' (He meant military policemen, not deselected back-benchers.) He sighed. 'If anyone asks you, you'd better say you were in the navy.'

Our role in the event of an attack was to scream as we were machine-gunned to death, reminding the Sheika inside to lock the door and phone for the police. McDuff's body-guards have never warranted a play like *Rosencrantz and Guildenstern Are Dead*. We were human alarm-bell reception-ists.

'She's gone out shopping,' Mike explained on my first morning as a bodyguard. 'She's the principal wife of the Sheik, see. So she gets to spend the whole of the summer over here. All the other wives are left behind in the Gulf state '. . . Oi!' He stopped in mid-sentence and looked up the corridor. 'Oi. I've told you, haven't I? Fuck off out of it.'

A shifty man in a grey suit had come half-way down the corridor. 'I'm just waiting until I can see the Sheika. I need to talk to her,' he whined.

'She's not going to see you. I don't want to see you. You'll have to talk to the embassy.'

This was Colin.

Until the week before, Colin had driven the Sheika around town in a limousine. He had been on contract to the hire company. 'But then his company went bust and he was laid off.' He couldn't explain what had brought about such an unlikely financial failure. 'But Colin has put a hell of a lot in,' Mike told me. 'I have some sympathy. She's going home the end of next week, and then the baksheesh will be flying around, and he's going to miss out, after all that work, poor bloke.'

Colin had gone and hired a limousine at his own expense. Whenever the Sheika left the hotel, he did his best to try to steer her into his car. Several times he had almost pulled it off, much to the annoyance of the embassy staff. They had hired a new limousine service and disliked the prospect of losing their crowned head to a pretender to the post of royal chauffeur.

'Do we go out with the royal party?' I asked.

'Not really, no,' said Mike. 'Sometimes, if it's an outing, perhaps, but our job is to guard the room, even when they're not here.' He lapsed into a determined silence.

So, we were paid to sit outside the door for twelve hours at a stretch, four pounds an hour; forty-eight quid a night. I had brought *Dombey and Son* with me. I cracked it open. Mike watched me. 'Is that a book, is it?'

'Yes.'

'You going to read that, are you?'

'Yes.'

'Oh right.'

As I started reading I could feel his eyes on me. Finally, he reached down and picked up a copy of the *Sun*. I applied myself to the first paragraph. Mike opened his paper, gazed perfunctorily at the inside page, slapped open the rest of the pages in quick succession, sighed and threw it aside.

He was looking at me again. 'What's it about then?' he asked.

'Well, I haven't got very far, but basically it's a description of the sun coming up over London, illuminating the houses and waking everybody up.'

'Right.' He shifted his massive bulk and plucked at his crotch. Then he settled back and sucked diligently at his teeth for a few seconds. 'So . . .'

'What?'

'What's happening now?'

'Well, Mike, the sun is still coming up, and the morning light is beginning to suffuse the city-scape.'

'Mm.' He cleared his throat noisily, sniffed and made a prolonged guttural hawking. He leaned over delicately and gobbed on the hotel carpet. He extended a foot and rubbed it in. He caught me looking at him.

'I expect you think I'm an animal, don't you?'

'No, no.'

'What's happening now?' He pointed at the book.

'Much the same,' I said and closed it. Mike was uncomfortable about reading, but then Mike was uncomfortable generally. Being a bodyguard involved long periods of doing nothing. Mike liked the totally undemanding 'work', but chafed against the inertia involved. He was not a great conversationalist. Nonetheless there were a few subjects he was keen to 'learn' me: the fact that this was not his real job (his real job was as a Hollywood extra – 'I shouldn't be doing this'), the way the hotel economy worked and what was 'proper'.

To pass the long hours he decided that we should play 'Spoof'.

'Ever played before?'

'No.'

'I'll teach you.'

Spoof is a game where you try to guess what combinations of coins the other player has hidden in his hands and match them with the ones secreted in yours. If you guess correctly then the money is yours: wrong, it is theirs.

I was a novice. To begin with, much to Mike's satisfaction, Mike won steadily. It vindicated his perception that students were as thick as pig-shit.

Spoof was not a difficult game. I soon got the hang of it. I also got the hang of Mike's 'system'. If he won, Mike would start again with 10p. If he lost, Mike would start with 5p. He never varied his foolproof technique at all, ever. I began to win money from him. It was difficult not to. Mike stopped chuckling. He became distinctly crotchety. But still, he never varied his system.

Mike chuckling was more bearable than Mike crotchety. Since Mike rarely tired of playing Spoof, to keep him relatively calm for the next six days we were to spend together, I had to pretend to lose for a while, and then pretend to win for a while. With a bit of care we would usually come out even. Hours passed in our bare hotel corridor playing an utterly pointless, mind-numbing game of total witlessness. Sometimes, I thought it might be better if I just read Dickens out loud to him.

There were bursts of activity, like flurries of snow. On the first day at about eleven came a sudden 'Grand Hotel' moment. 'Aye, aye,' said Mike. 'Here they come.'

The Sheika's entourage bustled down the corridor. The Sheika herself was short and hidden behind a burkha. Anna, an Anglo-Indian governess, was clucking over a three-year-old boy. He ran ahead of her up the corridor kicking the doors. They were accompanied by a number of small men in dark suits. Mike stood up. I did too. They ignored us, opened the door, and all went inside. The door closed. We sat down again. It was over.

Five minutes passed. A bell-hop (at least, I assumed that's what he was) in a tight pair of trousers with hussar stripes and a bum-freezer jacket (that's why I thought he was a bell-hop) came around the corner. He had a large trunk on his shoulder. He was followed by four or five more porters (in varying bottom-protecting lengths of jacket) with similar cases. They swung them around, balanced them on their heads and tossed them one to the other. They were empty.

'They've been to Harrods again,' Mike told me. He knocked, and the porters went inside. A few moments later they emerged empty-handed and went off giggling down the corridor, and ten minutes after that, they came back round the corner, this time laden.

'The Sheika's been to the food hall,' Mike observed. Several hampers of sandwiches, whole sides of salmon, platters of lobsters in mayonnaise, hams, sides of cold beef and towers of cream and strawberries were ferried into the room.

'They're going to eat that?' I asked.

'No, no. She's the number-one wife and she's the only one who's allowed to come to London and enjoy herself, so what she does is load all that food into the packing cases and trunks and has it flown straight back to the rest of the younger wives in the harem at home in Qatar, so that they can have a nice picnic. The Sheika is the main shareholder in Qatari Airlines.'

Did the Sheika really enjoy herself in London? She spent a lot of time in her suite, attended from day to day by her crown princes (the men in suits), which must have been slightly limiting. We once went out with her, when she wanted to have a picnic of her own. It was the only time she attempted any form of communication with us. She clicked her fingers and we hurried over. She motioned to us to go away and sit on the other side of a tree. We had been a little too assiduously playing at being bodyguards. The first wife of the Sheik of Qatar had found our presence, quite rightly, a little oppressive. Otherwise we played Spoof.

The little crown prince liked to come over and hit Mike very hard around the ankles with a piece of solid metal tube that he had found in a wardrobe. Mike's hugeness was clearly an object of fascination to the little fucker. Mike would take the full whack across his shins and bare his teeth.

Mike was philosophical. 'When they leave, that's when it's all worthwhile,' he told me. 'One bloke, he had chauffeured these sheiks around all summer and his last job was to take them to the airport, so he drove them there and hung about waiting for the tip, but they never gave it, so he followed them to check-out, carrying the bags all obsequiously, but they never gave him a tip. He went all the way with them to the departures gate, but no tip, no nothing. They just sailed on through. He called after them, 'Oi, what do you want to do with the car?' And they turned round and said, 'Keep it, my friend, keep it.'

Mike told this story to a number of people. He told the porters, when they flourished the fistfuls of fivers they'd just been given. He told it to Colin the ex-driver, who just looked ever more rueful. He told it to the plumber who arrived with a sink plunger. ('I shouldn't be doing this. I'm a trained heating operative.')

'You see, what he's doing,' Mike explained when the plumber had gone inside, 'is unblocking the toilet. They all go and use it, one after the other, and nobody pulls the chain.'

Unlike many, Mike was scrupulously non-racist. He never called them towel-heads. 'They have different customs to what we do. It's probably 'cos they live in the desert, they have to be very careful about wasting water.'

It sounded plausible to me. The plumber emerged looking happier. They'd bunged him for his un-bunging.

But Mike never told his stories of largesse beyond the dreams of avarice to the nanny. Anna was in her late forties, the daughter of a Welsh train driver. Her employers paid her twenty pounds a month, and she sent most of it back to her own husband and daughters in India.

In the end, disastrously, we missed out on the big bung.

I hardly deserved it. I had only been there for a week. They left in the early morning before our shift began. I met Douglas a little later. 'Mmm. Interestingly,' he said, 'she just handed me two hundred pounds without a word.'

Our team was broken up. The security company didn't want to let me go. They had other work for me. I was transferred to bomb-checking.

In the mid-seventies, the hotel had been blown up by an IRA bomb. As a result, a small table was installed in the entrance and two men in blue uniforms were stuck behind it to examine the hand-luggage of anyone entering the establishment. Another operative guarded the back entrance. The security company also manned a little booth at the staff entrance. A typical twelve-hour shift involved two-and-three-quarter-hour sets on the front desk, and two-and-three-quarter hours on the back and staff doors. The spare time was given over to 'breaks'. There were five operatives altogether: four to check handbags and one to stand in and supervise.

I was now in a blue shirt and wearing those rather cleverly designed uniform trousers with high waists, deep pockets and little buttons that seemed to be able to fit anybody. Nonetheless, this was a bit of a climb-down. I missed the erroneous status of 'bodyguard', but, more significantly, I missed the chair and, whenever Big Mike dozed, the reading opportunities.

At least on the front desk, when we weren't poking about in the bags, there were still two of us. Brett came from Bromley.

'I expect it can get quite busy about lunchtime.'

He turned and looked at me. 'I expect it can get quite busy about lunchtime?' He put quite a lot rudimentary satire into the riposte. It was neither an auspicious nor a particularly sparkling conversational gambit. I tried other sallies, but they were met with barely audible grunts. He had said enough for the next hour or so.

Brett was seventeen. He did explain later, in simple terms, that commentary on your surroundings or state of being was a waste of breath. He was more forthcoming with the supervisor, who turned out to be his uncle. The two of them agreed that only mugs would exert themselves to make money. At other times any challenge to the trance-like state of utter immobility was met with ferocious annoyance.

During the day there were bags to be checked anyway. Brett opened a case, and it was full of guns. The man looked him in the eye. 'The hotel knows all about this,' said the man. Brett's uncle came over and peered at them. With the natural regard that stupid authoritarians have for people with guns he waved him through.

I reassured hamburger-smugglers who were trying to avoid the exorbitant room-service prices that I didn't give a damn what they took up to their room and tried to calm Americans who became incensed at being called 'sir'. ('What is this? What is this British fake deference?') I referred people who wanted to see 'the general manager' about our intolerable intrusion to the concierge.

What they didn't realize was that 'the general manager' of the hotel was only ever seen in the lobby once a day at about eight-thirty. He descended in the lift, an elderly, French, fat man with the demeanour of a dowager in a lavender garden, and took his tiny white dog out to defecate on Park Lane.

At night, the hotel became more enjoyably sinister. It hosted boxing nights. Rather than the mug punters who came in during the day, these were attended by proper gents (not toffs – everybody hated toffs). The proper gents didn't tip more. It was sheer force of repellent personality that impressed. Our job became a major entertainment.

'Ha ha ha. Go on, darling. Let him have a look. If you find any money in there, let me know, my friend.'

Over three months I never found anything compromising of any kind in any woman's handbag but I spent hours trying to persuade heavily perfumed, twittering ladies to open the wretched things.

As the evening concluded and the ballroom emptied, the guests swept out to argue over taxis, new guests arrived to enjoy the '007' disco on the seventh floor and sometimes single ladies walked in. Brett enjoyed his duty to keep 'tom' out of the hotel. 'Where do you think you're going, darling?' he would ask salaciously. If unaccompanied, they were invited to leave the premises. He was indiscriminate. To Brett, any woman, even of a matronly demeanour, was bound to be on the game.

'No, I think you're making some mistake.'

'No, I tell you what. You're making the mistake. Whores are not allowed in here.'

The investment banker (something of which Brett, so it seemed, had never heard) stormed off, promising retribution. Brett was uncowed by 'the cow'. After all, in the early hours of one morning, just before Christmas, a manager escorted a well-spoken and expensively dressed woman to the door. She swung around in the entrance. 'Will you get your hands off me,' she snapped. He let her go. She addressed the lobby in a carrying voice. 'There's nobody in this place that could afford me, anyway,' and exited to a round of applause.

Our world was bounded entirely by the reception area: the white shining marble vestibule floor, with the porters' desk to the right, the entrance to the basement cocktail bar just by it, the jeweller's shop to the left that nobody ever looked at, let alone went into, and, behind us, the lower seating area. Opposite the reception desks, two staircases ran down to the hateful back entrance.

Brett's uncle usually stuck me down behind the lift shaft after midnight. Six hours, standing guard over nothing. Few used this entrance during the day, and after midnight almost nobody did. Originally, we had been allowed to sit down, but late one night, following a gruelling workout at the 007 nightclub, the boss, Mr West Junior himself, came down into the lobby and found his men lounging about reading. He was incensed. This was not the alert, twenty-four-hour bomb-proofing he had undertaken to provide. An order from above came down via Roy and Brett's uncle: 'No sitting, no lounging, no reading, ever!'

Do you ever feel that life is too short? I spent half my entire existence standing in that grim space. The muzak was switched off at 1.30 a.m. precisely. It came on again at seven, sounding, suddenly, as blaring as a colliery band. The rest of the time I was left in silence. I recited poetry, I wrestled with half-remembered philosophical problems, I followed the geometric pattern on the carpet, round and round, up and down through imaginary mazes, along imaginary paths until I knew it better than its designer, while the seconds crashed past like waves on a beach.

I used to ration myself. After I could stand it no longer, I would sneak a look at my watch. I was always disappointed. Disconcertingly, the last ten years have passed more quickly than one of those shifts.

But I knew I would escape eventually. It was an interlude. All I wanted was the money. In a few weeks I would be off back to Cambridge to fill up the time before I started proper work. There was a chance I might direct some more plays back there. It wasn't real professional work, but it would tide me over. Apart from Brett, all the other operatives were, like me, just putting in a bit of duty, a couple of tours.

Ken had been a journalist on the *Scottish Daily Express*,

which had recently been shut down. It wasn't bad, was it? Eighty quid a shift was a lot more than he got for writing up court cases in Glasgow. Come the summer he was going to be off. He was even hot-bunking with a friend in Bermondsey. They shared a bed-sit. He worked the night shift. His mate worked the day. He got into the bed that his mate had just got out of. They were thinking of sharing shoes. That way they could save even more. He already had a few thousand, plus his redundancy money stashed away. He was just waiting for the summer and then he was going to go camping in the South of France, and then he was going to find himself a proper job.

After Christmas, I left. I got another session as a bodyguard in the spring. But I never did handbag checking again.

But in the early eighties I had gone back to the same hotel for a big television awards ceremony. I was wearing a dinner jacket and was in an overexcited state. 'I used to work here as a security guard,' I giggled, and the other members of *Not The Nine O'Clock News* who were with me laughed in astonishment. 'Yes, yes, and Douglas too.' How they roared. We pushed through the revolving doors. The lobby was still bathed in the unearthly glittering white of dozens of pin-sharp spots. There was the jeweller's shop. The head porter's eyes flickered over me, but paid me no more attention than he did to the hundreds of other punters that he guessed wouldn't be worth that much in tips. But I let the others go on ahead a bit. The table was still there. And behind it, so was Ken.

'Hey, Ken.'

'Griff, how you doing?'

We greeted each other as veterans. I couldn't help myself. I asked, 'I'm just surprised to find you still here.'

'Oh yes. Yeah, well. Not for much longer,' Ken said. 'You know, it's good bread, and you get used to it after a while.'

19. Pigs May Act

It is Sunday, 20 February 2005. The temperature has fallen overnight to zero. My daughter has just celebrated her eighteenth birthday. It's her last day of half-term, so it's her choice, and she wants to eat sushi for lunch. I have grumbled halfway into Soho and all the way back about the sensation-less gastronomic experience of eating raw fish in a snowstorm.

Still hankering after nursery food, I take 'her' dog to the park for its run (and mine of course). As I pull up, I notice a man in a track suit leaning against the people carrier in front of me. It is John Chapman. As a returning old-boy director he made me wear a gold nappy and a pleated wing cloak as the Governor of Malta in his Marlowe production at the Cambridge Arts Theatre in 1974. Well, well. He is still in a state of resuscitation after his own health experience, and I have to remove my glasses before he is able to recognize who it is gesticulating at him through the windscreen. We pause in the chill Regent's Park air and talk about his TV work at Granada, our children's gap years and the perils of running, which we both do now we're getting old, and would never have done at all when we were young enough to enjoy it.

Later, half-way around the park, I nearly knock over a woman trying to stop her Labrador puppy eating a discarded sandwich. This is Hero. When I first moved to London, I lived in her house (where I now realize she must still live, since it is just across the way). We can't do much more than note that our dogs are related by a mutual interest in my ex-Cambridge girlfriend Charlotte's dog, Molly, because Jacob, the puppy, won't leave the picnic alone and because I don't like to stop for anything once I have got running, I jog on past the zoo, feeling bemused by my village connections in a city of ten million. It seems incredible that I can so casually bump into, greet or knock flying friends I had first made thirty years before. Had I kept on running I could have gone into Primrose Hill. I might have met Nick Hytner. I might pass John Makinson. I would see Jon Canter in a few days when I went to Suffolk. The night before I had talked to Clive Anderson. I still get daily text messages from Rory McGrath. All this jelly was setting in 1975.

It was a year of behaving badly. As I laboured in Park Lane pretending to be a bodyguard, Charlotte got a lowly job at Sotheby's, clerking in the Islamic Art and Antiquities department, and I busied myself ruining her life.

Twelve-hour shifts doing nothing at my bomb-checking work left little time to do nothing at home. My surroundings rather discouraged loafing, anyway. Hero had inherited a Nash Regency villa in Park Village East. It overlooked a big, sooty wall behind which mainline trains from Euston Station clunked up and down in a massive culvert, but inside Cassandra, Hero, Charlotte, Penelope and me – the grubby and frankly untrained interloper, tolerated and indulged like Jacob the Labrador puppy – padded about, drinking Earl Grey tea, eating wilted greens and listening to hearty soups plopping on the stove. Nick Hytner tells me I visited Cambridge one weekend, threw my hands in the air, and snorted, 'They spent all last week sewing a chair!' It was *Friends* as written by Jane Austen.

I can write all this with confidence because in 2005, after months of prevarication, it was time to open the last undisturbed research artefact of my past – a leather case I bought

for a quid in an Oxfam shop in the Kite and into which I
had shoved the residue of my life from the mid-seventies. I
must have lugged it away when Charlotte finally kicked me
out of her bedroom. The 'time capsule' was filled with
genuine detritus – little tubs of powder paint, gum arabic
and a squeegee for making screen prints. (I had designed my
own posters. I had forgotten that I attempted to manufac-
ture them too.) There was student flotsam: a bicycle bell (ah,
how sweet) and one of those flat spanners for getting at
wheels. There were two bow ties, one black, one white –
postcards of Monets, still dotted with the Blu-Tack that had
stuck them up behind my desk, and bank statements moni-
toring a permanent, fungoidly multiplying overdraft in
increments of four pounds or 'two pounds and three pence
only'. There was even a curled whitish card congratulating
me on my degree, from my college.

There were also, however, running-orders scribbled on the
backs of envelopes, a collection of hand-written sketches and
two bundles of letters. The biggest was a sheaf of thirty-one
rejections from theatres across Britain, brusquely setting me
straight. There was no work available for me as a director,
assistant or unpaid help, at all, ever, anywhere.

The second bundle was smaller. First, a note from Margaret
Windham, the president of the Marlowe Society. She told
me I had little chance of directing the society's main production in Cambridge, but Commander Blackwood was
meditating on employing me to do the Footlights. The others
were all from Charlotte. They invited me to step gradually
through the break-up of our relationship as if scripted by
Charlie Kaufman for *Eternal Sunshine of the Spotless Mind*.
They went backwards. On the top was a poignant farewell,
charged with all the awakening honesty that the end of a
relationship engenders. At the bottom was an account of

the joy of mixing paint for Hero's front room, the horrors of a mutual friend's motorbike which had dripped oil on a patio step, the dinner I had missed with her activist cousins and a paragraph begging me to ring – everything I wanted to run away from, in fact.

She was tied to her unrewarding new job, living 'with a canary with sinusitis', but trying to find a flat for us to live in and informing me about dinner parties with distant relatives who were angling to inherit her father's silver heirlooms. Mostly they were letters of heart-rending apology. She was sorry about her 'bates', guilty about her clinging, worried about her obvious frustration, about my lack of communication and her jealousy of my independence. They were only written because, despite Margaret Windham's note, I had prevailed with the Marlowe Society. They agreed to pay me two hundred pounds to direct at the Arts Theatre in the spring and the Footlights in the summer. Like a selfish junkie, leaving his girlfriend to go cold turkey, I had gone back to the party in Cambridge.

Shortly after Christmas my first call was to the white house in the Madingley Road rented by Peter Bennett-Jones and Nick Hytner. As I poured myself a drink I felt the first pangs of uneasiness. These people were as busy as I had been a year before. They rushed in and out of their house between feverish assignations and snatched academic work. Having talked briefly about our plans I was left to feel . . . what? Free? How was I going to deal with this sense of displacement? I was just beginning to feel that maybe this wasn't really my world any more when Jimmy Mulville and Rory McGrath arrived to borrow Nick Hytner's car.

It was rare to have a car as an undergraduate. I think it was actually illegal. McGrath couldn't drive, so Mulville was going to get him to Ely, and I suggested I tag along. I was relieved. This was the sort of time-wasting I respected. Perhaps I could have a look at McGrath too.

Rory tells me I had met him before he arrived at the house in the Madingley Road, but I didn't remember this. I knew who he was. He was at the same college. He had been for two years by then. Some time in his first term he started stalking me. I would look up from shuffling along to some self-important meeting to see an Afro hairdo peering at me from behind a pillar. He was always staring at me and eventually came to see me.

'I knew you were something to do with Footlights, so I wanted some advice.'

'What did I say?'

'You told me not to step on the poster you were designing.'

Jimmy Mulville I knew already but not well. As we slithered away in the borrowed car they talked up their ideas, and Jimmy kept turning round to make a point directly in my face, or he lifted both hands off the wheel to gesture, or buried his head on his chest and slewed over the road. He didn't see very well when he laughed. He had ginger hair and a twelve-year-old's mottled red face. His eyes filled with watery excitement when he had your attention. He usually had crusted eyelids.

In Ely we drove to a suburban street. Rory had an appointment with a girl he'd met in a bookshop. Her husband was an optician. Jimmy and I made a cup of tea. She and Rory went upstairs.

We left the house an hour or so later, but it had snowed while we were inside. Before we got back in the car, we had to search for long twigs and sweep our footprints off the drive, so that she wouldn't have to explain to her husband that three men had called at her front door while he was away issuing spectacles. And then we skidded off.

Jimmy was even more excitable on the way back. The road was covered with sleet. The windscreen wipers kept stopping. It was getting dark. We met the rush-hour traffic and almost slithered into a ditch. It was an ordinary day near the beginning of the Easter term. This was better. I felt more secure.

I couldn't stay in Madingley Road. There was no room. So I was put up for the next few months in the house of the highly 'imitable' Harry Porter, the senior treasurer of the Footlights (Harry had a fluting voice that everybody could impersonate). He lived in Warkworth Street behind the police station at the back of Parker's Piece.

My son lived in a house in the same terrace of Victorian villas in his second year. When I went to pick him up at the end of term I could stop to stare up at Harry's first-floor sitting room. The gentlest of men, shy, impeccably polite and always slightly distant, the legend was that Harry had been a young fellow of enormous promise in Tudor history. One night in London he had picked up some rough trade who had chopped his face to pieces with a broken bottle. His red face still bore the scars. His college, just to be helpful, had promptly kicked him out, but Selwyn took him in. He never really 'did History' again. His job now was to coach people in 'ordinary degrees', that is people who had failed the system, and were considered too hopeless to manage a third.

But Harry's life's work was to mentor the Footlights. If you appeared regularly in smokers you would inevitably find yourself invited back to his house. 'I rather think you might like this . . .' he would say as he wandered off to the shelves at one end of his womb-like sitting room and carefully put on one of his huge collection of Max Miller records. We drank his wine and prodded him.

'Well, the funniest person I *ever* saw in Footlights . . .' We would lean forward on the plush seats by the ivory-shaded lights hoping to learn. Was this Cleese? Or 'Cleass', as Harry liked to call him? '. . . was a man called Michael *Roberts*. And now of course . . . he's a *postman* in New South *Wales*.'

Harry was there to comfort. In the midst of gross failure, he could almost always remember a far worse disaster. 'Of course, the longest revue ever . . .' he might start with a serious look of alarm in his eye '. . . was mounted by John *Bird*. It was about the nuclear *bomb*. I think it was three hours *long*. Most of the audience had left before the *end* and they refused to cut a word despite the fact that Commander *Blackwood* was very *upset*, for some reason. I thought it was rather funny.' For Harry what mattered was the current lot. He was always perfectly happy to reassure them that legends were rubbish in their day.

But when I lived in his house I existed in a sort of limbo. Directing *Bartholomew Fair* only took up a few hours of the day. Rehearsals could only happen in the late afternoon or evening. I spent an astonishing amount of time in bed, dozing until late in the morning, in a half-world between sleep and wakefulness, disturbed by vivid examination dreams, breaking the surface relieved that I wasn't taking a French paper in the afternoon, tangled in bed sheets, trying to persuade my dreaming self that I wasn't reading French anyway. During the day I found myself becoming a townie. I would visit the municipal library to read the papers, or swim at the big glass-fronted city pool across Parker's Piece.

I might have been free to rehearse, but my cast weren't. They were all still involved in their university life. I had to wait until after lunch. So I clambered into bed with an actress, and then later into a bath with a comedienne. Charlotte was writing me letters about her gardening and apologizing for being so demanding in our relationship.

I loved *Bartholomew Fair* even if much of the demotic slang was largely incomprehensible. Jonson is to Shakespeare as Surtees is to Dickens, a celebrant of sex, swagger and the prosaic. The cast practised by swearing in their own language and then transferred the inflections to sixteenth-century blasphemies. We visited Petticoat Lane to watch traders run an illegal auction. Mike Arnold, the Arts Theatre stage manager, built a two-storey wooden scaffold. My enormous cast carried huge bundles of vegetables and bales of cloth on to the set during the first half and then carried them all off again during the second.

Nobody is in charge of university theatre at Cambridge. No professor of drama chooses favourites, encourages the unworthy or boosts the unwilling. It is a naked fight amongst the totally unqualified. I recognize the glint in the eye of the Cambridge Mafia today. It is a political glint. Successful directors learned to play the game at Cambridge, while still in a small, unthreaten-ing fish pond. *Bartholomew Fair* was my final stab at playing the game. Around this time BBC Radio Light Entertainment offered me a job, and I took it. It wasn't what I really wanted to do. I decided to work in radio for a few years. I thought I would get back to directing later – probably.

There was a party to celebrate the successful conclusion of *Bartholomew Fair*. I recall the huge numbers on somebody's stairs, and the exquisite feeling that this experience would have to give over to some mundane reality. In the event, it was nothing as predictable as work. Shortly afterwards a letter came from Charlotte. I have it here in the suitcase. It is a masterpiece of controlled anguish. It begins by telling me that my bank has been in contact. She has paid my outstanding rent. After dealing with these she almost casually mentions that she has crabs.

It would be difficult to conceive of less appropriate visitors to the studied gentility of Park Village East. In a dignified tone she doubted that she had introduced them, but explained in some detail (knowing me well enough) how I could get rid of them using Prioderm shampoo. Only then did she break down and fall to recrimination and despair. I decided to come clean – well, as clean as possible in the distinctly grubby circumstances. I confessed. She told me how she'd taken comfort with some bloke called Stephen, riding bicycles near banks of primroses and listening to Monteverdi in the pouring rain. Naturally, I became furiously jealous and highly contemptuous at the same time. She kicked me out.

During the Easter vacation, I joined Rory McGrath, Jimmy Mulville and Martin Bergman in the 'White House', a grim motel just outside Cambridge, to write *Tag* and go off the rails by way of compensation. 'One night we went looking for a jam factory,' Rory told me. 'All over north Cambridgeshire, looking for a jam factory in the middle of the night. And finally, after three hours, we found ourselves outside the biggest jam factory in the whole of Britain, Chivers', a huge place, in the middle of the night. And you looked at it and said, "That's not the one."'

The Footlights revue, *Tag*, was workmanlike. The staging was neat. I had a row of bathing huts, or changing cubicles, in and out of which, through swing doors, the cast popped to perform the sketches in quick succession.

I refused to have any discussion of the title during rehearsals. Every Footlights revue wasted half its rehearsal period in the search for an amusing title. *A Clump of Plinths*, *A Jug of Warm Water*, *A Big Hand on Your Opening*. The Arts

Theatre, a professional organization after all, had to produce advance publicity. Commander Blackwood, the general manager, dispatched his underling, the assistant manager called Melvyn, to the 'Prompt Corner', a tiny café in the passage round the back of the theatre. 'We have to have a title now,' Melvyn said.

Jimmy stirred his coffee.

'I know you haven't been able to think of one. I have. How about *Michael Foot Lights up the Room*?' Nobody even acknowledged that he had spoken.

Rory finally nodded. 'Melvyn, can you tell Commander Blackwood that we do have a title.' Melvyn got out a notebook. 'We want to call it *Twelve Inches of Hairy Cock*.'

'It's a¹ pun,' Jimmy explained. 'The poster would have a pair of trousers with its fly open and a cockerel's head sticking out.'

'A hairy cockerel, though.'

It was eventually called *Tag* because of the poster – a wrestling advertisement with pictures of the cast, including Robert Bathurst and Nick Hytner, in grunt-and-grapple leotards.

A bust-up makes everybody conscientious. It certainly made me caring with Charlotte: attentive letters and frank confessions. I went on tour with Footlights as far as Oxford and sat in the pub opposite the stage door playing Leo Sayer's 'When I Need You' on the juke box. It was that dismal.

But I had an appointment of my own. I couldn't continue. I had to start work at the BBC at the beginning of July. I had to drag myself back to London. Where did I stay, though?

'Oh, you went to live at home,' Charlotte told me.

Home? I went back to Epping? But I couldn't have done. Did I really?

I had seldom been back to Epping in those last three years.

If I did, it was unexpected. I would return from a tour to find the house locked up and them away on holiday. I would bring a pile of washing and a fellow member of cast to doss down and I encouraged them to bring their washing too.

I had been happy to assume that my parents were there when and if I wanted something.

I had taken this from my father, I suppose. In a sense, he was a hermit in his own household all his life: noisy at meal times, demanding and needy perhaps if he wanted attention but the rest of the time happy not to have a fuss (unless it was his own fuss), following rituals which he had ordained, apparently heavily burdened with his 'work', whether that was work on his boat or the rather more mysterious dignified occupation that he undertook in the hospital.

I took that from him – not, I fear, the necessity, but the self-importance. Like a child lost in its own intense play it freed my father and me to assume that somebody else would take care of the lesser things in life, even the decisions about what to do next. I had got busy and preoccupied. Just like him.

Had they missed me? There is no family as emotionally bound together as the family that takes that sort of thing for granted. If all we did, throughout my teenage years, was grunt at each other and get on with our lives then that was because we felt no need for comment. Nobody said 'love you' before they put the phone down. Nobody worried about their relationship and demanded kisses. We took it for granted that my father wouldn't want to attend prize-givings or moments of personal triumph. ('He works so hard, your father. You know he gets so little time to go on the boat.') Arguing was as much part of the status quo as the meal times, but so was resigned acceptance. My father never really interfered in my life after I left school.

The year before we separated, Charlotte and I had sat in the house in Epping on the blue fake-leather-covered sofa nursing a bottle of wine. It was one o'clock on New Year's Day and my parents had gone to bed. I looked around and felt all the oppression of Hartland Road and the London suburbs in the yellow wallpaper and the black Welsh inherited furniture ('the coffer') and the fake gas log fire and the Dralon curtains. What were we doing there? What was this New Year, then? When I got my own house, my parents could come to me, so I could open a second and third bottle of wine if I wanted, so I could switch the television off if I wanted, so that people could come and go as they wanted, so we could play loud music and dance until dawn if we wanted, not sneak around at midnight. I wasn't going to do this again. So I didn't. I live now in the middle of the West End. I have a house in the country. I avoid the suburbs and everything associated with them. But let's face it. I go to bed at half past twelve on New Year's Day. Some of us have work to do.

Apparently I went back to Epping and lived at home when I started my first proper job. Quite probably. I arrived by tube at Great Portland Street station, which is just opposite where I live now. I haven't travelled very far since.

The revue I had directed went on to Edinburgh without me. Just before it arrived at the Festival someone unearthed a letter from some fringe organization, inviting the Footlights to take part in the inaugural Festival parade. This honour was passed out on a rota basis. It had no significance. Nobody had bothered to do anything as civilized as reply to it. But on the day, a spruced-up coal lorry arrived. Peter Fincham and his band were loaded on to the back of the truck. They lacked a festive touch. At the back of St Mary's Hall, they found some bolts of silvery material. It was hauled outside, cut into pieces and draped on the lorry. Looking like a coal truck wrapped in Bacofoil, they joined the parade.

After a morning playing the numbers from the revue often enough to finally learn them, the coal lorry wound back up the hill to St Mary's Hall. Standing outside were Richard Curtis, Angus Deayton and their stage crew. When they saw the lorry they blanched.

'What the hell do you think you're doing?' the stage manager asked. He pointed to the shredded silvery material now dragging in the Edinburgh dust behind the lorry. 'That's our set!'

According to Rory McGrath, Jimmy Mulville said something on the lines of 'See that wall over there, if you come any closer I'll paint it red with your blood.' Then he walked away up the hill towards the pub.

The stage manager chased him. 'Oh, go on then,' he said. 'Punch me, then!'

Jimmy punched him.

The stage manager apologized.

Although 'the snake pit', which emerged from 'the Camden Town Boys', provided a number of leading light-entertainment figures of the early eighties, including a cross-section of both Oxford and Cambridge; although it numbered people as diverse as Richard Curtis, Angus, Stephen Fry, Hugh Laurie, Rowan Atkinson, Helen Fielding, Douglas Adams, Clive Anderson, Philip Pope and Mel Smith, and writhed with producers Geoffrey Perkins, Peter Fincham, Jon Plowman, John Lloyd, Andre Ptaszynski and Peter Bennett-Jones; although the two sets which had first met or mingled at this grubby church hall were to go on holiday together, inter-marry, send their children to the same schools and meet frequently over the next thirty years, I never felt that the first sharp thwack of that initial meeting was ever forgotten.

The game was on. But as for me, by then I was just visiting. I waited about three months before summoning Rory and Jimmy to come and join me at the BBC.

Just before my father died he was brought home to his house in Woodbridge, and my mother made up a bed in a low-ceilinged den just off the kitchen. This was where he had made his cabinet for his hi-fi and his special boxes to hold all the classical music tapes. It was where he had painted his cartoons and drawn his garden plans, constructed more doll's houses for his grandchildren, cranes, sand pits and cars and started writing scenarios for novels and sit-coms. He was quite content to organize a busy playtime for his retirement but he was diagnosed with cancer at the age of seventy and died of it two years later.

We gathered for his final moments. His breathing became more laboured. He was linked to an automatic morphine injector that clicked regularly, a low rhythm of efficiency ticking out the end. Only a week before, he had walked as usual to get his paper. A few days after that, as they increased the doses of painkillers, my mother told me how he suddenly got frisky and stood and held her, giggling and trying to dance. But when I got there he was drifting in and out of lucidity. 'Talk to him,' the Macmillan nurse said. 'The hearing is the last thing to go.' She wasn't to know that we never really chatted, this father and son. 'What can I say that wouldn't sound trite?' he had written to his elder brother when Joan, his wife, died. I probably talked about jobs I was doing, just to reassure him that I was employed. And then I took his hand in mine. He was barely conscious but he withdrew it. I saw it as a last refusal to accept intimacy between us. My wife was rather more straightforward. 'You exaggerate all these things,' she told me, 'he was probably just in pain.'

Yes, I do exaggerate all these things.

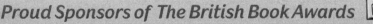